ARTHUR O'CONNOR
UNITED IRISHMAN

Jane Hayter Hames was born in Devonshire and studied at Oxford. For twenty years she ran her family's farm on the edge of Dartmoor. She is author of *A History of Chagford*, her native town, *Madam Dragonfly*, a biography of Cynthia Longfield, naturalist, dragonfly authority and indefatiguable traveller, and *To Capture those Who Dart and Sing*, an account of her African journeys. She also contributed to *The Rough Guide to World Music*. She returned to Cork in 1998 to write the biography of her kinsman.

ARTHUR O'CONNOR
UNITED IRISHMAN

Jane Hayter Hames

The Collins Press

PUBLISHED BY
The Collins Press, West Link Park, Doughcloyne, Wilton, Cork

British Library Cataloguing in Publication data.

ISBN: 1-898256-88-8

Printed in the UK by Creative Print and Design

Jacket design by Upper Case Ltd

CONTENTS

List of Illustrations

1. Anne Conner, née Longfield, mother of Arthur O'Connor.
2. Richard Longfield, Lord Longueville.
3. Roger O'Connor, brother of Arthur O'Connor.
4. Daniel Conner of Orme Square, Bayswater. Born 1754, brother of Arthur O'Connor.
5. Charles James Fox, by Thomas Day.
6. Richard Brinsley Sheridan by John Russell.
7. Sir Freancis Burdett, 5th Baronet, by Sir Martin Archer Shee.
8. Edmund Burke, from the studio of Joshua Reynolds.
9. Theobald Wolfe Tone (1763-1798).
10. The Dublin Volunteers, College Green, 4 November 1779, by Francis Wheatley.
11. Lady Pamela Fitzgerald and her daughter, by Mallary.
12. Arthur O'Connor introducting Charles James Fox to Napoleon, cartoon by James Gillray, 1798.
13. Fort George, Inverness, Scotland.
14. Lord Edward FitzGerald, by Hugh Douglas Hamilton.
15. Henry Grattan, by Gilbert Stuart.
16. Robert Stewart, Viscount Castlereagh.
17. John Jeffreys Pratt, Marquis of Camden, by Thomas Lawrence.
18. William Pitt the younger, MP, British Prime Minister, by John Hoppner, G. Clint.
19. Eliza Condorcet O'Connor, bronze relief by David D'Angers.
20. Arthur Condorcet O'Connor, bronze relief by David D'Angers
21. Chateau de Bignon-Mirabeau.

Nos 1-4, 19, 20 by kind permission of the Conner family.

Nos 5-8 copyright courtesy of the National Portrait Gallery, London

No 9 copyright courtesy of the Ulster Museum.

Nos 10, 11, 14, 15, 17, 18 copyright courtesy of the National Gallery of Ireland.

No 13 c. Crown copyright courtesy of Historic Scotland.

No 16 copyright private collection, by permission of the owner and the Ulster Museum.

I would like to thank Comtesse de la Tour de Pin for allowing me to use Arthur O'Connor's papers and to quote from them. Her daughter, Marie-Liesse d'Abouille gave me invaluable help. It was a privilege to visit Bignon. I am very grateful to the Comtesse and all her family for their assistance and hospitality. Without their generosity, this book could not have been written.

Mrs Patience Fawsitt gave me invaluable information, access to her papers and pictures, as well as every encouragement. I would like to thank her and her daughter Diana most warmly for all their help and hospitality.

My grateful thanks to Leonard Deas who read the manuscript and gave so much time and attention to suggesting improvements.

I am very grateful to Con and Oriana Conner for all their help and access to their papers.

For help with research and access to papers I would like to thank the following people: Kenneth Ferguson, Professor Roy Foster, Iain McIvor, Dick Douglas, Lt-Col A.W. Scott Elliot, Lt-Col A.A. Fairrie, Bertie O'Connor, Desmond Longfield, Richard Longfield, Michael Longfield, Arthur Earl of Bessborough, Brigadier Dennis FitzGerald, Anne Duchess of Leinster, Lord Rayleigh, The Hon. Guy Strutt, Dr Gerald Lyne, John McCabe, Dr D.D.C. Pochin-Mould, Nan Conner, Patrick Holohan, Dr L.G. Mitchell, David Cole and Tom Bogue.

For translation I would like to thank Brigitte Lemoult-Wasserman, Matthis Osterman and Steven Dodd.

I would like to thank Finnuola McCarthy for the picture of Arthur O'Connor. For help with picture research I would like to thank Jill Newhouse of New York, the Witt Gallery of the Courtauld Institute, the Victoria and Albert Museum Art Library and Pat McLean at the Ulster Museum.

I would like to thank Fiona Spencer-Thomas and Stephen Pearce for help with publication.

Many people were kind and hospitable while I researched and

wrote this book and I am grateful to them all. I would particularly like to thank Arlene Hogan, Miles and Alison Duncannon, Lana and Bertie Pringle and Elizabeth Neave.

To the Allen family of Ballymaloe I owe a debt of gratitude I cannot repay. Anyone who has experienced the hospitality of that great house will know with what joy I was taken into their family, fed delicious meals, lent books, introduced to helpful contacts and made welcome. To Myrtle, Hazel and to the late Ivan Allen, I am especially grateful.

Rory Allen took me out night after night, guitars in hand, splashing through the rain to pubs, clubs and houses where he and many other fine musicians sang the history of Ireland into me. Many thanks to Rory and to all those musicians and singers.

For permission to quote from original sources I would like to thank the following: the Board of Trinity College, Dublin for the Madden Papers, Ms 873; the Council of Trustees of the National Library of Ireland for Ms. 886-7, Ms. 10,961, Ms. 18,994, Ms. 35,005; Lady Marie Bury for the Londonderry papers, also the Deputy Keeper of the Records, Public Records Office of Northern Ireland who also gave permission for T/765, D/1759, D/2707, T/3393; the Duffin family for permission to quote from the Drennan letters; to the Bodleian Library at the University of Oxford for Ms. Eng. lett.c.144, Ms. Eng lett.c.60, Ms. Eng lett.c.64-66; *The Journal of the Cork Historical and Archaeological Society* for the account of the penal colony, Le Bibliotheque de L'Institut de France for Ms. 2475; Le Ministere de la Guerre, Archive Vincennes in Paris for quotations from O'Connor's military dossier and Archives Nacionale in Paris for Pol. Ang. 590 fos 217-23 and AF111 186B.

For the use of illustrations I would like to thank the Conner family, The Lady Mairi Bury, the National Gallery of Ireland, the Ulster Museum and the National Portrait Gallery in London.

To the staff and management of the following libraries I am most grateful: the British Library, the National Library of Ireland, the Bodleian Library at the University of Oxford, the manuscript department and the library of Trinity College, Dublin, the Royal Irish Academy with especial thanks to Siobhan O'Rafferty, the

National Archives in Dublin, the Registry of Deeds in Dublin, the Public Records Office of Northern Ireland, Jonathan Armstrong at the King's Inn Library in Dublin, the Public Records Office in Kew, Cork City Archives, Cork City Library, Boole Library at University College Cork, Bristol Public Records Office, the Linenhall Library in Belfast, the Family Records Centre in Islington London, Archives Nacionale, Bibliotheque Nacionale, Bibliotheque de L'Institut de France, all in Paris, the Archive Department de Loiret and to Naimh Cronin and Tim Cadogan of Cork County Library.

I have given the quotations as they were originally written. Double 's' was written as 'sf' and this I have changed. Otherwise spelling and punctuation are as in the original.

Place names and states have changed. I have used names which O'Connor and his contemporaries used and, if necessary, indicated this. I use Britain to refer to the island containing England, Scotland and Wales. Great Britain is the state which includes those three countries. The United Kingdom is the state which was created by the Act of Union in 1800. Before 1707, Scotland was a separate state from the rest of Britain and, regarding political events for that period, I have used England to include Wales. The crown was then the crown of England, of which Wales was a principality.

Dr Derry McCarthy gave me a splendid lunch and told me that my kinsman, Arthur O'Connor the United Irishman, might have been made King of Ireland by Napoleon. He said that I should write O'Connor's story, that it was an important one. It was good advice.

For Dr Derry McCarthy

"AWAKE, MY LORD, OR ... SLEEP FOR EVER"

PROLOGUE

Towards the end of his life, Arthur O'Connor sat down to complete his memoirs. Outside the library window, flat parkland lay between stands of mature forest. Beyond were fields of wheat. It was fine land for tillage, the soil fertile and deep. In winter, cold fog lay over it; in summer the crops grew tall, the woodland put on heavy leaf. It was better land than any he had had in Ireland.

O'Connor bent to his task, begun years before. He had already written of his boyhood, his education, his early years in Irish politics. As he wrote his hand never faltered, as he looked up his eyes retained their brilliant hawk-like stare. He was writing about Ireland at the close of the eighteenth century and the old gall began to rise in him. Rage still possessed his powerful body. The tragedy and loss of life became vivid to him again as he wrote. Muscles in his shoulders went taut but the hand that held the pen moved on.

'I am now arrived,' he wrote, 'at the moment when it must be proved either, that I have been the author of the greatest mass of evil, or that it is Pitt who has been the real cause of it. Much human blood has been lavished, seventy thousand souls are said to have perished in the struggle, millions have been made to suffer unspeakable cruelties. Pitt on one side, or I on the other must bear the load of all the crimes which have been committed; it is on the examination, which he or I is the Guilty man. If the proofs I produce in my vindication and in his condemnation are incontestible, I must succeed and he must fall, but if my proofs are doubtful, ambiguous weak, nay I will say if there can exist a possibility of their being refuted, let all the guilt fall upon my head and let my name be handed down to posterity as the greatest enemy to Ireland and doomed to infamy.'[1]

O'Connor was not a moderate man. Looking back to the critical moment in his life, he saw it as a lawyer might. After all the arguments, there was only one judgement: guilty or innocent. He expected his memoirs to be published. They never were, but remained dormant, read by a few scholars while his name attracted strange reverberations in the history of Ireland – and began to fade.

Once hated and feared by the Anglo-Irish establishment, loved by the radicals of Ireland, Britain and France, the memory of Arthur O'Connor began to diminish. Until, two hundred years after the rebellion of 1798, I pick up my pen to tell his story that you, posterity, might judge.

---- Chapter 1 ----

THE ORIGINS OF CONNER AND O'CONNOR

As with many individuals, Ireland's greatest strength has also been her principal weakness. Her isolated position, as the outer of two islands at the edge of a continent, allowed an ancient culture to live on into the modern age. But that peripheral situation left her dangerously unprepared when the modern age trampled in.

Europe has been settled by successive migrations of peoples originating in Eastern Europe and Asia Minor. Only occasionally did they reach Ireland. Some arrived by sea from the Mediterranean, others from northern Europe. Once settled in Ireland, they remained unmolested for centuries. For this reason, Gaelic speaking peoples retained an unbroken Celtic culture for centuries after it had disappeared from mainland Europe and low-land Britain.

Vital events in the political evolution of England left Ireland untouched. The Romans gazed across the Irish Sea but never crossed it. The Saxons seldom penetrated the hill country of west-ern Britain, let alone Ireland. Only the Norsemen, first from Scandinavia, much later when they had become Normans, crossed to Ireland and imposed their will. In England, Norman French was spoken alongside Saxon English. To the Irish these were the alien tongues of an infrequent invader. Until the Age of Discovery, the Reformation and then the Age of Revolution created waves on the continent which rolled out of Britain and engulfed Ireland.

Even in the face of these political storms, Ireland produced her own unique response. Until the steamships opened up the routes to America, the Atlantic was hard to cross and Ireland was the end of the continent. In that fertile, misted island, the last remnants of the old order stood obstinately on the land and did battle with modernity. When that battle seemed irretrievably lost, the young gentlemen of Ireland overleapt the ideas of early modern Europe, embraced the Enlightenment and produced a vision which, even in the last years of the millennium seems far-sighted. Throughout the world, multi-culturalism is yet to be achieved.

Arthur O'Connor was formed by this critical period. His name, ancestry and ideas all reflected the confusion of Ireland's history and the outstanding features of the age. He was born Arthur Conner on 4 July 1763 at Mishells, near Bandon in County Cork. His father, Roger Conner, had substantial estates in west Cork. His mother, Anne Longfield, came from an Anglo-Irish family settled at Cloyne in the east of the county.

Arthur was the fifth and youngest son. He had four sisters, two of whom died as infants. His younger sister Mary was the family favourite, 'disinteredness personified in this Angel;'[1] but she died at the age of six. The five sons and eldest daughter Margaret grew up at Connerville, their father's mansion near Ballineen. Daniel, the eldest son, was born in 1754, then came William, followed by Robert. Margaret was several years older than Arthur but only one year separated Roger from the youngest son.

Arthur was a strong, vigorous child. 'In general,' he later wrote, 'the Irish are an athletic comely race, the climate is peculiarly propitious to the human race, never hot nor ever cold it is always moderate. Nature had been most bountiful to our family, all my brothers were tall, well made and all had good capacities, but they were too rich to be in the necessity to seek professions.'[2]

Their father Roger was immensely wealthy. In the century which had elapsed since Cromwell came to Ireland and the Protestants became firmly ascendant, large fortunes had been made and the face of the country had changed. Land had been drained, hedges built, pasture ploughed and stone mansions constructed with large windows and slate roofs. The dispossessed hissed in Gaelic at the new landlords in their airy slated mansions, cursed them as foreigners, Saxons, English but among them were many Gaelic Irish. The right to land rested not on race but on religion.

The Irish were not racially homogenous. Oral history records that the Parthelon, giant Formorians and conquering Firbolgs were supplanted by the Tuatha de Danaan. They were then subjugated by the Milesians, said to have come from Spain around 500 BC.[3] The last two peoples probably spoke the language known as Gaelic, called after Gaul where many invaders originated. They had migrated across Europe; their ancestors were known to the Greeks and Romans as Celts and the name survived. In central Europe, the Celts ceased to be a distinct race. Only in Brittany, Galicia, Wales, Scotland, Cornwall and Ireland did the language and culture of the Celts survive. It was based on semi-pastoral cattle herding. On the Atlantic fringes, they hung on while agricultural peoples triumphed. In Ireland, cut off by the sea, they were least disturbed. Princes and Chieftains fought their neighbours for territory. The island was divided into four provinces: Leinster, Munster, Ulster and Connaught. One High King was to rule over all from Tara but it was a heavily contested office.

The provinces were a natural division and lasted, despite the upheavals of the centuries. Gaelic was the language of the whole island. The people carried ancient stories forward into Christian times and written records. Even in the eighteenth century, after profound catharsis, the Celtic past was vivid and treasured. It was a rich heritage of myth, music and poetry. The *Táin Bó Cúailnge*, the Cattle Wars of Ulster, was a great European epic. Exquisite jewellery was found in the tombs of the Kings. When Christianity infiltrated, a new flowering occurred. In the abbeys, illuminated manuscripts became a fine art. Within the monastic libraries, old pagan sagas were recorded and stored safely.

Ancient names survived too. The O'Connors of Munster and Connaught claim descent from Milesius. They retain memory of the King lists, the feats of the early Christian princes of their line and their struggle to hold the High Kingship. They remember how one of the Kings of Leinster married the daughter of the O'Connor High King but conceived a passion for her sister. He pretended his wife dead and obtained the hand of the second daughter. The two women met in his house: 'astonishment and vexation put an end to their lives'.[4] The O'Connor monarch invaded, a heavy tribute was laid on the son-in-law and his line, in perpetuity. 'To the exaction of this odious and oppressive tribute was ascribed the commotions and disorders of ages.' Conn, one of the succeeding monarchs, lived in constant turbulence attempting to extract this tribute. He died with the title Conn of the Hundred Battles. His grandson Cormac O'Conn was a renowned monarch and now the name of the ancestor began to recur. From this Conn of the Hundred Battles, another line moved to Scotland in the sixth century AD and established the Kingdom of Dalriada which was the origin of the Lordship of the Isles, a kingdom which once stretched from Antrim, to Ross and the Hebrides.[5] Conn of the Hundred Battles was the warrior ancestor of great men.

It was the Ostmen, the Scandinavians from the east who built the towns of Dublin, Waterford and Cork; it was the Danes and Norsemen who took the eastern seaboard, developed an external trade and created what would become the Pale. The Gaelic tribesmen fought them, Brian Boru beat them and by the twelfth century, Roderic O'Connor was High King of Ireland. He was the last.

The Middle Ages saw a slow erosion of the power of the Gaelic Kings. The O'Connors had six distinct lines, among them O'Connor Kerry and the senior sept, O'Connor Connaught.[6] Roderic came from the last. In 1169 Norman knights from Pembrokeshire in Wales came at the invitation of the King of Leinster to contest Roderic's throne. Henry II of England soon followed and claimed the Lordship of Ireland. His knights, Norman by ancestry, speaking old French were assigned much of the traditional tribal territory of the Gaelic princes. As the Normans confirmed their position, territory was ceded. In Munster the FitzGeralds and FitzMaurices squeezed O'Connor Kerry and his principality of Iraghticonor until only the southern shore of the Shannon, surrounding the castle of Carrigafoyle, remained of his former kingdom.

In the eighteenth century, the Rev Charles O'Conor wrote 'there was besides one obstacle peculiar to Ireland, which rendered political improvement extremely difficult, and it originated in the very nature of the country – Level, open, and firm ground opposes no natural barrier to the speedy execution of the will of the magistrate; it affords no retreat to the insurgent, and no shelter to the obnoxious; but mountains, woods, and morasses, intersected by deep rivers and extensive lakes, seem to be the natural seats of boisterous independence.'[7]

It was into such countryside that Arthur Conner was born. The Bandon river rises in the hills of west Cork and flows east to the estuary of Kinsale. Arthur's father had inherited substantial estates in the valley of the Bandon. To the west of his land, the hills rose towards the mountains of Kerry, with peat bog, fast falling rivers and deep valleys opening into wild and beautiful sea lochs. The Conners had land near Ballineen, in and around Bandon town and on the promontory above Kinsale. In medieval times much of this land had been held by Clan Carthy but they had lost it in the confiscations. The neighbouring dynasties were the O'Briens and the various lines of the FitzGeralds. During the Middle Ages, these great families knew little check or hindrance. The monarch and overlord was in England. Left without a resident King, the Norman knights became lax in their duties, did not enforce a feudal system, were not committed to primogeniture, did not adhere to English common law, began to speak Gaelic, to foster their children, to practise coshering and to war with each other over castles and land.

The King, kept occupied by alarums and usurpations in England, marching towards Jerusalem on Crusade, struggling with the English barons and early parliaments, had no time for Ireland. The Irish Normans became chieftains; great families emerged in the four provinces, of both Gaelic and Norman ancestry, harpers played in the great tribal houses and bards collected the stories of the great lord's doings. Occasionally efforts were made in London to bring Ireland into the English system, settlers would be encouraged to take land in Ireland and farmers bearing English names began to move to County Cork, to the eastern seaboard and to the Pale. In England, French and English began to fuse. In Ireland, the new settlers began to learn Gaelic and made only slight impact on the culture of Ireland. The values of the heroic age lived on, embodied in verse and song. Until a red-headed Welsh family called Tudor ascended the throne of England.

It was Arthur O'Connor's reading of Leland, the eighteenth-century historian, that prompted him to declare Queen Elizabeth I as jealous of Ireland's potential, for with the Tudors came internal peace in Britain, giving the monarch time to consider overseas concerns. Devonshire sailors set out with rude maps, improved navigation instruments and rumours to come ashore in America, the Caribbean and West Africa.

The Age of Discovery transformed the economies of northern Europe. The rush and excitement would not leave Ireland in her previous isolation. While monarchs and priests contested who finally should make the law, while generals carved out the territories which would be modern nation states, sailors and merchants took advantage of social upheaval to lay the foundations of big fortunes.

Cork is one of the finest natural harbours in the world. Deep, sheltered from the Atlantic storms, it is a natural base for trade with America. Waterford is good, Dublin Bay easily navigable, Galway Bay well positioned but unprotected. Cork surpasses them all, is more convenient than Liverpool, more accessible for shipping than Bristol, larger than Plymouth, has a better anchorage than Southampton. London is a useful port for trade to Europe but Cork is the obvious harbour for trans-Atlantic trade.

Cork had little immediate opportunity to benefit from her natural advantages. With England and Wales firmly united under their rule and a marriage alliance made with Scotland, the Tudor monarchs were still the rivals of France and Spain. As Spain developed an empire in America, she became England's enemy. Ireland was the dangerous back door through which Spain might attack England. Ireland might develop a competitive advantage with America. Queen Elizabeth I sent her generals to bring the wild Irish noblemen to heel. Titles were awarded, deals were struck but Elizabeth could not guarantee her Irish noblemen protection, her overlordship was useless to them, the treaties did not hold. To secure Ireland for the English system, a new wave of plantation began in Ulster and Munster. Rebellion followed rebellion, the FitzGeralds in Munster and O'Neills in Ulster resisting Elizabeth's armies. English forces conquered and in 1607, after the Battle of Kinsale and the death of Elizabeth, the flight of the Earls to Europe left Ireland in the grip of England.

The O'Connors fought for the old Gaelic order with Hugh

O'Neill, Earl of Tyrone but did not flee with him to Rome. During this war, O'Connor Kerry's son Donough Mael was killed, in 1599, by a party of soldiers of the Earl of Desmond, (a FitzGerald), 'and that slaying was deemed a great misfortune by the Earl, for O'Conor himself was his ally.'[8] It was a war of strained loyalties and painful racial divisions. Afterwards, John O'Connor, Prince of Kerry received a pardon from James I and retained a part of his ancestral land.[9]

Yet now the rivalries of Europe were not only strategic or racial, but religious. The Tudors were Catholics from a Welsh background when they took the throne. Elizabeth died the Protestant Queen of England. Rome considered her a bastard. A much deeper struggle underlay the burnings and executions of the Reformation; the struggle for modern nationhood against the old, cohesive dominance of Rome. Who was the law-maker, to whom was allegiance owed, to Pope or monarch? Which was the ultimate law, the Common Law of the state or the law of the Roman Catholic church?

In Ireland, where land holding had never been brought fully into the feudal system, where a merchant class had not developed as it had in London and other English cities and where much property was not held under the Common Law of England but on the old Gaelic system, this struggle was not relevant. The monarch in any case was absent; if the Pope was absent also, what harm?

But for Irish landowners with an eye to the signs of the times, Protestantism was modernity; it was the way the wind was blowing in the court at Whitehall. Whether from conviction or from necessity, some of the Irish nobles, both Gaelic and Norman, began to convert and to marry the new English settlers.

Then came the final convulsion. War broke out in Ireland in 1641 when a confederacy of Gaelic Irish revolted against the power and privileges of the new settlers. England's Treasury was weak. An army was required to subdue Ireland. To finance it, grants of Irish land were promised in advance, as surety on loans to fund the war. Before the conflict in Ireland was resolved, Civil War broke out in England. The King, autocratic, disdainful of parliament and with Catholic sympathies was challenged by the noblemen and merchants who claimed their rights in parliament. Towns and even families were split, the countryside was ravaged. This complicated the Irish war, where many Catholic rebels supported the King, some looked elsewhere for the Roman Catholic interest and the Protestants began to see parliament as their best guarantor. Civil war in two sister kingdoms was a protracted, ruinous condition which tore apart the society of both islands. Costs mounted. By the time that Charles I had been beheaded, and England subjugated by Cromwell's parliamentarian army, the war in Ireland had created enormous debt. It had to be finished quickly. Cromwell, puritan and anti-papist, at the head of the New Model Army arrived in Ireland in 1649 and put two towns to fire and the sword. With iron will, he ended the conflict. He was in Ireland for nine months and he conquered. The settlement imposed on the island was dictated by two things, a determination that Popery would never again threaten the English constitution and the extraordinary debts created by eight years of Civil War.

Now confiscation and transplantation began. The great majority of Catholic landowners were dispossessed and exiled to the poor bogland of Connaught. Only a few great noblemen retained their positions if they proved no threat to the new order. The peasants largely remained where they were, as tenants or labourers, but the disposition of their lives was entirely altered. The Catholic landowners were given notice, the men would leave in autumn, the women in the spring. In heavy carts, on horseback, on foot, the people of substance left their ancestral land and set out west – 'for hell or Connaught'. The fine pasture and arable land of Leinster, Munster and Ulster was put into the freehold ownership of Protestants, those 'Soldiers and Adventurers' whose debts must be paid, as well as the many, including Frenchmen, who were rewarded for service to the winning side. The new landlord was loyal to the English constitution and he was a Protestant. Only the Catholic grandees retained their lands and position. The Irish population, decimated by war, struggling to survive on ravaged land, went through a harrowing social upheaval. English soldiers enforced the order to quit the land causing a rage and bitterness never forgotten.

Anglicisation of Ireland now really took hold. Towns were

given English names, the administration was run in English, the gentry spoke English, and even many of the Gaelic Irish, keeping abreast of the times, anglicised their names. Conchobor became Cornelius, Donough became Daniel, Sean became John, Ui-Niall became O'Neill, O'Conor became Connor or Conner. The new gentry learnt sufficient Gaelic to speak to their tenants, labourers and servants, but through daily contact the grooms and maids, shepherds and ploughmen began to speak some English.

John O'Connor Kerry did not survive this last attack on Gaelic, Roman Catholic society. He fled from besieging Cromwellian forces to John FitzGerald, Knight of Glin but FitzGerald trapped him, he was imprisoned and executed at Tralee in 1652. There was not another O'Connor Prince of Kerry.

In England, the Protestant landed interest and merchant classes obtained their object, a Protestant ruler and a parliament with real power. When James II married for the second time to a Roman Catholic wife, he was ejected, and his daughter Mary with her Protestant husband William placed on the throne. In Ireland, the population remained mainly Roman Catholic and Gaelic speaking, with their traditional gentry and clan leaders dispossessed. As a version of the English constitutional system was set up on the shattered remnants of Irish society, it was the new landowners, the Protestant Ascendancy, who took their parliamentary seats in Dublin. After the labourious business of allocation, much land was re-sold, Ireland was a doubtful investment.

By the end of the seventeenth century much land had changed hands or been leased. The purchasers were land speculators, merchants, men who had profited from war, from the new trade with America, from smuggling and from the now-growing trans-Atlantic slave trade. All those who had survived the eruptions of the century might take a chance and buy estates in Ireland, hoping there would be no more tumults and confiscations. There were English, Welsh and Scots farmers looking for land, clerks and merchants from the English cities looking for new prospects, Huguenots escaping Roman Catholic France and Gaelic Irish themselves who, swept out of the patterns of medieval Ireland, saw opportunities for trade and self-advancement among the chaos, made a little capital and speculated in land.

Cork city began to grow. East Cork with flat, fertile land and modest rainfall was attractive to settlers. In west Cork the rainfall was higher, peat cover more extensive, the soil more acid. The Hollow Sword Blade Company had supplied the English government with military hardware throughout the Civil War, their bill was enormous, the allotment of land vast.[10] Much of this was re-sold, some of it to the Conners. The Earl of Cork held considerable acres from before the war, much of this was leased, later sold. The Conners bought Drumtelagh in the parish of Kineth and Murrogh.

Cornelius Conner was settled in Bandon by 1675 when he leased land there from John Baldwin.[11] He and his son Daniel sat in the Jacobite corporation of Bandon in 1689. This was part of the administration under James II before he was overthrown by William III at the Battle of the Boyne. At his death in 1720, Cornelius Conner was possessed of several ploughlands in the Barony of Muskerry and a lease from the Earl of Cork for his dwelling house and other properties.[12]

His son Daniel prospered. He was a merchant in Bandon, owned land in his own right and acted as agent to Henry Boyle, later 1st Earl of Shannon, with regard to both land and the parliamentary seat of Kinsale.[13] He asked Boyle to recommend his son William Conner to manage the nearby Bernard estates. William went on to marry Anne Bernard and became MP for Bandon. In his generation the family property greatly increased; his brother's will mentions estates in County Kilkenny and in England.[14] The Bernards lived in a Queen Anne mansion called Palace Anne and were a branch of a family newly created Earls of Bandon. The house was named for one of the Bernard brides; the Anglo-Irish had a vogue for naming their houses after themselves or their fiancées. Palace Anne, nine miles east of Bandon, was a neighbouring property to that of the Conner family who were buying large tracts of land in the area.

On the ploughland of Drumtelagh near Ballineen, William built Connerville. He might have chosen a site to the east of his property, near the town of Bandon or Kinsale. The Conners had built up a large land holding in the Bandon valley from Mishells, just north of Bandon town to Manch, west of Ballineen, to Ballinspittle near the Old Head of Kinsale. But William chose a site near the western extremity of his property and constructed a fine Georgian mansion which he named Connerville in the prevailing fashion. It was large and commodious. William proceeded to plant the domain and to construct offices for the estate.[15] William and Anne Conner had two sons and three daughters. William Conner died in 1766 and was buried in Kilbrogan cemetery, Bandon. His eldest son Roger, born in 1728, now married with children, inherited Connerville. His brother William had Mishells near Bandon.

Roger was heir to a mansion, thousands of acres of land as well as property and business interests in England. In 1753, he had married Anne Longfield, the only daughter of Robert Longfield of Castle Mary, Cloyne. It was a propitious time for the Anglo-Irish, the country was settled, trade was increasing, agriculture improving and their own position was advantageous. Queen Anne had died in 1714 and a Protestant Hanoverian had succeeded to the thrones of Great Britain without any major disruption. The Protestant constitution seemed absolutely secure. Penal laws still bore down heavily on the Roman Catholics but many believed, as Jonathan Swift in the generation before had done, that Roman Catholicism would die out, that with the law so hard against it and with modern ideas infiltrating the population, Roman Catholicism had had its day. In his mansion among the lush pasture of the Bandon valley, Roger Conner had no need to look back, the present was bucolic, the future seemed splendid and his children were robust and lived in luxury.

But robust, well-educated children ask questions.

---- *Chapter 2* ----

CHILDHOOD IN WEST CORK

'You know our characters are formed for us not by us, we are what our early impressions have made us. It is education that makes the man and this comes from the laws, customs, institutions, family and neighbourhood in which we are born and bred and the books we have studied,'[1] wrote Arthur O'Connor.

Arthur the youngest had a naturally intellectual mind and it was given powerful stimulation by his mother. He was clever and quick to learn, and was responsive and genuinely interested in what he was taught. 'It was my good fortune to have a mother who was not only capable to instruct me but that had for me all the affection which could induce her to take pains of doing it. To this adored mother I owe that the foundation of my education was laid on the most liberal principles.'[2] Anne Conner educated her children herself, teaching them the philosophical ideas of the age. She taught them history and geography, then the great seventeenth-century philosophers, Tillotson, Hoadly, Sherlock, Prideau and Locke.[3] Her fourth son, Roger, was very bright but he had a disorderly imagination which undermined his quick comprehension and excellent memory. Roger was a red-head and had a volatile temperament. The older boys showed less interest in their education. Daniel was capable but William and Robert preferred riding, hunting and sport. Margaret, 'lovely and beloved'[4] was given a gentlewoman's education, learnt French and was taken to France by her mother.

Anne Conner was in the Protestant tradition but she was a Deist by personal inclination. The certainties of medieval Christianity were shattered by the Reformation. In the seventeenth

14

century, speculation filled the vacuum, as people struggled to find a new vision. Far greater emphasis was now put on the conscience of the individual and the power of human reason. Anne Conner had read and understood many of these ideas.

Her husband Roger, Arthur's father, was altogether different. He had a fortune of £10,000 a year and he expended it in the most generous manner. 'All in my father's house was the broadest scale of genuine Irish hospitality. The money was all spent at home,' Arthur says, '200 workmen of all descriptions were daily employed, 50 servants dined in the Great Hall, hounds horses carriages, all gave movement and animation to the country round.'[5]

One might have thought Roger Conner an old Gaelic chieftain in the midst of his clan and indeed, that was the heritage he claimed. Early in their lives, his children learnt from the traditions of the family that they were descended from the line of O'Connor Kerry and that O'Connor Kerry was a younger branch of the line of Roderic O'Connor who reigned over all Ireland before the coming of the Normans.

Roger claimed to be descended from a widow and her O'Connor son. There are several versions of the story. This is Arthur's:

The last of those Princes [O'Connor Kerry] married a Protestant of the house of Pembroke which so offended his bigoted subjects that they burnt him alive in his castle of Carrickafoile. I mention this to show that such inhuman treatment must have made his widow detest the popish religion and educate her children in the same sentiments, she escaped with an only son in her arms taking all the treasure in the palace. She made for the town of Bandon so known for its aversion to popery that over the gate was written: 'A Turk, a Jew, an Atheist, May enter here but not a Papist.' She concealed her name, until her son had arrived at the age of manhood.[6]

Arthur tells another story to illustrate his family's religious attitudes.

An anecdote I learnt from my great grandfather's old butler; the housekeeper asked my great grandfather what should be done with a servant of one of his guests who was beastly drunk and insulted the women. 'Throw the papist rascal in the river', was the answer. 'But', said the housekeeper, 'he is no papist, he is as good a protestant as yourself.' 'Then put the little protestant rogue to bed'.[7]

Other versions of the Conners' ancestry occur in later histories. In these, Arthur O'Connor is descended from the last O'Connor Kerry, murdered by Cromwell's soldiers from whom his widow fled. She took gold coins sewn in her skirt and arriving in Bandon, a protestant town, she changed her name to Conner and brought up her son Cornelius as a Protestant.[8] In the nineteenth century Dr John O'Donovan wrote that the Bandon Conners were descended from Philip Conner to whom his relative John O'Connor Kerry conveyed Asdee by deed, dated August 1598.[9] Dr O'Donovan had apparently seen the deed. Local tradition claims that this Philip was the illegitimate son of John O'Connor Kerry and a Spanish mother.

Nineteenth-century historians poured scorn on Arthur O'Connor's story of his ancestry but they had many reasons to denigrate his reputation. They said he was descended from a London merchant called Conner who got land after the Cromwellian confiscations. Nineteenth- and indeed twentieth-century historians have not always recognised that considerable numbers of Gaelic Irish became Protestants, were engaged in trade both with and in Britain and were able to hold and buy land after Cromwell. But clearly they were.

There is an English name Conner meaning examiner or inspector, especially an ale-conner. As early as 1596, one William Conner was sufficiently wealthy to leave a will proved in Exeter.[10] There were apparently several Philip Conners recorded in the port area of London at this time. The name Conner appears in London parish registers and in East Anglia from the time of the Civil War and there were Conners in America by 1674.[11] Some of these may be of Irish origin. Their Christian names do not prove their background; Brian, Anne and William were common in both countries at the time. Equally the Irish name O'Connor was frequently given as Connor, Conor or Conner. Spelling was not standardised in the seventeenth century.

There is no evidence to prove that Roger Conner was of English stock and there were many of his relatives living in west Cork at the time, all of whom were Protestants and any one of whom could have contradicted him.

Assuming that some version of the story is true and that the Conners were the descendants of the O'Connor Kerry bloodline, what had happened? In 1580 Sean Cathac, John O'Connor Kerry was vassal of Gerald FitzGerald, Earl of Desmond.[12] Sean Cathac fought with Desmond and his cousin FitzMaurice in the Munster rebellion. It was a war of religious character fought with guerilla tactics in the mountains of western Munster against the army of Elizabeth Tudor. The Catholic Irish were beaten, O'Connor lost Carrigafoyle and retreated north to Clare. In the 1590s he fought with O'Neill but after the Battle of Kinsale he appealed to James I, to whom he was related and got back Carrigafoyle.[13] In the intervening years, in 1598 he had granted his fortress of Asdee to his kinsman Philip[14] or Fedlim. Sean Cathac, John of the Battles remained head of his sept until his death in 1640.[15] He was succeeded by his brother, Donough Mael's son Con, then Con's son Con, succeeded by his son John the last O'Connor Kerry, executed by Cromwellian forces at Tralee in 1652.[16]

The leading men of the sept had for generations married into the powerful local families of the Norman Irish or Gaelic Irish clans.[17] Philip's wife may have been a Protestant from a Norman Irish family. The Munster Rebellion was a religious war for supremacy by the Gaelic Catholics and families had split dangerously over it. Carrigafoyle was sacked. Asdee was close by. O'Connor Kerry and his men were Catholic. Perhaps the tribesmen turned against John's relative and his protestant wife. Whatever happened to Philip, his wife took her son and what gold she could hide in her clothing and fled to Bandon, a well-fortified protestant enclave. She was careful, called herself Conner, gave her son's name in the English form. When he grew up, he had no land and he went into trade. He knew the story of his mother's flight and he told it to his son. They remained staunchly, angrily Protestant. But they kept the old family names, Donough became Daniel, Conchobor Cornelius.

The widow's son reached manhood in the 1620s. James I was King of England, Scotland and Ireland. There had been peace in Ireland, trade had greatly increased.

In the sixteenth century wool and woollen cloth, hides, tallow, fish and timber were exported from Munster,[18] most commonly from Cork to Bristol. In the early seventeenth century the volume of trade grew, live cattle were exported in large numbers and between 1600 and 1640 the population of Cork city almost doubled. The outports of Youghal and Kinsale were involved in this trade and they grew and prospered.

British ports were growing even faster. Europeans were building colonies in America and the Caribbean. Sugar plantations on the islands would create large fortunes both in the new commodity and its derivative, rum. Ships from British ports landed in West Africa to trade in ivory, gold and Guinea pepper.[19] They supplied the new colonies of Virginia and New England bringing back furs, gold, silver, tobacco and sugar. Soon they were trading in slaves.

New companies were set up to finance these voyages but many people in port towns had a small investment in the ships and their cargoes going in and out. By 1660 the company of Royal Adventurers to Africa monopolised the African trade from Britain.[20] The Hudson Bay company was incorporated in 1670 for trade to New England. Before the regulation of the Atlantic sea routes, great fortunes had already been made. In 1662 one of the Royal African Company's ships sailing for Gambia was called *Kinsale*.[21] Irish merchants traded slaves in the Caribbean; in Monserrat, negroes spoke Irish Gaelic. Cork city became prosperous from the provisions trade to the West Indies. Smuggling became a problem for the Customs as ships from Cork and its outports crossed to the West Country of England and the ports of north-west France such as la Rochelle.

Ireland felt the effect of this burgeoning trade. Daniel Conner was a merchant, as was his son Cornelius. They remembered their traumatic family history but Ireland was changing, Cornelius went to Bristol to do business. The ports of the 1600s were the hub of a colourful and adventurous world. Into harbour came the heavy caravels, stinking of salt and livestock, fat and wool. Sometimes the larger, long distance vessels hove into view, their masts a billowing mass of sail until they crunched on the wharfs, the men shouting, swearing, telling tales of the black men of Africa, the naked women with earrings of gold, the heat and danger, the awful vicissitudes of the planters in the West Indies; throwing down bear skins from America, reeking crates of salted cod.

There were plenty of opportunities for men with quick wits and a little capital to make a profit. Cornelius Conner did well in Bristol, probably traded both there and in Cork. By 1675 he had returned to settle in Bandon.[22] In 1670 he had married Mrs Joan Splane.[23] There was a large family of Splanes in Bandon. Cornelius' son Daniel was active in business. Father and son both sat in the Jacobite Corporation of Bandon in 1689; they were of some standing in the town. In 1698 Daniel married Margaret Slone,[24] they had four sons and four daughters. Daniel did business for Henry Boyle, but principally he was a merchant.[25] He travelled to London where he traded in tallow and lived in St Swithun's Lane in the city.[26]

Cornelius died in 1720, a respectable man of property. His will was drawn up in 1719, leaving to his grandsons the land in the Barony of Muskerry which he had bought from the Hollow Sword Blade Company.[27] His son, Daniel, leased townlands in Carbery from Hugh Lumley of Ballymaloe.[28] Daniel's eldest son died in 1737 but his second son William inherited and built on the achievement of father and grandfather. William Conner bought six properties from Henry Lumley of Ballymaloe for £5669 in 1762,[29] a considerable investment.

Although the eldest son carried the family name Daniel, the second was named carefully with an eye to the times. William of Orange had triumphed at the Boyne in 1690, the name now signified protestant loyalties.

The Irish records show the Conners accumulated a large land holding in three generations. But there were parallel business interests in England. The Conners had turned their trading profits into Irish land. They had found their place among the Anglo-Irish gentry.

William built a mansion, became an MP and married Miss Bernard, the cousin of an Earl. If his son Roger was a squanderer, that was all too common in the generations after the wealth had accumulated.

The link between O'Connor Kerry and the first Daniel Conner may not be possible to prove. The recurring eruptions and scarcity of records between 1580 and 1652 obscure a period of fast change and recurrent violence in the affairs of Ireland. Nonetheless, for some people, sailing carefully on a stormy and changeable wind, it was a period of advantage. There are several reasons why the story of Arthur O'Connor's descent from O'Connor Kerry rings true. All the versions of the story overlap but are not identical, a characteristic of family traditions passed on in childhood. There are curious details such as the deed to Asdee, Daniel's address in London and a recurring connection with Bristol. The family Christian names are traditional O'Connor Kerry names. There were red-heads in the family, far more common in the Celtic countries than in England. William built his house at the western end of his land when the eastern would have been more fashionable and more convenient for Cork city or Kinsale. Perhaps the west was closer to his roots. Arthur had a passionate antipathy to primogeniture, a system alien to the old Gaelic way. Primogeniture was not practiced by Roger, Arthur's father.

Whatever the facts, Arthur took the story of his origins very seriously; he and his brother Roger reverted to the Gaelic form O'Connor when they became young men.

The passionate hatred between Protestant and Catholic in Arthur's story of his ancestors was characteristically expressed by burning. A hatred of popery was then handed down by the family; the butler's anecdote shows that Cornelius despised Catholics. But in his generation there was no religious security. The Protestant succession was not secured until William III was safely installed, when Cornelius was already a middle-aged man.

Arthur O'Connor was led to abandon this ancestral hatred. When he was born in 1763 the Protestants felt more secure and the vengeful attitudes towards Catholics began to moderate. The penal laws were still in force but men of influence had begun to question them.

Arthur's father was a bon viveur and displayed little interest in politics or religion. 'Unfortunately,' wrote Arthur, 'the passion of my father for employing workmen was not accompanied with discernment of what was useless from what was productive and hundred thousands he expended added little to the fortune of his children.'[30] Roger had curious notions. At a Cork assize he walked across the table in the court-house in the presence of the judge,

> conceiving that his personal importance gave him privileges from which meaner mortals were properly excluded. The judge, who did not know him, gave him a sharp reprimand. Shortly afterwards, the judge received, to his great surprise, a note from Mr Conner, which was handed to him by Lord Longueville, requiring either an apology, or 'satisfaction' at twelve paces. The judge was a man of peace; and as no hostile meeting occurred, it is not improbable that he apologised.[31]

Duelling was common in eighteenth-century Britain and Ireland. Very little provocation was required. It suited the style of the Anglo-Irish to cut a dash, be easily offended, choose seconds and 'blaze'. Sheridan, playwright and politician had a famous duel early in his career and Arthur O'Connor's nephew killed his cousin, Captain Daunt, in the last duel in the south of Ireland.

'Intellectual is not a word that springs to mind in describing the Anglo-Irish gentry of the eighteenth and nineteenth century. One thinks of them as, at their best brave, dashing and witty; at their worst drunken, dissipated and illiterate,' wrote Mark Girouard in 1965.[32]

They certainly had style. The lovely country houses, the elegant lines of Georgian Dublin are proof of that. In the eighteenth century, wit and oratory were at a premium. The Anglo-Irish had picked up much of the delight in verbal skill, the music and intonation of the native Irish and wound it into the language of Georgian English. Their speech could be entrancing. The clothes of the period were flattering, breeches, frock coats and ruffled shirts were worn by young men, with long boots, greatcoats, wide-brimmed hats with feathers and cockades. Dashing they undoubtedly could be.

Roger Conner had also the obnoxious side of the species. 'Being asked by a guest at his table what description of wine they were drinking, Roger replied that it was Pontick wine ['Pon tick], thereby implying that it had not been paid for.'[33]

His wife Anne was very different. Her youngest child, Arthur adored and respected her; he was disdainful of his father. Anne was one of three children of Robert Longfield who was settled on a substantial estate at Cloyne, to the east of Cork city. Her ancestor John Longfield had come to Ireland in 1652 and in 1666 was Usher of the Exchequer in Dublin.[34] His son John was tax collector at Mallow, where he married Mary Hawnby. In 1698 John bought Garrymaconwy from Bartholomew Purdon. On this land, Longueville House was built. In 1715, his nephew William took a lease on Carrigacotta near Cloyne from William O'Brien, Lord Inchiquin[35] who had been awarded it in the Cromwellian settlement. William then made it over in trust to his uncle John Longfield[36] who renamed it Castle Mary for his wife.

John Longfield had three sons. Like the Conners, the Longfields had been building up their land holdings, financing this by well-paid positions in the new civil administration. Longueville was a pretty Georgian mansion. Castle Mary was originally a Norman fortress, strategically placed in the valley between Cork harbour and Ballycotton Bay. A Georgian house was constructed around the Norman tower by the Longfields. John's eldest son, Robert, settled at Castle Mary. Inchiquin had mortgaged the property; in 1759 Robert Longfield bought the mortgage and gained the property outright. It was in a key position and excellently placed for Cork city and harbour, where trade with the Caribbean was a vital part of the fast growing Irish economy. The second son, John, lived at Longueville, though both properties were in the gift of the eldest son.

Robert had three children, John, Richard and Anne. John married Alice Tilson and had a son. Separate arrangements were soon made for her income and John was last heard of in Martinho, Portugal.[37] Their only son Robert married but died soon afterwards without children. On his nephew's death, the whole estate passed to Richard Longfield. His cousins were settled on the family property at Mallow. His sister, Anne, married Roger Conner and moved to west Cork. Richard Longfield married Margaret White of Bantry. Their country seat was at Castle Mary and their Dublin house was in Fitzwilliam Street Lower, one of the recently built Georgian terraces.

Richard Longfield became a typical country squire and pillar of the establishment. Either by nature or because his elder brother had let the side down, he was very sensitive to insult, to being overlooked for preferment or to losing any political influence he considered his due. He was an anxious and humourless man, though a diligent and responsible office holder. He had no legitimate children. Richard Longfield certainly showed no interest in the liberal philosophy which his sister taught her children. But he did take a keen interest in her youngest son, Arthur.

The scene at Connerville was a lively one. Daniel, William, Margaret, Robert, Roger and Arthur grew up with a father who walked on tables and a sophisticated, intellectual mother, in a large house full of builders and servants which grew every day.

But Arthur was sent away to school when he was only three. He relates how he went to Lismore at this tender age, so long a journey from Bandon that it must have been more like fostering than schooling. In Lismore, the Rev William Jessop, a graduate of Trinity College, ran a school for Protestant children. Arthur had an uncle in Lismore Castle. From here, he went on to a school at Castle Lyons and afterwards to Bandon, only nine miles from Connerville, where he was a weekly boarder, coming home on Saturday and returning on Monday morning. As a teenager, he went back to Dr Browne's school at Castle Lyons where he was a boarder with 60 or 70 other boys.

'My school education did me great service from the powerful control it exercised over me, the constant rivalship between such numbers on the same footing made each individual estimate his worth with his equals and still oftener with his superiors.'[38]

---------— *Chapter 3* —---------

GROWING UP WITH SOLDIERS

Arthur O'Connor was twelve when the American War of Independence broke out, eighteen when the Americans won. During his adolescence, war raged in the Atlantic and ideas on governance were hurled about the English-speaking world. He had been taught to read, think, enquire and ponder by his mother. The war was provocative to a clever young mind.

'The beloved mother who made my early education deeply impressed on my mind that of all vices lying was the meanest and the most contemptible.'[1] He learnt from her to examine his own conscience. As he grew he came to believe that noble, generous independence sprang from self-examination and self-correction. The conscience of the individual was answerable to no man but only to 'the Great Spirit', to God. It was a thorough protestant upbringing.

When he was at school at Bandon, aged about nine or ten, he came home on Saturday morning, the nine miles quickly travelled by the boy on a pony or driven by one of the grooms in a light trap. On Monday morning he returned to school and his mother always gave him little commissions, to take gifts to families who had fallen on hard times. At first he made these visits out of duty to his mother, but when he began to feel the pleasure he gave and the warmth with which he was greeted, 'I came to taste the exquisite delight of sympathy and that the pleasure I gave to others became my own.'[2] Then the visits became a genuine delight to the boy, he looked forward to them. 'I never failed to raise contributions at the card table among the numerous guests of my father's hospitable house by a little bank or totery which enabled me to add to my

24

stock of presents.'[3] Once when his mother gave him five guineas for some verses he had written, he resisted the temptation to buy whips, spurs and pen-knives but used it to relieve the need of a family in deep distress. A long time afterwards, his mother discovered this and pressed Arthur to her with deep affection. He was very moved.

Nonetheless, Arthur O'Connor was a child with a very strong will, with competitive instincts, clever, vigorous and inquisitive. 'Man is born with such strong propensity to self that of all the virtues, abnegation of that self is the rarest. Among the thousand obligations I owe my beloved mother, the estranging me from this vile passion is the greatest.'[4]

He had plenty of outlets for energy and competitiveness, not least four older brothers. Arthur was intended for a military profession and raised 'in all the manly exercises, swimming, hunting, riding, shooting, in all which I attained a considerable perfection at a very early age, long before others began to learn them.'[5] The children might bathe in the river Bandon which flowed past the grounds of Connerville, or in the sea at Kinsale when their mother took them down to the coast. Horses were essential; pulling the carriages, the plough, the carts of turf and firewood. There were fine horses for gentlemen's transport and hunting. Children rode ponies. Donkeys drew garden carts of vegetables or dung. The stables were a vital part of country house life.

Family friends took a part in the education of the children. There was a bigoted attitude against Roman Catholics in the Conner family, arising from memories of civil war. The children could not help adopting it. But other influences made an impression on Arthur when he was still young. A man named O'Mahony frequented the house, 'a great proficient in the Irish language [who] possessed a store of old Irish manuscripts which all passed under the title of Ossion's poems. To hear these translated into English, perched on O'Mahony's knee was the delight of my boyish years'.[6] Sitting by the fire, he heard the man's musical voice recite the tales and the old heroes came alive with their battles, their magic. The boy was entranced. It was like having his own *seanchaidhe* in the house, relating the history of the warriors. The stories were all to the glory of the Irish and against the oppressors.

In rural Ireland, the poetic tradition in Gaelic was still alive. The ancient stories and verse included the tales of Fionn and Oisin. A minor Gaelic revival occurred in the eighteenth century. After the sharp trauma of the Cromwellian settlement, the new society began to look back and remember the ancient culture. The new Ascendancy absorbed some part of the native tradition, often in a romantic form. The northern Presbyterians actively studied and encouraged the Gaelic inheritance. In Scotland, James MacPherson produced the poems of Ossian, supposedly translated from ancient Gaelic sources; later shown to be his own work. To nineteenth-century scholars this invalidated the work although Gaelic tradition had always been a living one, in which old sources were taken up and re-worked.

What version O'Mahony recited to young Arthur is unknown. It had a powerful effect on the child's imagination. Excited by the flavour of an older, heroic world, Arthur was also curious. He began to read history for himself and discovered a tale of cruelty, plunder and oppression by the Protestants. He was shocked. The prejudice against Catholics which he had absorbed in his family was dissipated and a real horror of such prejudice entered his heart. Instead he felt bitterly sorry that his own countrymen should have been degraded 'by slavery and ignorance, superstition and bigotry'.

Taught by his mother to use his reason, he 'read the best histories nearly all by Protestants and of the prejudices of Englishmen, yet even in those I acquired the conviction that the system by which England had constantly governed Ireland had been unjust, tyrannical and as impolitic in the interest of England as ruinous for Ireland.'[7] It seemed to Arthur, sharp-witted and with the clarity of innocence, that England's rule in Ireland was stupid. What good did it do England to break Ireland's spirit? He was a proud Irish boy and prejudice against his country nettled him.

Not that he approved the Papal religion. He had been taught to think for himself, approach God directly, to be the guardian of his own conscience. For Arthur, the obedience of thought as well as action required by Roman Catholicism was the death of mental liberty. He would spend the best years of his life fighting for the political rights of Catholics. He would never accept their state of mind.

Arthur O'Connor, child and man, believed in liberty of the mind as much as liberty of the person.

O'Mahony and his manuscripts had a great influence on young O'Connor. Appolos Morris had a more obvious and immediate one. 'My education of the heart I received from my mother and from Major Morris.' Appolos was the descendant of a Cromwellian soldier from Shropshire. There were Quakers in his family. They were successful merchants with several properties in Cork.[8] Morris was a family friend, a soldier in the British army and a good one. 'In his time the discipline of the regiment was the office of the Major, the higher officers were the creature of political interest, Morris's regiment was esteemed the best disciplined in the British service.'[9] But further promotion depended on connections which Morris lacked. He left the British army.

If Arthur had been his own son, Appolos Morris could not have put more care and effort into his education. A graduate of Trinity, he was a clear-headed man, unhampered by prejudice. Morris repeated to the growing boy that he should concentrate on the laws of nature for those were certainties. Newtonian science had made a great impact on eighteenth-century thought. Science was both exciting and useful. Morris was a Christian because he saw the laws of nature as the way God directed the Universe. For him, Christ's teaching coincided. Arthur thought him wonderful – noble, liberal and generous. The soldier was kind and forgave the faults of others, except lying which Appolos Morris would not tolerate. A guest of Roger Conner's was much given to telling extravagant tales. Morris said to Arthur 'what esteem can I have for a man on whose word I can have no reliance? If I had the misfortune to detect you in a lie it would be impossible for me to love or esteem you.'[10] This made a deep impact on the boy. The thought that he could lose the affection of this fine man, whose love and attention meant so much, alarmed him. His mother had taught him contempt for lying, Appolos Morris completed the lesson.

Busy with his studies, the classics, mathematics, history, the modern sciences, Arthur had not forgotten O'Mahony and the tales. Despite Cromwell's Act of Settlement, many Gaelic families populated their once tribal lands. O'Callaghan, McCarthy and O'Brien were common names in Munster. Some family heads retained their position. Arthur O'Connor was interested in history. He also had a taste for poetry and wrote verse, although later Major Morris and his parents discouraged it. Gaelic verse history and stories of his ancestry had stirred him. He met a man who embodied them.

'I remember in my youth the first interview between Charles O'Conor and my father, it was at a dinner given by a common friend to bring them to an acquaintance.' Charles O'Conor of Belenagare was the descendant of Roderic O'Connor the last High King of Ireland.[11] Charles was the acknowledged O'Conor Don, head of the O'Conor Connaught sept, a learned and thoughtful man, author of *Dissertations on the History of Ireland*.[12] He was a scholar of the classics, as well as of Irish and English. Like most of the O'Connors he had remained Roman Catholic. Though he was a man of standing, like all his co-religionists he was subject to the penal laws. His situation was very different from the freedom and opulence of Roger's. 'At this meeting they regarded each other like two brothers who had met after a storm which separates them in a shipwreck, Charles broke the silence by feliciting my father on his having obtained an affluence after the ruin of their house.'[13] The evening went well and the two men treated each other openly and with affection.

Arthur, much impressed by seeing this man, the living descendant of the O'Conor warriors and a scholar in his own right, had approached, taken Charles O'Conor's hand and put it to his lips. The old man was 'much affected' by this gesture from a boy, embraced Arthur and asked what he had studied. The youngster gave the names of the Irish histories he had read, including O'Conor's own *Dissertations* and Dr Curry's review of the civil war. Charles O'Conor 'turned to my father and said, "you have given us a fine boy to aid us in rescuing our wretched country from its oppressors. Nature has done its part, it is you will have to do the rest"'.[14]

'Charles O'Conor was the head of the papist population of Ireland, he represented the Regal Irish State which all his religionists so ardently wished to see reinstated in the place of the English intruders.' Arthur never could understand how a man of Charles

O'Conor's intellect could have accepted the dogmas of Rome. Much later, he conjectured that O'Conor's family position explained this. He was head of the leading Gaelic sept and could not abandon their religion. Arthur also supposed that once a religion had been persecuted, no man who called himself a man could desert it for fear that others would brand him coward and say he had converted for personal advantage. He had a deep respect for Charles O'Connor and for the position he upheld with such dignity.[15]

In 1765, when Arthur was twelve and George III was on the throne, conflict began in America. The colonists were demanding the full rights of Englishmen. Early the following year, in 1776, a pamphlet entitled *Common Sense* was published in America, written by Thomas Paine, the son of a Quaker from Norfolk. On O'Connor's thirteenth birthday, the American Declaration of Independence was published. The British army fought in the Atlantic and along the eastern seaboard of America. Early in 1778 France made a treaty with America and entered the war. Fighting was on both sides of the Atlantic, spread into the colonies of the Caribbean. It was not over until 1783. During that time, the colonists teased out modern ideas on how they should be governed; this set minds alight elsewhere.

When the war broke out, Arthur O'Connor was at boarding school at Castle Lyons. Appolos Morris, like the famous French General, Lafayette, went to fight under Washington. 'No taxation without representation' struck a cord in Ireland. The Irish, like the Americans, expected the rights and freedoms of the British constitution. Often loyal to the monarch, they expected George III to guarantee those rights. That was why the Hanoverians had been granted the throne. Despite appeals to King George, the Americans received no support in their contest with the British government.

Morris had an independent fortune in lands in Ireland which he would not jeopardise, so he concealed his service with Washington, using a feigned name. Even so, he was arrested on his return to Ireland. There was no proof against him and he was freed. He had property at Clonkeen, but he was unmarried and took up residence with his old friend, Roger Conner. He particularly asked to oversee Arthur's education.

Ireland was defended by Volunteers. The British army was stretched to its limits in the American war. Ireland was unprotected from French invasion. Spontaneously, the leading citizens raised a Volunteer army. Starting in the north, soon there were Volunteer companies throughout the country. Under a statute of William and Mary, citizens could arm to defend their property. Catholics were forbidden arms under the penal laws. It was therefore an army for defence of the property of the protestant nation. But the Volunteers had a profound effect. They proved that Irishmen had the rights of the Glorious Revolution of 1688 and they were visible proof that Ireland was a nation. As a result, they received money from Catholics and exerted pressure for constitutional change. The Lord Lieutenant was nervous but knew he could not disarm them.

The American war raised questions of loyalty, both in Britain and Ireland. Irish families, both Catholic and Protestant, had young men fighting in British regiments. Leading citizens questioned the London government's position. A medical student from Belfast, William Drennan, studying in Edinburgh, wrote to his sister Martha, 'it is probable that future historians will date the fall of the British Empire from the 16th October 1777'[16] (the defeat at Saratoga). Yet, the war dragged on.

At the school in Castle Lyons, the boys took sides. In general they followed the principles of their parents. Arthur O'Connor knew where he stood. After reading Irish history, horrified by English oppression and with the example of Major Morris foremost, O'Connor had 'imbibed republican ideas, was a decided American'. The majority supported England. Young Arthur, his teenage mind excited by ideas of freedom, was combative. 'I was on the Republican side, we were in minority but having more energy we kept the upper hand.'[17]

Morris had formed a Volunteer company from Roger Conner's tenantry. At home from school, Arthur trained with them. 'Nothing could exceed the rapidity and exactness of our movements.' Morris taught him military skills and mathematics, important for calculating territory, explosives, logistics and rations. He learnt to assess by eye the space a thousand men would occupy in line three deep. Morris would mark it out with a chain to correct him. O'Connor's eye grew more exact. By extending the space for larger bodies he could fix the space for a whole army. 'During the time we were engaged in these exercises there was not a military position round Connerville we had not made an object of my instruction.'[18]

Arthur O'Connor had a strong constitution. Morris could see he was growing into a tall, well-made man. Arthur was already adept at swimming, riding and hunting. He found the military training exciting and now understood the Major's concentration on mathematics. They calculated every detail, plotted strategy. Seeing its practical application, O'Connor's respect for science increased.

Later, O'Connor described the American Revolution as 'the greatest epoch that has happened from the fall of Liberty in Greece and Rome.'[19] Although the Volunteers sprang into being to defend Ireland against Britain's enemies, they quickly became the guarantors of Ireland's rights. Arthur O'Connor experienced Republicanism and Volunteers together. If there were underlying contradictions, he did not see them. He was heart first into liberty, patriotism and military athletics.

Appolos Morris was a paternal influence on the boy. His uncle, Richard Longfield took a warm interest. Longfield was MP for Charleville and spent much of his time in Dublin. He would later become Lord Longueville. One of the leading landowners in east Cork, he was cautiously advancing his position in the county. This depended on patronage. Paid positions were awarded by the Dublin administration. Parliamentary seats could be bought; ownership was power. Like every landowner, he was concerned for the security of his property. With no sons of his own, Longfield was attentive to his sister's, especially Arthur.

Of his brothers, Roger was closest to Arthur in age and outlook. He could have 'risen high in science'[20] but was too volatile. Arthur thought him the most talented of the brothers. They shared many interests. Daniel, the eldest, was nine years older than Arthur and went away to University at Oxford with a large allowance. There, according to Arthur, he learnt to live like an English aristocrat but was not prepared for life in Ireland. The second son, William, was left a considerable fortune by his grandfather and namesake; he took no more thought of a profession. William was mild tempered, never ruffled, utterly unlike the younger boys. Robert was destined for business in the West Indies but broke his hip just as he was due to depart, stayed in west Cork and became a country squire.[21]

Margaret, the only daughter to have survived childhood, had been carefully educated by their mother. 'Never was nature more lavish than in her bounty to this angel sister.' But 'at the age of eighteen in all her youth and beauty, we lost her.'[22] Arthur was twelve. Margaret had gone to an out farm visiting some pet lambs. To return home she had to pass a mountain stream which had swollen between the time of her going out and returning. Her foot slipped, she fell, was swept into deep water and drowned. Arthur had loved his sister and was utterly grief-stricken. Her image haunted him. He would get up at night and go to the gloomy, solitary spot where she had drowned. The river ran through bog, dark peaty water seeped out and coloured the river giving it an even more forbidding hue. 'Here did I pass night after night inviting my adored sister to come and speak to me.'[23]

It must have been a shocking blow for Anne Conner. Her five sons were vigorous but she had lost all her daughters. This accomplished woman now had no female companion in the family. Connerville rang with the footsteps of young men. Outside, companies of Volunteers put on their uniforms of Irish cloth and drilled loudly, clattering their weapons.

Anne Conner's views on politics are not recorded but her ideas on religion were clear. Arthur learnt them.

> I was made to understand that for religion to be true it must coincide in every jot and part with all God's attributes and with his code of laws which are called the laws of nature. Of all the laws of God, the most important for mankind is that which forces him to receive the impressions which objects make upon his senses. Christ has taken special care that it is to God only he shall give an account of the impressions objects have made, in nothing is he more positive than that all man's moral and religious accounts should be between him and his God.[24]

Arthur would never comprehend how people could abandon their reason to the dictates of a priesthood. Only coercion like the Inquisition or temptation like the wealth of the Papacy might explain it. Science insisted on empirical observation. So did the new philosophy. Knowledge was acquired honestly through the senses, and by rational thought. The superstitions of the medieval world were contemptible to him.

With these liberal, empirical, republican and Deist ideas forming in his mind, in June 1779 and just before his sixteenth birthday, he set off for the College of Dublin.

Chapter 4

STIMULATING IDEAS

The College of the Holy and Undivided Trinity of Queen Elizabeth, near Dublin, first admitted students in 1593. Like the University of Oxford, Trinity College was to provide educated men for the clergy and as teachers so that the sons of the gentry might increase in learning. Under the 'care and bounty' of Elizabeth, the University of Dublin would provide scholars versed in Irish but educated in the Reformed Faith. The College was built on the site of a ruined monastery near the mediaeval city of Dublin which clustered round the Castle.[1] It grew, was supported by the monarch and after Cromwell, was endowed with grants of confiscated land.

Near Dublin in Elizabeth's reign, by the time that Arthur O'Connor arrived at the university in 1779 it was at the heart of Georgian Dublin. The western gate of Trinity opened out to College Green and was directly opposite the Parliament House, an elegant and impressive building begun in 1729 and once completed, finer than that in Westminster. In the Parliament House the Lords and Commons of Ireland exercised their wit and struggled for the interests of the kingdom and for their own ascendancy. To the south the wide streets and large squares were lined by newly-built houses with dimensions based on the golden mean. Light fell from long windows and curved fanlights into elegant rooms.

Trinity College was intellectually lively. Students from a variety of backgrounds, the sons of landed nobles and businessmen, gave it a breezy air. The university trained men for the ministry of the Established Church and was the intellectual focus of the second city of the Empire. The library had received important gifts. There was a laboratory and an anatomical theatre for tuition in the sciences. Trinity was solvent. 'The cheapness of its education, and the prevailing distaste for industrial life which induced crowds of poor gentry to send their sons to the university, when they would have done far better to send them to the counter, contributed to support it',[2] wrote the historian Lecky in the nineteenth-century. Arthur O'Connor arrived in a city of new buildings and modern ideas.

Now just sixteen, the boy 'never was more isolated than I was in the midst of the capital'. The only person he knew in Dublin was his uncle, Richard Longfield who had a house at 11 Fitzwilliam Street Lower but was not then in town.

> This state formed a great contrast with the paternal house where I took a lively interest in such numbers and where such numbers took so great an interest in me. I shall never forget going from the college up Grafton Street the first day of my arrival, where I saw a brood mare with its coalt, the little animal had been separated by some carriage from its dam which made it neigh most bitterly. Methought I was like this little foal crying for its mother. It went to my heart. I felt I was separated from all I loved.[3]

O'Connor was a precocious and serious student. He had read *The Wealth of Nations* by Adam Smith before he went to college and was so impressed by 'economical science', its lucid exposition by Smith, that he returned to it again and again, determined to master all it contained.

New ideas were developing in northern Europe. Vital contributions were made by the universities of the British Isles. For the new philosophers, the individual was the beginning and judge of all knowledge. It was a heady concept. The Revolution of 1688 had proved to the British that their constitutional rights could be maintained without dogma or bloodshed. Parliament had inalienable rights, even regarding the monarch. The terms of the succession had been set by the representatives of the people. This became an important part of O'Connor's political ideas. With a firm constitution, property was secure, commerce expanding and science offering enormous possibilities. The merchants, as well as the intellectuals of Britain and Ireland were in confident mood.

The Enlightenment was the expression of that confidence, of a belief in reason. It was a time of scientific progress based on prosperity. It was both practical and philosophical. In France, Descartes developed important new methods in mathematics and philosophy. In the British Isles, Locke, Berkeley and Hume developed a philosophy of empirical knowledge, drawn from the senses. Locke wrote convincingly on the terms of the social contract. In particular, the intellectual advances in Scotland were important for O'Connor. Adam Smith shaped his adult thought. David Hume was frequently discussed by his contemporaries. The Scottish Enlightenment was the philosophical basis from which the United Irishmen would grow. O'Connor read this philosophy as a schoolboy.

At Trinity he studied for the degree of Bachelor of Arts. He read the classics in the original and in English translation. He learnt the speeches of Demosthenes and Cicero by heart. He read and memorised the work of Milton, of Shakespeare and the English poets.[4] The cadence of the language moved him. His ear became tuned to the patterns of political oratory. He was being educated for public speaking. Many students crossed College Green to represent constituencies in the parliament.

O'Connor learnt science, with the exception of political economy, in his view the most useful but not taught at Trinity. 'Of all the college courses the science of Astronomy pleased me most. The grandeur and the vast expansion it gave my ideas rescued me from all those blasphemous atheistical grovelling notions on which imposture has founded superstition and idolatry. As I advanced in the knowledge of the milliards and milliards of Worlds that filled the skies which made me imagine it was more to be believed the Universe was Infinite; than that it could be bounded.'[5]

O'Connor was a Fellow Commoner at Trinity. He was entered as a pensioner[6] but his status changed. He took his degree in three years. The young men had rooms in College and took their meals in the dining room. The Fellow Commoners were a small group with privileges, paying higher fees than the Pensioners. Noblemen paid a great deal more and wore splendid gowns. The sizars paid no fees at all, wore plain gowns and did menial duties to pay for their tuition. O'Connor disliked the social ranking at Trinity, so clearly displayed by the different gowns and privileges.

> I had not been long at college when I was remarked for my Republican principles, a trivial circumstance was remarked. As Fellow Commoner I dined with the Fellows whose table is served by the sizars in the capacity of waiters, my feelings were hurt at seeing students on a level with the best of us for education and often our superiors in science reduced to endure such humiliation. Instead of suffering a Sizar to take my plate I instantly rose and placed it on the side board. This little act of republican equality did not draw on me any censure from the Fellows for it was before the French revolution.[7]

The provost of Trinity was John Hely-Hutchinson, a liberal-minded politician from the government benches who was committed to Catholic emancipation. Hely-Hutchinson had introduced dancing, fencing, riding and language classes to prepare the young gentlemen for adult life. The syllabus included classics, mathematics and philosophy, as well as Newtonian science then quite new. Examinations were oral, public and in Latin, as they had been at Oxford for centuries. The atmosphere was competitive and trained the young men for public office, whether as clergymen, teachers or politicians.

The students had free ingress to the parliament building where many of them listened to debates with keen attention. It was a highly charged moment in Irish politics. 'Few senates ever possessed more genuine eloquence than the Irish Commons especially at the epoch when I began to frequent it, for the great vital questions of National Liberty which were agitated, served to diminish the damaging effects of the corruption which pervaded this assembly more than any national representation that ever has existed.'[8] It was indeed shockingly corrupt, even by the standards of the day. Power was owned by a tiny minority of the population, free to indulge their designs on offices, pensions and preferments. Eloquence was highly valued. Since the Middle Ages, parliaments had been called in Ireland, making it one of the oldest parliamentary democracies. They became regular only in the reign of Anne.[9] In one century the Irish legislature had established effective systems and traditions. Now, in 1780, the Irish parliament was determined to gain legislative independence from Britain.

Henry Grattan entered parliament in 1775, where his eloquence quickly brought him the leadership of the patriot Opposition. Curious adjustments had been and were frequently made to try to solve the constitutional problem of Ireland. The Lord Lieutenant was now resident in Dublin Castle, previously absentee. His role as head of the Executive was thus firmly established. Appointed by the 'British Minister',[10] the Irish parliament had no power to dismiss him. However, the Lord Lieutenant had uncertain support in the Commons where allegiances constantly shifted. The House was made up of members for boroughs and for county seats. Most of the former were bought and sold, many were rotten. Government in the Castle could usually rely on place-holders, while the Opposition was firmly patriotic, but the country gentlemen might go either way. Elections were stormy affairs. The county seats were genuinely contested but only men with 40 shilling freeholds could vote. The great landlords tended to march down to the elections, their tenants following to vote as the owner decided, as if he were chief of a clan and the election a tribal ritual. Catholics could neither vote nor stand for election. Presbyterians, although not repressed by Penal Law, were barred from public office by the Test Act of 1704 which insisted that office holders should celebrate the sacraments according to the Established Church. But as O'Connor arrived in Dublin, all that began to change.

Britain was fighting the American colonists and France. The Volunteers, now a strident patriot force, made demonstrations for free trade. The British government was pressed militarily and financially. The Anglo-Irish Ascendancy now identified themselves as wholly Irish. They had a great deal in common with the English Whigs except that there was far greater social mobility among the Anglo-Irish. For a member of the Established Church in eighteenth-century Ireland, great opportunities were available.

The Catholic Relief Act of 1778 removed landowning

restrictions from the Roman Catholics. In 1780 the Test Act was repealed which let the Presbyterians into local corporations and parliament. In 1779 Henry Grattan achieved a great success when restrictions on Irish trade were removed. O'Connor, fired up with the ideas of Adam Smith on free trade, the use of capital and economic growth, was a student in the public gallery, eagerly following the debate.

Dublin was a city of fast growth and shocking contrasts. Students at Trinity lived with the banging of builders and construction site mud, as new additions were made. The Georgian mansions were still under construction. A short distance from Trinity were the Castle and old medieval streets. Nearby were the Liberties, an area of weavers, small shopkeepers, industry, prostitutes and beggars where the buildings were rotten, theft common and the stench of slaughterhouses and distilleries foul. Behind the Parliament House was the River Liffey where ships unloaded; a constant reminder of the trading potential of Ireland. If only the nation had full control of her affairs, what a prosperous, influential country she might be.

In 1780 Grattan and the Opposition began pressing for full legislative independence for Ireland. The Kingdom had a mature parliament. They intended to use it fully. No longer would they tolerate laws being initiated for them in London, nor passed through the British parliament. The Privy Council was not to suppress Irish bills. They would send their bills direct to the monarch for his assent. The Borough-monger party would benefit; 'in making the Legislature of Ireland sole law maker for her, the property of the Irish borough monger was made more valuable.'[11] The owners of the boroughs would also become vital to the British Minister, only through them could he initiate Irish legislation. With the almost unanimous support of the Irish parliament, the Opposition pushed the bill through. A Volunteer Convention at Dungannon lent military support to the measure. The Whigs were in government in London and they acquiesced. In 1782 an Act granting Ireland the right to make her own laws was passed. O'Connor was impressed. He noted the effect of the armed Volunteers on the argument, the eloquence in the Parliament House and the persuasive, unswerving dedication of men such as

Grattan to Ireland's interests. 'I found Ireland on her knees,' Grattan said. 'I watched over her with an eternal solicitude; I have traced her progress from injuries to arms, and from arms to liberty ... Ireland is now a nation. In that new character I hail her, and bowing to her august presence I say "*Esto perpetua*."'[12]

The press and pamphlets were vital. Skill in political debate was matched by the potency of the pamphlets run off by booksellers and publishers. Cities had influential newspapers. Those who could not read might hear articles read out in the ale or coffee houses where they were debated by the assembled company. Ideas, often complex concepts of constitution and governance, were couched in a language emotional and poetic. Like Shakespeare, the pamphleteers had a mixed audience and had to appeal to all. O'Connor began to submit anonymous articles, directed against the corruption of parliament, to the Opposition journals and had the satisfaction of reading complaints against his work in the government owned public prints.[13]

'The parliamentary debates, the theatres, the public newspapers were so many hotbeds to one endowed by nature with such a vigorous frame of mind and body as I possessed.'[14]

He had been at College for two years when he attended the assizes of Cork 'where all the Country gentlemen assembled for their jobs and peculations and where hundreds of the handsomest women in the world filled the ballrooms with their charms.' Henry Boyle, now Lord Shannon was the great Borough-monger, monopolised the nomination to several boroughs and received all the government patronage of County Cork. Arthur O'Connor watched as the local gentry fawned on Lord Shannon, hoping for local offices with the attached salaries. Among them was his own uncle Richard Longfield who owned important estates at Cloyne and Mallow, as well as Lord Kingsborough, a man of equal if not greater property. O'Connor was inflamed. How could these men of fortune display this 'vile servitude'? He wrote an article calling on these gentlemen to stop their fawning and come forward in defence of the liberty of their country by placing themselves at the head of the liberal men of the county. He took it to the box of the local journal at midnight. The following day, at the Merchant's Coffee House it was the cause of great agitation. At breakfast with Richard Longfield at his lodgings, the discussion was all of the article. The youth was not discovered as author, and the country gentlemen were not brought to expressions of liberty. But Arthur O'Connor's first shot had been fired.[15]

He left Trinity in 1782 with the degree of Bachelor of Arts.

At the moment I was leaving college I was to encounter the greatest misfortune that could befall me, I lost my adored mother. The first information I received was that she was in imminent danger. I set off from Dublin, without stopping night or day until I reached Kinsale where I arrived just time enough to press her to my heart. I found her in the plentitude of her reason but so weak that she felt she was at the point of death, her last words were 'I have neither the strength nor the time to give you advice, my last words are remember and practice the principle I have taught you.' It seemed to me as if she had struggled against death to be able to utter these last words, for she instantly after closed her eyes and sank to death. I felt as if the reason which had hitherto supported me had failed me. The thought that she is the companion of my life has supported me throughout all its events and often have I dreamt she gave me advice in my most trying moments.[16]

Roger Conner did not try to keep up life at Connerville without his wife. He was 54 years of age and had led a self-indulgent life. He began to divide his property among his sons. Arthur was not of age when he was put in possession of a considerable fortune. Among Roger's bequests was an advowson, the right to nominate a clergyman to a living. Arthur might have taken orders and had a secure profession but his ideas on Christianity were too 'simple and sublime' for the Established Church in Ireland. He considered it aristocratical and opulent. He sold the advowson. He also became the owner of land, of a forest of fine timber, of large flocks of sheep and herds of horned cattle.[17]

Neither did O'Connor mean to be a British soldier when England dominated his country and had a standing army there. So he settled on the law. Eager to see England, he arranged his affairs so that he could 'eat his commons', and study law at Lincoln's Inn in London. He was far more interested in England than in being a lawyer; 'supporting right and wrong indiscriminately and for money was never to my taste.'[18]

Appolos Morris died in 1783 and left Arthur Conner a legacy of £100.[19] Without his mother and Major Morris, he had lost his two strongest influences within one year. He left Ireland soon afterwards to study and travel.

England made a strong impression. At that time, the country was more highly developed than any other in Europe. The land was well farmed, the towns bustling. To O'Connor's astonishment, everything was the opposite of what he had left behind; 'cleanliness for filth, order and neatness in the appearance of the country for disorder and slovenliness, comfort and abundance for misery and wretchedness; but what was the most striking contrast was the religious respect for the law and its total absence in Ireland, where men were as strongly given to violate it as the English were to observe it.' O'Connor saw how centuries of oppression had curbed and crippled Ireland. 'It is in the pride which the possession of liberty creates that England is superior to Ireland, for in Ireland the heart fails and the soul sickens for want of the recompence of industry.'[20]

Adam Smith had influenced O'Connor profoundly. *The Wealth of Nations* explained the dynamics of a national economy in scientific terms. Smith identified industry, capital, trade and growth, efficiency in production and increased wealth. If any country needed advice on economical science, it was Ireland. It seemed to O'Connor that only he had read the seminal work.

'It was not that England was superior in fertility or in harbours, in navigable rivers or in the beauty of her women nor the courage, vigour or intelligence of their men ... it is in the pride which the possession of liberty creates',[21] he noted. He judged England on the principles of Smith. Obviously, class interest still undermined productivity at the expense of the mass of the people but that, he supposed, was an error that would continue for a long time.

Once in London, in lodgings, and enrolled at Lincoln's Inn he applied himself to study. The principles of law interested him. He read Montesquieu's *The Spirit of the Law* and was impressed by his ideas on checks and balances, but O'Connor thought Montesquieu should have studied political economy. He read and re-read Blackstone. He frequented the King's Bench and watched the Judge focus the process so that the case became clear. O'Connor studied the doctrine of evidence carefully, how to present it so that truth is revealed. 'But the Old Bailey was the theatre of all my experiments, after two years study there, I could form an almost unerring opinion of the testimony of a witness, of its truth or falsehood. This has been the greatest use to me through life.'[22]

In London, he could watch political debate. Pitt's first Reform Bill had just failed. George III, raised in England unlike his father and grandfather, seemed keen to regain lost powers for the monarchy. The Whig noblemen and merchants had not put the Hanoverians on the throne only to find them stealing back parliamentary power. George III was young when he came to the throne; his mother's friend Bute was said to have greatly influenced him. Now, Jenkinson had the King's ear. It was the talk of the town. George III was not a clever man, but he was able to grasp main points and was very assiduous in what he believed to be his duty. He had the dogged mentality of a country squire, loved livestock and was known by his English subjects as Farmer George.

In contrast, the intelligentsia among his subjects were reading and debating the ideas of the Enlightenment. With religious wars over, with the Greek and Roman classics widely studied and with wild economic growth from Atlantic and Asian trade, thinkers in Britain, France, Holland and Germany addressed great questions: What is matter and what laws govern it? What is human knowledge? What are the proper laws of reason and logic, how is this expressed in mathematics? What is God and how do we recognise God in matter? What certain knowledge does man have? How should man be governed and who owns power? How can such knowledge be put to practical use? Ideas of democracy and the development of modern science inevitably followed.

While O'Connor studied law, met his Irish friends to enjoy the theatres or frequent the coffee houses, while he became familiar with London, war still raged in America. A speech of Pitt the elder, Lord Chatham made a great impression on O'Connor. It was delivered after the defeat at Saratoga but was still in print when

O'Connor got to London. Negotiations, sooner or later would have to be entered into. Chatham had told the house,

> You have been the aggressors from the beginning. You ought therefore to make the first overture. I say again my Lords you have been the aggressors, you have made descents upon their coasts, you have burnt their towns, plundered their country, made war upon the inhabitants, confiscated their property, proscribed and imprisoned their persons, you have injured, oppressed and endeavoured to enslave them; America is therefore entitled to redress. Let then reparation come from the hand that has inflicted the injuries.[23]

It was too late; the colonists had outgrown reconciliation. In 1783 a peace treaty was signed and Britain recognised the United States of America as an independent nation. George III was inconsolable.

Britain also concluded a treaty with France. Travel was possible and in 1784 O'Connor, with two Anglo-Irish friends, set out to visit France. Standish O'Grady and John Waller of Castle Waller, were two 'most amiable and honourable men' who also came from Munster. They crossed the Channel in a smack crewed by a man and boy, landed at Dieppe and spent a few days at Rouen. France was as different from England as Ireland was. The three young men went by post to Paris, 'where we entered with a clatter, descending the Champs d'Eleyes full gallop with cracking of whips of our Avant Courier and postilion and the neighing of seven Nerman stallions including those our servants rode.' The *ancien régime* was tottering. O'Connor was struck by the clear divide between the nobility who paid no taxes and seemed above the law, and the people who were splattered and charged by their horses on the streets.

Britain had experienced two revolutions, that of the 1640s and that of 1688. In France, the monarch was absolute, the source of law, head of the administration and grantor of all offices. The King was consecrated by the Roman Catholic church, the clergy were powerful and rich. The feudalism which England learnt from the Normans and had outgrown, lived on in France. It was the intellectuals who challenged the old order. 'France at this time contained a great number of men who devoted themselves to the study of sciences which had been greatly encouraged by the establishment of the Encyclopedia',[24] which was being compiled by Diderot and d'Alembert of the Academie de Science.

O'Connor, O'Grady and Waller went on to Dijon, to pass the year in perfecting their French, as well as fencing and dancing. They travelled in a large, heavy wagon, laden with luggage fore and aft with enclosed seats between. O'Connor thought it barbarous, vehicles in England were of a much more modern design. 'I was forcibly struck with the inferiority of the state of culture during all my journey compared with what I had seen in England, it approached nearer the disorder and slovenliness of Ireland.' Cattle grazed on the verges, sheep seemed to have neither grazing nor roots for feed, grass was not managed, there was no means of getting manure on to the fields, wheat and oats were very inferior to the same crops in England, probably poorer than in Ireland and the people in the countryside looked ill clad and ill fed.[25]

On the journey they met a Dutch businessman of republican principles who saw a great deal of Europe, 'he said he could estimate the liberty, morality and ease of every nation by the degree of influence the Papal priesthood exercised over the public mind, he began with Rome where the seat of all the evil lay, here in the finest country in the world he saw the lands uncultivated, the people sunk in idleness, superstition, ignorance and misery.' The Dutchman explained the excessive power of King and clergy, but said that increase in commerce and education, as well as the American Revolution, were changing the public mind of France.

Dijon was cheaper than London. The Irishmen took lodgings, applied themselves to their studies and to the amusements of Dijon. A few months later, Waller and O'Connor made an excursion to Switzerland. On the journey, O'Connor was astonished to see two monks leave the coach with two prostitutes. The conducteur said 'oh but you are young, you will see ...' In a jewellers, Waller was offered an inlaid box with a hidden picture of a Bishop and a woman in a shocking position. He refused it. They crossed the lake and travelled up into the mountains. O'Connor loved Switzerland, a true republic where despite poor land, the industry of the people created income all their own, bought them comforts. 'Here for the first time I saw the fruits of Equality. Every citizen possessed the consciousness he was a free and independent man.' Switzerland had no import tax on foreign goods: 'the nations which adopt this liberal economical principle are those whose industry is most profitable and that has fewer beggars.'[26]

They rejoined O'Grady in Dijon where Waller returned to his studies, while O'Connor and O'Grady set out for London. O'Connor's agent in Ireland had £3,000 in hand but failed to get it to the bank in Paris. An Irishman stopped O'Connor in the park in Paris. He said he had French Louis d'Or he wanted to exchange for English money, that he knew O'Connor's family in Ireland, that O'Connor should accept the French money without giving a receipt and pay him in English coin when he came home. O'Connor was astonished and delighted. The 30 Louis d'Or just paid their lodgings and got them safely to London.

Back in England, the Whigs were out. Charles James Fox, their leader, was one of the powerful Holland family and cousin of the great Irish FitzGeralds. The Fox-North coalition had presided over American independence and Irish legislative freedom. George III was delighted to dismiss them. William Pitt, son of Lord Chatham, had become British Minister. In the Commons, two Irishmen made a lasting impression. Both would later befriend Arthur O'Connor. Edmund Burke was a man of great intellect, friend of Fox, champion of Ireland and adversary of Thomas Paine. Richard Brinsley Sheridan, playwright and theatre owner, was a magnificent orator and Mr Fox's close associate. The British House of Commons rang with the speeches of these men: on the administration of India, on Ireland, on trade, and, underlying all, the defining of the Constitution.

The rights and duties conferred by that constitution affected the making of law, the terms of trade, the income of public servants, the holding of land, the distribution of wealth, down to the potatoes eaten in the cabins of Connemara. The American colonies were lost but the battle for the British Constitution had once more been joined.

Arthur O'Connor did not linger in London but set out for Holyhead and took the boat to Ireland.

Chapter 5

HIGH SHERIFF OF CORK

By his early twenties, Arthur O'Connor had grown tall and strong boned. He stood well and moved with the physical confidence of a man who rode and swam naturally. Red shone in his curly brown hair. His high cheek-bones, oval face and straight pointed nose were in proportion. His hazel eyes were arresting; they had an intense, piercing gaze. There was a hint of humour in the face but it could be watchful, brooding. He dressed carefully in the style of London where he often bought his clothes, had his hats made.

In Dublin he saw a great deal of his uncle Richard Longfield. Arthur's father had made Connerville over to his eldest son, Daniel, and lived there with him. Old Roger was never an influence on Arthur. Since the loss of his mother, Arthur had no female guidance and Morris was also dead. His childhood had been severed. There was no one to confide in but his brothers and his uncle. His brother Roger had coincided with Arthur at Trinity and had been called to the Irish Bar in 1783. Roger had now formally changed his name from Conner to O'Connor.

On returning to Ireland from London, Daniel became intimately involved with a married woman, Mrs Gibbons.[1] The affair became known and a scandal ensued. The couple ran away together, the injured husband sued and a prosecution followed. Daniel had to pay heavy damages. He married Mrs Gibbons and they settled near London, at Orme Square, Bayswater. They had one daughter. After a time, Roger married Louisa Anna Strachan[2] and Daniel sold him Connerville. Louisa gave birth to a son and a daughter. This family, with old Roger, filled the rambling mansion at Ballineen.

Without his mother's presence, it was no longer a family home to Arthur. He turned to his uncle, who became his mentor. Active in politics, Richard Longfield was cautious by nature, loyal to the King and generally supported the government with an eye to the landed Irish interest. In that respect he considered himself a patriot. He advanced gradually in prominence in County Cork. He was now head of the Longfield family and proprietor of large estates, while his wife had brought property in Bantry to their marriage.[3] Arthur was able, and would do well in politics. Longfield was grooming him as his heir.

Despite Arthur's precocious article which criticised Longfield's fawning on Lord Shannon, Richard knew better than his nephew how business was done. He saw his job as the maintenance of firm government under a Protestant dispensation and the security of his own property. As he acquired patronage, he awarded offices to his associates. His nephew noticed that, despite good salaries, his uncle did not keep all the positions himself. Longfield had served as High Sheriff for County Cork in 1758 and had a borough seat in the Commons but was aiming to become MP for the city of Cork.[4] The second city of the kingdom was an expanding international port. The merchant princes of Cork city were exporting fine produce, especially smoked foods which remained wholesome during the trans-Atlantic crossing.[5] These merchants were the men who Longfield hoped to represent.

Arthur O'Connor recognised this dogged sense of responsibility in his uncle and approved it. He was fond of his mother's brother, for her sake and for the kind attention the older man bestowed, but O'Connor was slightly in awe of Longfield's aloof and unquestioning paternalism. He did not argue, confront or challenge his uncle's views. But as he gained confidence and spent more time with Longfield and his associates, he gave himself the freedom to express his own views on equality and commerce, patriotism and liberal economics, though he would speak steadily and argue out his points. He did not play the angry young man with uncle Longfield.

On 3 May 1785, 'Arthur Conner, fifth son of Roger Conner of Connerville' was admitted to the degree of Barrister at Law in the

Kingdom of Ireland, at the King's Inns in Dublin.[6] He went back to London to complete his training and on 23 May he was entered at Lincoln's Inn.

Ireland by now had gained the right to trade freely throughout the British Empire. In the House of Commons, Mr Pitt put forward Commercial Propositions to regulate the trade between Britain and Ireland. This new measure was to clarify the terms between the two kingdoms. Ireland and England did not manufacture on equal terms, England was more developed. But free trade was a vital principle and the Propositions would remove duties, or equalise them. They had to pass parliament in Dublin and in London. Two principles were at stake in one measure, free trade and the legislative independence of Ireland. Did the Bill guarantee Ireland's right to trade freely or did it infringe on Ireland's new freedom to make her own laws? On College Green, frock coats swung and swayed as gentlemen gave full voice to their views. Grattan supported the measure and it passed. In London, it met formidable resistance. English manufacturers did not study Adam Smith and liberal economics. They believed in monopoly, so strengthening to one's profit margins. They lobbied in London and sent petitions. Burke raised some objections. Most distressing to Arthur O'Connor, Fox opposed the measure as ruinous to English commerce and infringing Ireland's independence. The Bill failed. This was a blow for free trade and for Irish exports and it was a heavy blow to the working relationship between Britain and Ireland. They could agree to share a common monarch. They had agreed who should initiate law. But trade and money were fundamental; the terms between the two islands had not been settled.

Arthur O'Connor wrote an anonymous article on the subject published in a London paper, 'which like a hundred others I had written on Economical principles fell like the leaves in autumn'.[7] Britain had an attraction for O'Connor. It was prosperous, London a fashionable capital and he was a rich young gentleman. In Ireland he was constantly reminded that corruption among the ruling classes and bad governance, imposed or supported from Britain, produced the squalor and poverty which he recoiled from, both in city and countryside. Many of the Irish were dispossessed people in their own land. Where once they had lived in large tribal groups herding cattle on ancestral land, where families had farmed under the franchise of the great man of the locality, now many scraped food for their children by growing potatoes on tiny plots, sub-let without security from men whose language they could not speak. The result inevitably was poverty, poor cabins, children with rags for clothes, handsome women aged before their prime, men without self-respect whose manhood had been stolen. O'Connor, proud by nature and engaged by the possibilities for commerce, found the state of his own country a constant thorn in his side. In Britain, at least he experienced a nation of confidence, prosperity and workable law.

He followed parliamentary debates from the gallery of the House of Commons. Although by temperament he was with Fox and Sheridan, whose eloquence 'was more congenial to my heart, and soul, more frank, more true and honest than Pitt in whose best speeches I could never defend myself from the idea that he sought to deceive',[8] yet O'Connor had to admit that Pitt had studied Economics under Dr Price and it showed. But Pitt had only absorbed the commercial aspect, he forgot the lessons regarding harvesting the resources of the nation through free and liberal policies.

'That Fox, whose mind was so strongly formed in the mathematical rigour of logical precision should have neglected to a great degree this first of sciences is most extraordinary yet we may account for it – from his being the Chief of an hereditary party and he must have found opposition to the pretensions of this party in every principle of Economical Science.'[9]

Primogeniture, feudalism, a society run by aristocrats, a dominant priesthood, all these O'Connor hated. In Greece and Rome, he believed there had been democracy.[10] In Saxon England, the people had voted in their Witenagemot, or early parliament. But democracy had been broken in Europe in medieval times by feudal, Roman Catholic monarchy.[11] Starting from patriotism and the Volunteers, O'Connor had read the current ideas and was now committed to democracy, free trade and equality of succession in families.

Britain was at the heart of a worldwide trade system. Ireland, the sister kingdom, was closely involved. Yet England was wealthy and well farmed, Ireland had areas of appalling poverty and a chaotic cultural system. It was imperative that rulers should understand modern thinking on trade and commerce, capital and labour. O'Connor felt that most of them had not even read the books.

Such modern thinking came from Scotland. Adam Smith studied at Glasgow, taught at Edinburgh where David Hume had been educated. Edinburgh led scientific thinking, produced leading historians and poets. It was also the era of MacPherson and the Celtic revival. Lowland Scotland was peopled by Presbyterians like those who had moved to Ulster under the plantations. These hard-working people had an egalitarian religion and high standards of education. They had built a successful linen industry using the port of Belfast to export. Their children frequently completed their education in Scotland, William Drennan became a doctor in Edinburgh. Their daughters were well-educated and exchanged ideas of politics and philosophy freely with the men.[12] O'Connor had grown up with similar ideals. The ideas of Hume, Smith and Locke were central to his education.

While O'Connor was listening to debates in London, returning to his property in west Cork or visiting Dublin to keep up with his uncle, his friends and the Irish parliament, Theobald Wolfe Tone was gradually arguing his way through Trinity College. Due to a love of adventure, an antipathy to prolonged study, high spirits, romantic engagements and an early marriage, not to mention his uncertain finances, it was 1786 before Wolfe Tone finally obtained his degree although, like O'Connor he was born in 1763. O'Connor matriculated at sixteen and took his degree aged nineteen. Tone dropped out, returned to Trinity aged eighteen and took five years to finish. Later, their paths would bring them to the same high political focus in France in 1796; their temperaments and the roads they travelled were different. O'Connor was intense, scholarly, passionate, impressive and obstinate. Tone was humourous, brilliant, brave, vivacious, mercurial and charming. Two things brought them together, an ungovernable love of Ireland and the awful inevitability of events in Irish political life.

When he returned to Dublin, O'Connor heard from Richard Longfield of Flood's failed Reform Bill and the continual agitation over the position of the Catholics. The Relief Acts of 1778 and 1782 had dismantled most of the Penal laws, Catholics could practice the professions, own land, receive education but they could not vote or sit in parliament. Catholic emancipation and franchise remained as two unresolved and vital issues. The century of penal law had made Catholics fearful. In terror of further land confiscations and repression, the Catholic gentry kept a quiet, if not servile attitude to government. They tended to be monarchical, waiting for a day of deliverance when a Gaelic Catholic king would once more rule Ireland. Arthur O'Connor had lost the prejudice of his family against Catholics and took a protective, paternalistic attitude to the Catholic population although their beliefs and outlook were at obvious variance with the new ideas which inspired him.

Many Irish Catholics had emigrated to France, an estimated 450,000 in the first half of the eighteenth century. The population of Ireland was now approaching five million of whom well over three million were Catholic. The population of Britain, according to O'Connor, was twenty million where only a tiny minority were Catholic.[13] The two islands, bound together by their ancient and painful marriage, moved through the centuries on wholly dissimilar dynamics.

It was at this time that O'Connor met one of the leading British Whigs, a circle in which he would later move intimately. He met Lord Suffolk by chance in 1787. They were on a passage boat from Dublin, travelling to Cork together, Suffolk going to join his regiment. Waiting at a lock, they walked by the side of the boat and got into conversation. Lord Suffolk was struck by O'Connor's gentlemanly manner and 'that kind of diffidence which I have always admired in his character'. Suffolk thought him a young man of extraordinary ability.[14]

There were rumours that France was restive. Curious, O'Connor crossed the Channel in 1787. 'The American Revolution and the part the French government had taken in it, and the expenses that had been incurred had at this time begun to produce their effects'.[15] O'Connor had been struck by the words of Harrington, author of *The Oceana* in 1737, who said that France, Italy and Spain were still in the dregs of the Gothic empire. Whichever awoke first to the ancient principles of Equality should 'govern the world'.[16] He says little about his journey to France in 1787.

He was back in London in time to hear the Warren Hastings trial in Westminster Hall, when Sheridan's oratory set a standard for British governance in India. Britain's Governor-General in India was accused of cruelty and extortion in Oudh. If Hastings was brought to trial in London, there were reverberations for Ireland. Although India was a colony and Ireland the sister kingdom, both looked to London as the source of government.

> Of all the delightful sensations I ever felt those which the hearing my beloved Sheridan on this occasion conveyed to my mind, was the greatest. I did not know him at that time but his matchless speeches on this occasion gave me the greatest desire to converse with the man that could make them and they contributed to the formation of the indissoluble love and friendship which united our hearts and souls together some years later.[17]

Sheridan's brilliance lay in supporting Indian armed rebellion against British soldiers, on the grounds that British justice must be beyond reproach. He changed many minds and carried both conservatives and radicals. As Sheridan ended with 'My Lords I am done' and sank into the arms of Burke, everyone present knew they had experienced great theatre and brilliant intellect. Of all lessons in oratory this was one of the finest. At 25, Arthur O'Connor noticed exactly how this impact was achieved.

O'Connor had been abroad for over four years and had made only occasional visits to Ireland. Roger's wife had died in 1787 and he married again, to Wilhamena Bowen of the family from Bowen's Court.[18] In the same year, the middle brother Robert began building a mansion on his own land, close to Connerville. He named it

Fort Robert.[19] The following year he married Anne Eliza Madras. They had three daughters. Arthur now felt he wanted to go home and digest all he had learnt. He had kept his eight terms at Lincoln's Inn and was qualified for the law.

He was in Dublin at Michaelmas 1788 where he confirmed his membership of the Honorable Society of King's Inns under the name of Arthur Conner. In Ireland, his name was more than his personal identity; it was an issue of race and culture. He appeared in court on 25 November to take the oaths of allegiance and the Declaration to prevent the further growth of popery which accompanied entrance to the Irish Bar. He took them under the name Arthur O'Connor.[20] Enrolled as a barrister, he did not practice.

'I sought retreat where I might be whole master of my time and studies.'[21] There was a property near Kinsale which had been mortgagèd to his grandfather for more than it was worth. Arthur's father, no businessman, had allowed it to become entangled with conditions and his brother had a share in it. Arthur untangled the legal claims, purchased his brother's share on a mortgage and became owner of the whole estate.[22] Here, at Ballinroe in the Barony of Courcy's he built himself a fine house, known as Mount Arthur, or Fort Arthur.[23] He built offices for the estate and several farm houses. He studied agriculture, introduced break crops between cereals and took a detailed interest in the management of his domain. Here too he studied Irish history, the sciences of legislation and political economy. He made friends in the neighbourhood. A rich old bachelor called Mr Karney with £6,000 a year lived nearby, 'a good, hospitable, generous, honest man'. A clergyman called De Courcy, brother of Lord Kinsale, was O'Connor's most intellectual company. Lord Kinsale was a 'most excellent citizen' and President of a Sea Water Club which O'Connor joined. 'In this retired state forgetting the World and by the World forgot I passed two years in study when a circumstance awoke me from my passive life to enter on the duties of an active citizen.'[24]

Our [sea water] club had met under a cliff near the entrance of the harbour of Kinsale, scarcely was dinner over than we perceived a dark inflamed cloud which denoted an approaching storm. At once the pleasure boat got under way to gain the harbour and I ran off for my house at two miles distance. I had not gone a half a mile when a most violent tempest assailed me on a barren heath. I passed a wretched cabin from which I saw a woman issuing who, with scanty clothing and long dishevilled hair blown by the winds, set violently to tear the thatch from her house. I followed her in and never did I witness so great a scene of wretchedness; two fine boys, two and three years old naked as they were born, on a most cold clay floor without an atom of furniture but an iron pot full of raw potatoes. I asked her what induced her to uncover her cabin in such weather. She showed me her little ones and told me she had no other fuel to boil the potatoes for their supper and her own and that if it was not for the storm she would have picked up some scraps of turf in the bog. The mind cannot conceive a scene of greater misery than that which offered itself to my view. Yet the sufferer was of those celestial forms that might have been the ornament of the highest station. She might be twenty or twenty two, her babes were like two cherubins entwined in each other's arms. They seemed unconscious of their wretchedness, a cord which supported the mother's light peticoat that descended but to the middle of her calf, marked a waist of a form the greatest sculptor would have sought for model. She told me she had been married very young. I learnt after that she and her husband were the handsomest couple in all the country. It was easy to see that adversity had made invasion on her youth, but her vigorous constitution retained the strongest lines which constitutes the angelic sweetness that forms the matchless beauty of our Irish women.

The cause of the profound misery of the family was the untimely loss of her husband, who was drowned in attempting to save a shipwrecked crew that leaped overboard to reach the shore.

The ship had been forced between rocks in a small creek on O'Connor's estate and the crew abandoned it. In attempting to save them, the young woman's husband died. Her neighbours built a cabin for her. O'Connor now gave money to re-roof her cabin, enclose and plough some part of the heath and to buy her clothes and utensils, 'which raised her state from the lowest depths of misery to be on a level with the ordinary wretchedness which has been so long the lot of the mass of the Irish'.

'This lowest scene of the lowest misery of the greater part of my country of Munster, Connaught and a part of Leinster, made such an effect on my feelings that it made me form the resolution to devote my life, fortune and efforts to change this state of Ireland.'[25]

1789 was a critical year. In Paris the Estates-General defied the King, riots broke out, the fortress of the Bastille was stormed for arms and fell before the onslaughts of the people. British radicals looked to France to establish modern democracy. Irish Protestants were astonished to see a Catholic nation reach out for liberty and reappraised the possibilities. In England, the King was recovering from a period of insanity during which his son, George, Prince of Wales had almost become Regent. MPs in London and Dublin wavered between George III and the Prince of Wales. When the King recovered, those who had deserted him were dismissed. Lord Shannon found himself in this disagreeable position. Longfield and Lord Kingsborough, loyal to the King throughout, now found themselves close to government. Longfield became a Privy Councillor. Leinster, Charlemont and Connolly had led the Princely negotiations.[26] George and William Ponsonby were Whig grandees and were closely involved. Shannon was Ponsonby's brother-in-law. This group was now out of favour.

A new constitutional item had arisen. If Ireland was a separate kingdom from England, she had the right to chose a Regent independently of London. The Whig Clubs were formed in Ireland to maintain the integrity of the constitution of 1782. Achieving parliamentary reform was the vital issue now. Grattan, the hero of 1782, the Ponsonby brothers, Leinster and Conolly, Curran and Flood, would all keep working for reform.

Arthur O'Connor awoke from his Tolstoyian seclusion to take a part in the 1790 elections for Cork, acting as Lord Kingsborough's lawyer.[27] Kingsborough was standing for one of the two county seats, Longfield for the city. Elections were long events, something between a market, a festival and a court hearing. The electors had to prove their right to vote and fraud was a high art.[28] Patronage and influence were traded. Leases produced to prove voting rights might lead to increased rents. The emotive use of patriotism, the rise and fall of local families, bartering of interests; all these made the parliamentary elections a lively affair. Local elections were even more byzantine. In 1790 the Cork elections lasted three months, O'Connor working eight hours a day on sorting out voter eligibility and taking the votes. His legal training and sharp eye made him a terror at catching vote riggers and fake evidence. The High Sheriff ran the election but his probity was not guaranteed.

Since the Regency crisis, Shannon was estranged from government and had lost some of his power. O'Connor capitalised by reminding the electors of the ruinous measures previously supported by those now in Opposition. The Opposition was a fragmentary group, but always known as patriots since the government was always British-led.

Richard Longfield was delighted with his nephew's public speaking, 'pressed me to his heart before the whole assembly'.[29] As Longfield and Kingsborough were triumphant they chose the new High Sheriff. They nominated Arthur O'Connor.

O'Connor was now in charge of the next round of elections. 'The first day of the new elections the immense Court House was cram full. I addressed them by remarking on the disgrace the secret practices of the late election had brought on the County.'[30] He assured them he would run a straight election. To spare time and expense the electors agreed on two independent candidates and everyone was pleased.

Besides holding their own seats, Kingsborough and Longfield owned borough seats themselves. There was always concern that they would be contested. The Earl of Shannon, the largest borough-owner of the locality, wrote to his son on 25 May 1790, 'As to the elections I met not the least opposition in any of my Boroughs – the contest for the city of Cork is over. Longfield and Hutchisson are returned but a Mastiff who could bribe as desperately as the former did would also have succeeded.' '... Government are afraid that

Ponsonby will defeat Foster for the chair – I know they never yet bribed higher.'[31] Ponsonby was a powerful Whig in Ireland; in London, his relations were at the heart of Whig society. But government would hardly let the Opposition get the chair; John Foster was Speaker when the new parliament sat in 1790.

Arthur O'Connor, High Sheriff of Cork in 1791,[32] was greatly in favour with his uncle. Richard Longfield offered him a borough seat for Philipstown in King's County and in 1790 he entered parliament. Other new members included Arthur Wellesley, later the Duke of Wellington and Robert Stewart, later Viscount Castlereagh. Charlemont gave Stewart some advice, 'Remember the excellent precept of Lord Camden, that English politics should be totally forgotten by an Irish member of parliament'.[33]

William Drennan wrote to Sam McTier:

I have just seen Grattan and FitzGerald proceeding to the hustings at the head of more than 1400 men, eighteen of the corporations bands of music playing. Grattan advancing on his light fantastic toe, hope elevating and joy brightening his crest, his eyes rolling with that fine enthusiasm without which it is impossible to be a great man. FitzGerald is a fine tall young fellow bending to hear what Grattan is saying.[34]

In January 1791, the new parliament got down to business.

---------- *Chapter 6* ----------

IN GRATTAN'S PARLIAMENT

In 1790 Wolfe Tone met Thomas Russell in the public gallery of the Irish House of Commons. An important friendship began at once. Below in the Chamber, Arthur O'Connor was taking his seat for the first time. George Ponsonby had engaged Tone as lawyer and pamphleteer to the Whig Clubs but Tone was impatient. He was outgrowing the Whig position. Russell was a soldier. His religious principles wrestled with his drinking and promiscuity but he was an effective political thinker. Tone was a gifted writer and Russell sparked his ideas. Reform was not enough, the society of Ireland was divided. Tone began to see that only by the full inclusion of the Catholics could Ireland's political system work. Catholic emancipation was essential.

Arthur O'Connor had accepted the seat in parliament that his uncle offered, on the understanding that he would follow his own principles. 'I leave you,' said Longfield, 'to your entire independence.'[1] O'Connor's friend Sir Laurence Parsons MP had made two important speeches against government corruption and the relationship with England. 'True,' he said, 'we are an independent kingdom; we have an Imperial Crown distinct from England; but it is a metaphysical distinction, a mere sport for speculative men ... Who governs us? English ministers, or rather the deputies of English ministers.'[2]

When O'Connor entered parliament, the big borough-mongers and the Prince's party were estranged from government. Longfield and the independent country gentlemen supported the government warmly, expecting preferments previously awarded to the big magnates. It was a dispiriting chamber. O'Connor followed Longfield's line, made a speech on entering parliament to find his feet. Lord Shannon wrote to his son: 'The Irish Session has opened very quickly. The Lord Lieutenant's speech was perfectly harmless and unalarming ... In the Commons two Country Gentlemen moved the address, but that to the Ld Lt was seconded by O'Connor the nephew of Longfield and the fellow that Burr flogged.'[3] O'Connor's speech criticised the Opposition but its main content was how to control undue aristocratic power in government.[4] He was taking a careful line between his own views and his loyalty to his uncle. O'Connor soon realised that the aim of the independent members was to acquire patronage. He regretted having spoken.

'Sir Laurence Parsons was the honestest member in the house; we were collegiate friends. Dining together tête à tête at my house we discussed what men in our situation could do to serve Ireland. We concluded that the part of honour was a private station.'[5] For a year he sat in the house but kept silent.

Tone and Russell were as active as O'Connor was passive. The French Revolution was in full flood. The Declaration of the Rights of Man, published in August 1789 declared:

> The National Assembly doth recognise and declare, in the presence of the Supreme Being, and with the hope of his blessing and favour, the following sacred rights of men and citizens:
> 1. Men are born, and always continue, free, and equal in respect of their rights ...
> 2. ... these rights are liberty, property, security and resistance of oppression.
> 3. The nation is essentially the source of all sovereignty; nor can any individual or any body of men, be entitled to any authority which is not expressly derived from it.[6]

Democratic monarchy still seemed possible. In the Assembly, the charismatic Mirabeau was ascendant. The big idea of the Revolution was that sovereignty belonged to the nation, but who exactly made up the nation, who was to represent them? In Paris, great men argued out the terms of the constitution, who could vote, under what system? The arguments were idealistic, often abstract. Later, the people realised that if they had sovereignty, whatever that was, they had power and they took it. Meanwhile, the public finances of France were critical which caused fundamental instability.

The American and French declarations of rights excited Tone and Russell. New ideas were thrown up. The two men argued them out at the seaside during the summer. In Dublin, that winter, Tone founded a debating club which included Joseph Pollock, William Drennan and Thomas Addis Emmet. It was William Drennan who suggested to Sam McTier, his brother-in-law in Belfast, the forma-tion of a Brotherhood.

21 May 1791.

I should much desire that a Society were instituted in this city having much of the secrecy and somewhat of the ceremonial of Freemasonry ... A benevolent Conspiracy – a plot for the peo-ple – No Whig Club – no party Title – The Brotherhood its name – The Rights of Man and the greatest happiness of the greatest number its End. Its General end – real Independence to Ireland and republicanism its particular purpose. [7]

Belfast was ideal; a prosperous linen town with a well-educated middle-class, home of the Volunteers and the egalitarian Presbyterians. In September, an editorial committee was formed for a new paper, the *Northern Star*. Its aim was to promote parliamen-tary Reform and Union among Irishmen. The Society of United Irishmen was established on 14 October 1791, with 28 members. The 'Secret Committee' of William Sinclair, Sam McTier, Samuel Neilson, William McCleery, Thomas McCabe, the brothers William and Robert Simms, Henry Haslett, John Campbell, Gilbert McIlveen and William Tennent, was almost exactly the same group of men who formed the editorial committee of the *Northern Star*, which became their mouthpiece.

Drennan wrote the declaration, Tone composed the resolutions.

DECLARATION AND RESOLUTIONS
OF THE SOCIETY OF UNITED IRISHMEN OF BELFAST

In the present great era of reform, when unjust governments are falling in every quarter of Europe; when religious persecution is compelled to abjure her tyranny over conscience; when the rights of man are ascertained in theory, and that theory substantiated by practice; when antiquity can no longer defend absurd and oppressive forms, against the common sense and common interests of mankind; when all government is acknowledged to originate from the people, and to be so far only obligatory as it protects their rights and promotes their welfare: We think it our duty, as Irishmen, to come forward, and state what we feel to be our heavy grievance, and what we know to be its effectual remedy. WE HAVE NO NATIONAL GOVERNMENT, we are ruled by Englishmen, and the servants of Englishmen, whose object is the interest of another country, whose instrument is corruption, and whose strength is the weakness of Ireland; and these men have the whole of the power and patronage of the country, as means to seduce and to subdue the honesty and the spirit of her representatives in the legislature. Such an extrinsic power, acting with uniform force in a direction too frequently opposite to the true line of our obvious interests, can be resisted with effect solely by unanimity, decision, and spirit in the people, qualities which may be exerted most legally, constitutionally and efficaciously, by that great measure essential to the prosperity and freedom of Ireland. AN EQUAL REPRESENTATION OF ALL THE PEOPLE IN PARLIAMENT.[8]

There was no mention of separation from England though Tone was already thinking of it.

Two other publications caused a stir in 1791. *Rights of Man* by Thomas Paine was published in London under the guidance of William Godwin. By the summer it was all over Ulster. Paine had sailed back from America, breathless from one revolution to plunge into a second in France. *Rights of Man* opens with an argument against Edmund Burke who, doubtful about the revolution in France, had written: 'the effect of liberty to individuals is that they may do what they please. We ought to see what it will please them to do, before we risk congratulations.'[9] Paine was impatient. The book was dedicated to George Washington, 'that you may enjoy the Happiness of seeing the new World regenerate the Old'.[10]

In September of the same year, 'A Northern Whig', alias Wolfe Tone was author of *An Argument on Behalf of the Catholics of Ireland*. It was a best-seller. The previous year the Belfast Volunteers had agitated for abolition of tithes for Catholics and Dissenters. Hands of friendship suddenly stretched out towards the Catholics. The leaders of the Catholic Committee saw their best hope in Britain. They had always received a more reasonable reception from London than from other sects within Ireland. The London government saw that the majority of Irish subjects would only remain loyal to the Crown if they were included in the political nation. In Ireland, the Protestants lived with a single terror. If Catholics became dominant, the constitution of William of Orange might be overturned. If that happened, they could lose their land. No compromise seemed likely to remain stable.

In Britain, the Glorious Revolution was seen as the guarantee of constitutional rights and O'Connor took this view. It was the Whig position. In Ireland, after the victory of William III at the Boyne and Aughrim, the Treaty of Limerick had been drawn up, in which it was stated that Roman Catholics 'shall enjoy such privileges as are consistent with the laws of Ireland' ... 'a parliament ... will endeavour to procure the said Roman Catholics such further security in that particular as may preserve them from any disturbance on account of their said religion'.[11] Irishmen believed that the Treaty of Limerick had been savagely broken and that the penal laws were in violation of that treaty. O'Connor certainly considered William III a just King whose pact with Ireland had been ruptured by a small Protestant governing class. In Britain, Edmund Burke argued that the rights of the British constitution had been built gradually over the centuries and were the inheritance of the people. The United Irishmen were less dependent on tradition or the past for the rights they claimed. The Glorious Revolution was a divisive memory in Ireland and tradition treacherous. Sampson and Russell considered the Glorious Revolution an exercise in aristocratic domination.[12] The basis for the constitution could be more safely argued from Locke and the concepts of the social contract. The people were sovereign and made a compact with government. Should government break that compact, their legitimacy ended and a more democratic government could and should be formed.

O'Connor took his duties as High Sheriff of Cork very seriously that year. There was constant agitation. He had leave from the government to go to England on private affairs. According to O'Connor the Shannonites took this opportunity to recommend themselves to the government by putting down a Papist insurrection. First they had to instigate one by exciting the Catholics to nocturnal meetings. O'Connor was just getting on the boat when news reached him of this and he hurried back. First he confronted an illegal meeting of Shannonites. Then with the help of his Steward, he found the secret meeting of Catholics near Macroom, who were planning a show of strength to get a reduction in their rents and tithe; paying for the Established Church was a terrible grievance. He told these men they had been duped; an agitation would provide an excuse for refusing indulgences in the coming parliamentary sessions. He impressed upon them that he was their real friend and would vote for them. O'Connor persuaded them that they should obey the law. The leaders acquiesced and dispersed, abandoning their plan. On the following Sunday, as High Sheriff he addressed the population of Macroom. Without soldiers to support him, as might have been usual, but with only his Steward in attendance, he gave a short speech pledging his friendship to their cause. He then hurried back to Cork to reassure the commercial men and to stand guarantor for the good conduct of his Catholic countrymen.

O'Connor received many letters of thanks, including those from the Catholic Committee of Ireland and of Dublin. The Catholics of Clonmel wrote: 'we lament that men of your honour and Philanthropy have not been always appointed to the important trust to which you have added such luster. If that had been the case we should have been always considered what we wish to be – loyal and faithful subjects – good citizens and zealous defenders of the laws.' O'Connor thought he had been just, as any public servant should, and that such acclamation proved how infrequently the Catholics received ordinary justice.[13]

In fact when Langrishe's bill for repeal of the remaining penal laws was debated in March 1792, O'Connor did not speak.[14] The Catholics petitioned for their right to vote to be included in this bill but were refused. O'Connor did not vote for the electoral franchise.[15] His support of Catholic rights was still a measured one. Langrishe's bill was passed easily, without the franchise. Lord Shannon gave a pithy account to his son:

> the Bill brought in by Sir H. Langrishe for removing certain restraints to which the Papists were subject has engaged not only the attention of parliament but the whole conversation, or rather wrangling of private society – the Bill ... has, after producing a great deal of heat, passed unanimously and is to come before the House of Lords on Wednesday where I am sure it will not be altered ... I hope we shall now be quiet for some time tho' the Papists are by no means satisfied.[16]

In July Wolfe Tone became secretary to the Catholic Committee. He worked tirelessly for the cause of Catholic emancipation and to improve their relationship with other sects. By refusing the Catholics entry to politics, parliament had thrown them into the arms of the Ulster Presbyterians and the young but growing Society of United Irishmen. Naturally Tone brought them into contact with his new Brotherhood and several leading Catholics joined. Yet still the Catholic Committee thought that London might be a safer ally.

Before the Relief Acts, Catholics could only bear arms under licence. This hindered them from joining the Volunteers. In disturbed times, the Dublin government worried that weapons were being imported for the Catholics. It was a highly emotive issue; the right to bear arms was the right of free-born men.

While these issues worked away like yeast in the guts of Irish life, O'Connor's only contribution in parliament was on the India Bill, a measure designed to prevent Ireland from trading with India.[17] The night before the debate, 25 government members, including the Speaker John Foster, came to dinner with Mr Longfield where

Arthur O'Connor did the honours of the house. They bewailed their lot at having to support a measure ruinous to Ireland. O'Connor ventured to disagree. Uncle Longfield chortled and said in that case, his nephew would be obliged to support the government. After dinner, O'Connor went round to talk it over with Laurence Parsons. Troubled, he rode out next morning to the Wicklow mountains to think over his position. Inadvertently, government had taken a sound economic move. It would so delight uncle Longfield if his nephew spoke for a government bill; but O'Connor despised the government for its abject corruption.[18]

In the House he began by stating it was not a question of right but of utility. What was in Ireland's best interest? If she invested capital in trade with India, it would have to be withdrawn from agriculture or manufacturing, both of which groaned from lack of capital. The Indian trade would not pay for several years, the home trade or that to Britain gave returns within the month. Ireland could not afford it.[19] O'Connor spoke well, Parsons backed up the argument, uncle Longfield was delighted and the Castle very pleased.

The independent members who had secured much government patronage after the Regency crisis were in danger of losing it. Beresford and Fitzgibbon had been staunch in supporting the King and were still very much in favour. A Privy Councillor for Ireland and England, John Beresford was Commissioner for the Revenue and had the ear of William Pitt. John Fitzgibbon, now a Baron and Lord Chancellor of Ireland was inalienably a government man. These two men, with John Foster the Speaker, were the three Johns so despised by the radicals as crisis developed. They had enormous power in Dublin.

Beresford and Fitzgibbon were busy trying to restore their friend Lord Shannon and the other borough-monger grandees to their former patronage and offices. The independent country gentlemen would soon be squeezed out of their newly acquired positions. Longfield consulted his bright young nephew. O'Connor told him to despise government, remember his own fortune and lead the independent men on behalf of Ireland. Longfield sighed, said he too had been a patriot in his youth but parliament was too corrupt. Now he tried only to secure the position of himself and his friends. In that case, said the nephew, deal directly with the English ministers, nothing worthwhile can be achieved with the crowd of scavengers in Dublin.[20]

Accordingly, the two men set out for England. O'Connor was determined to go on and see what was happening in revolutionary France. In London they called on the Marquis of Lansdowne, an old friend of Richard Longfield. The two men had been to school together near Kilkenny. The talk at Lord Lansdowne's house was all of France. 'The Marquis observed,' says O'Connor, 'that it required the aristocracy in England should abate somewhat of its lofty pretensions and make some approach to equality.'[21] He sought liberal and republican friends for his son. Richard Longfield answered merrily that his nephew had been a republican from childhood. 'He never knew me swerve an iota from Republican principles or ever acknowledge any rightful government but that which was in the interest of all.'[22] Republicanism included democratic monarchy, as long as it was at the will of the people.

At Lord Lansdowne's house, O'Connor met a young Englishman who became a close and loyal friend. Sir Francis Burdett was 22, O'Connor seven years older. Burdett came from an aristocratic family of Norman descent. They had a family seat at Foremarke in Derbyshire. Francis Burdett's ancestors had sat in 23 parliaments, he was the heir to two estates, had been educated at Westminster School and Christ Church, Oxford. He was liberal minded and well meaning. With such advantages by birth, he had no need to seek places and pensions but was concerned for the public good and had modern ideas of social welfare. He took a great interest in O'Connor and his ideas, was impressed by the Irishman's intellectual confidence and breadth of study. O'Connor was a good speaker which also impressed Burdett. With him O'Connor formed

> ... one of the most intimate friendships that ever bound man and man, together we dined at the Marquis's with a young and beautiful French duchesse. The Marquis brought on the subject of political economy and put some question on the science to me. I excused myself in saying it was too serious a subject for

the entertainment of a young and beautiful woman like the duchesse. 'You are mistaken', said the Marquis, 'she occupies herself with the sciences.' The Marquis advanced some opinions on the old principles founded on monopoly and exclusions. I was called on to refute them which led to a discussion of the science as founded by Thurgot, Condorcet and Adam Smith. The next day I was walking down St James's Street when a young man jumped from his horse and ran up to me, this was Burdett. He told me he had been seeking me all the morning, that he had a request to make me. On answering how happy I should be to oblige him, he said it was to grant him my friendship and to instruct him in the science we had discussed at the Marquis's table. I was so struck with the frankness of the young man that I readily granted all he asked. For years we studied together and such was the unity of our hearts that neither had a secret from the other.[23]

In that age, when sentiment was highly valued, men and women considered it vital to show their feelings. Friendships between men developed tenderness and intimacy, which might become affected but could be warm and deep.

Lord Lansdowne meanwhile, gave Richard Longfield advice on how to deal with Mr Pitt and helped to arrange an interview. Pitt received Longfield politely. O'Connor suspected that the British Minister needed other Irishmen of influence 'in his immediate dependence', the more so because Beresford and Fitzgibbon were so powerful and close to Jenkinson, personal friend and confidante of the King. Longfield gave the Minister a good account of his nephew and his skill in debate, of the service he was capable of rendering to government, 'that he had just discumbered it of one of its most embarrassing questions', over the India Bill. Mr Pitt agreed that if this nephew understood economics, he was in a tiny minority in the Irish parliament. Uncle Longfield was encouraged and suggested 'the place of Chancellor of the Exchequer for me but Pitt objected I was too young. It was agreed I should have the post of Commissioner of the Revenue with a promise of the place of Chancellor of the Exchequer at a future time'.[24]

Longfield came away delighted, and in the street met his friend Lord Lucan to whom he imparted his happy news. Lucan hurried to tell General John Knox who knew O'Connor well. The General told Lucan that Arthur would never follow this plan as he despised the government. Leaving Lucan to puzzle this out, Knox went to warn O'Connor.

> When my uncle told me what had passed between him and Mr Pitt I don't know that in all my life I felt more sensibly than on the occasion, the sense of affection for the evident intentions with which my uncle had acted towards me, and the disappointment my refusal must cost him entered into my heart like a dagger. I took hold of both his hands and pressed them to my bosom.

O'Connor impressed on Longfield his gratitude and love but said he could not act in a way incompatible with his own self-esteem. Longfield tried to persuade him, he offered to pay off his mortgage of several thousand pounds. O'Connor was in great distress. He wanted their relationship to be disinterested, honest, based on respect and natural affection. He impressed this on Richard Longfield. His uncle, he felt, took this remarkably well.[25]

But a space had opened up between them that could only widen. For the moment O'Connor breathed a sigh of relief. He now felt free 'to take a view of the French Revolution'. John Hutchinson, 'a red hot democrat'[26] and son of the Provost of Trinity, joined him. In the early summer of 1792 they bought two fine riding horses and a good carriage and set out.

The philosopher and mathematician Condorcet had been elected to the National Assembly of France the previous year, now he led the Executive. Condorcet was a man of intellect, who applied scientific thinking to social affairs. He believed that the more truth spreads, the less societies need to be governed. This gentle idealist was the only one of the *philosophes* to play an active role in the French Revolution. That revolution, once begun could not be controlled or halted. Jacobin clubs had sprung up in Paris where debate raged about power and law. Robespierre was emerging as leader of the

Jacobins. Meanwhile, the Assembly had declared war on 'the King of Hungary and Bohemia', who was also Emperor of Austria.[27] Prussia entered the war. The French army was on the German front. Here General Lafayette, a close associate of Condorcet, was stationed near his troops.

Condorcet and Lafayette were family friends, Lafayette had signed the marriage certificate when Condorcet married Sophie de Grouchy in 1786.[28] Both men were landed and titled. Both were in the service of the emergent democratic France, Condorcet as a highly idealistic politician, Lafayette as a General. As Commander of the National Guard, Lafayette had ordered his men to shoot into a mass demonstration in Paris in 1791. He was already a marked man.

O'Connor and Hutchinson had introductions to several leading men in Paris and to Generals on the German front. Their first stop was at Lille where O'Connor experienced a Jacobin club, full and in uproar, 'hundreds bawling, no-one listening'.[29] At the Camp of Sedan, the young men presented themselves to General Lafayette. Like Appolos Morris, he had fought in America under Washington, was at ease with the Irish and 'a stranger' with the English. To Lafayette, Hutchinson's near-sightedness gave him the appearance of the extreme reserve of the English. But O'Connor had the Irish manner and the General took to him. The young man's early military enthusiasm had re-awoken and he was reading avidly on strategy. O'Connor introduced himself as a Colonel in the Irish Volunteers.[30] Hutchinson was a Colonel in the British Army. Lafayette received them kindly but was more cordial with O'Connor than with Hutchinson, a soldier of the British Crown. Here, at Sedan they met several officers of Irish extraction who helped them to see the campaign.

On 7 August 1792, Commissaires arrived, sent by the government where Lafayette had been indicted. Lafayette arrested them, against the advice of O'Connor who told the General that in a revolution 'popularity was a weather cock that veered at every blast'.[31] The General should not be confident that the people still supported him, as they had when he was a leading figure of the events of 1789. Lafayette felt secure in his position. Within days this had changed. On 10 August mobs forced the abdication of the King in

Paris. News reached the camp at Sedan. That night, O'Connor and Layafette dined together. The Irishman saw that the General realised now that his army might not be loyal to him, an aristocrat who had supported a democratic monarchy. O'Connor also saw that Lafayette did not realise that the Revolution was a tidal wave, sweeping all before it. Forming parties, making intrigues was useless before this torrent.[32] Lafayette imagined that once the *ancien régime* was overthrown, order would be restored, a new system set up. They had talked in Paris of ending the Revolution – as if it were a once and for all event. This was not so. The tide of the revolution had rushed on, taken more extreme and violent turns.

But Lafayette did see the realities of his own situation, that he would be arrested if he stayed. He was already preparing to leave France.

In Paris a provisional Executive Council was formed; a new Assembly was to be elected on universal suffrage. Condorcet no longer held a leading position. Lafayette left for Luxemburg and on 19 August fell into the hands of the Austrians. Hutchinson, meanwhile, had been mistakenly arrested in Sedan as a German spy and this, together with the mob rule developing in Paris, had turned him against the Revolution.[33]

After Lafayette's departure, Hutchinson and O'Connor left for Belgium where they introduced themselves to the other side. Their main idea was to experience the military campaign. An Irishman called General O'Brady introduced them to the Prince of Wurtembourg, commander of the Austrian forces. The Austrians argued over whether O'Connor and Hutchinson, from a neutral country, should disclose French positions to their new hosts. O'Connor absolutely refused and the Prince agreed with him.[34] The honour of war was definitely to be upheld.

In Paris, Louis XVI had been deposed and a Republic proclaimed with a new calendar to begin from that date. Hutchinson was deeply disillusioned about the Revolution. O'Connor was in haste to get back to Ireland. The next parliamentary session would begin early in 1793. Hutchinson and O'Connor parted and sold their horses. Travelling through England in December 1792, O'Connor discovered London in an uproar.[35] Goaded by King

George who was alarmed by events in Paris, Pitt was preparing to enter the war against France. O'Connor felt it was entirely wrong to interfere in the internal affairs of a neighbouring state. Britain would be far better advised to enjoy blessed neutrality. The American war had been ruinous. A second conflict would drastically undermine the public finances. George III was adamant. Ideas flew through London like frantic birds. The London Corresponding Society was a radical democratic group, its membership grew rapidly. Prosecutions for sedition became common. Pamphlets whirled from the presses. There was an air of panic. Fox, Sheridan, Grey and the Opposition spoke of the liberties of the British constitution, the right of other nations to such liberty, but reason was not driving the public mind. The government had extra troops brought to London, the Tower was in a state of defence. There was talk of restoring the French King to his throne, talk of war.

On 21 January 1793, the French executed Louis XVI. On 1 February, France declared war on Great Britain. O'Connor was in Dublin, parliament was in session and he the only member not in deep mourning. Why, they asked? His reply was typically idiosyncratic. He claimed to be the only man there who had the right to condemn the killing since he had always maintained that Society had no right to take the life of any of its members. The Quakers in America had shown that all men could be reformed. Was not this parliament, here in Dublin, the result of the execution of Charles I? These ideas did not satisfy the Dublin parliamentarians.[36]

Grattan had been talking to Hutchinson and was unnerved by the development of the French Revolution. O'Connor invited him and Forbes to dinner and talked it through, reassured them. He told them that the inevitable was happening, the overthrow of long despotism had unleashed a torrent of human energy and grievance. It would take its course. He hoped he had convinced the Opposition leader to remain calm about events in France. 'Grattan was a perfectly honest man, a sincere lover of liberty'.[37] But O'Connor also said that Grattan did not understand science and by that he included the science of government.

Deeply despondent about the state of the Irish parliament, O'Connor was delighted to receive an invitation to stay with

General John Knox on the Isle of Wight that summer. Here his ideas buzzed like angry bees. Knox suggested a pamphlet.

Signed 'A Stoic', it was entitled, *The Measures of Ministry to prevent a Revolution are the most certain means of bringing it on*. It discusses the background to the French Revolution and what Britain's attitude should be. 'What is the lesson a wise people would learn from the French Revolution? ... The Constitution should be founded on such impartial principles, as will occasion the least possible temptation to violate their dictates.' He gave figures for the national debt which war would increase. He said that monopoly of property in the hands of the few caused poverty in the many. War would increase that poverty. Ideas could not be contained by troops. 'Silly, silly, silly nation! In the midst of your joy for having destroyed France itself, you destroy a considerable part of that trade on which your precarious existence depends, commerce must have buyers as well as sellers!' He predicted an increase in taxes likely to cause revolution.

The pamphlet was published by Eaton in 1794. By then, the war effort had made criticism of the government unpatriotic, even treasonable. Reason, not truth, seemed to be the first casualty of war.

But before O'Connor set off for the Isle of Wight that summer to visit his steady friend the General, he had already met a man of more radical views. Lord Edward FitzGerald had been in France, had lived in the same house as Paine, had married the beautiful Pamela, daughter of Madame de Genlis and, society supposed, child of that lady's lover, the Duc d'Orléans. Louis-Philippe, cousin of Louis XVI, had supported the abolition of the monarchy and was dangerously, deliciously republican. Lord Edward FitzGerald was the fifth son of the Duke of Leinster, the adored child of the Duchess and had served with the British army in the American war. Afterwards he had travelled in the wild interior of North America and grown passionate about the Iroguois; Lord Edward was a romantic. Charles James Fox was his first cousin, as was Lord Holland. His English grandfather had been Duke of Richmond, now his uncle had the title. He had entrée to all the finest drawing rooms in London, the Whig grandees were his relatives. Edward FitzGerald was good-looking, emotional and impulsive. No one had ever refused him anything and he had the charm of someone who knows that not only his mother, but all the world love him.

Following his marriage, he was back in Dublin in time for the parliamentary session of 1793, loudly supporting the Revolution in France even after the King was executed. One of the first acts of the new session was to ban further assemblies of the Volunteers. The government was as alarmed in Dublin as it was in London. The Volunteers were declared some of the King's worst subjects. Lord Edward leapt to his feet and shouted to the Speaker, 'Sir, I give me most hearty disapprobation to this address, for I do think that the Lord Lieutenant and the majority of this House are the worst subjects the King has.'[38] There was an uproar. The older men of the parliament reprimanded him, cautioned him. It was to no avail. Lord Edward was fired up with revolution. It was not a fire that was likely to go out; the young aristocrat was not a man of reason, caution or moderation.

Lord Edward FitzGerald came from that great family which had held so powerful a position since the Normans first came to Ireland in the twelfth century. FitzGeralds had been Earls of Desmond and Kildare, had taken the land of O'Connor Kerry, had fought against Elizabeth I in the Munster rebellion. The Earl of Kildare had subsequently become a Protestant and supported William of Orange. Lord Edward's father inherited this title and was elevated to the Dukedom of Leinster in 1766. He had died in 1773 when Lord Edward was ten. His mother then married William Ogilvie who had been her children's tutor and had become her lover. They lived in France until Edward joined the army when he was sixteen. Lord Edward's brother was now Duke of Leinster and one of the grandest of the borough-mongers, although a patriot in the Irish parliament.

Lord Edward FitzGerald was as loud and emotional in his contempt of Ascendancy politics as Arthur O'Connor was incisive and analytical. Lord Edward had a dynasty behind him which gave him a confidence which O'Connor did not have. FitzGerald had been an MP since 1781, since when he had spent much time in London society. He had been the lover of Sheridan's wife. That fragile songstress had since died. Pamela was said to much resemble her.

FitzGerald was far more drawn to a military career than a political one but could not get preferment in the army. In the Irish House of Commons, his ideas were radical. Striding about the city with his lovely French wife, he was a controversial figure, noticed and commented on. He and O'Connor soon became close friends.

It was in the 1793 session of the parliament in Dublin that the Catholics at last received the right to vote. This was at the instigation of the government in London which wanted the full loyalty of Catholic Ireland at this critical moment. War with France was looming when the Speech from the Throne was delivered to open the new Dublin session. The proposed measure was a sweeping one, including Catholics in Grand Juries, giving them full educational rights, the right to bear arms with a property qualification and to become magistrates. Most important was the right to vote. Grattan had supported Catholic enfranchisement the previous year, now Ponsonby gave his support and only a few diehards like John Foster held out against it. Sir Laurence Parsons said what many knew: 'The extent of what you give the Catholics depends upon the reform, and the effect of the reform depends upon the extent of the franchise you give to the Catholics.'[39] For the right to vote was a great thing but not as great as it might be. Most of the seats in the house were already owned by borough-mongers who gave them to their friends, ensured themselves of a majority in the house and thereby controlled the parliament. Peers were created by the monarch. Public offices were often in the gift of government, appointed by Ministers in London.

O'Connor did not speak. After years of wrangling and worrying, the House of Commons passed the Bill in March 1793 with few changes and almost no opposition. There were two more issues for the Irish parliament to face, it would have to Reform itself and admit Catholic members. Reform and Catholic emancipation were the two big hurdles still ahead.

Meanwhile, the British army and navy mobilised for war against France.

---— Chapter 7 ——---

A DECISIVE SPEECH

At the end of the eighteenth century, rural Ireland spoke Gaelic while urban and political Ireland spoke English. They danced to different tunes. Music was central to Gaelic culture, the harp its ancient instrument. But the ruptures of the seventeenth century had almost broken the harp tradition. It was typical of Ulster that the Belfast Library were the organisers of a harp festival in 1792. The Presbyterian linen merchants saw that tunes and airs should be collected before they were lost. Edward Bunting was the transcriber and went on to collect the tunes handed down aurally in the big houses or country gatherings of the four provinces. Among these, only one pre-dated Cromwell. Harp music had undergone a metamorphosis, along with all else in Ireland. It had been adapted for the new gentry, had received influences from the continent. The great harp composer O'Carolan, who died in 1738, had heard and absorbed the music of Vivaldi.

Now in Europe, the measured beauty of Vivaldi began to give way to the turbulence of Beethoven, whose work expressed revolution and individuality as no music had before. France was the centre of Europe. From France influences and energies spread across the continent. After the King was guillotined, wave after wave of revolution broke over France like convulsions in a fever. The crisis came with the Terror of 1794 in mass executions in Paris, war on every border. Beyond that crisis, a new France struggled into being. The young Republic had a power vacuum at its core, soon to be filled by the victorious General, Napoleon Bonaparte.

France descended into a nightmare whose images haunted all Europe. Ireland spun into a similar vortex. The forces acting on her internally were complex but she could not spin freely, attached to Britain.

In the spring of 1793, the outlook in Ireland was not without hope. Both London and the government in Dublin Castle realised that divisions within Ireland could only jeopardise the British Empire as it entered war with France. To heal those divisions, Catholics and Dissenters had been relieved of severe disabilities. A start was made in regulating public pensions and bringing the public finances under the control of the Irish parliament. However, with concessions came restrictions. The government was afraid of unrest, of French influence and of disaffection during war. The military presence was increased and a militia raised from within Ireland. Heavy restrictions were placed on the importation and ownership of arms. The Convention Act banned public gatherings, such as that planned by the United Irishmen for the spring of 1793. Assemblies of pressure groups which had previously aired grievances and debated issues now became illegal. Suppressed, the pressure increased.

The North was restive. The Dublin Society of United Irishmen was active and very much against the war. The Belfast Society was more worrying to the government. In Ulster the large Presbyterian population was culturally egalitarian and in sympathy with republican ideas from France. Ulster had a well-established middle-class which was not represented by the Ascendancy parliament in Dublin. For so important a social group to be alienated from the establishment was a dangerous situation. There were also sectarian vigilante groups, the Catholic Defenders and Protestant Peep O' Day Boys, neither of whom government could or would control. As the Defenders became more active, they became potential recruits to the United Irish movement.

It was to unite all these groups that the Society of United Irishmen pledged themselves.

The honour of the liberal generous enterprise of strengthening Ireland by uniting Protestant and Papists in the noble cause of Ireland's freedom and independence is due in General to those staunch lovers of liberty the Presbiterians of the North, and in particular to the fathers of that pure, that enlightened Press, the *Northern Star*, edited by my dear and excellent friends the two Simms brothers Robert and William, and Samuel Neilson. These staunch patriots with William Tennent, were with Wolfe Tone the fathers of the Union of Irishmen. It is a justice Ireland owes to Tone to record in her eternal register that to the talents, the high honour, the unflinching sacrifice of all that man values most, Ireland will be for ever indebted to him.[1]

Lord Edward FitzGerald had already met the United Irishmen in Dublin. Drennan first became acquainted with FitzGerald in 1793. 'Lord Edward called on me this morning but I happened not to be at home. This I suppose has been done by Rowan's friendship.'[2] Archibald Hamilton Rowan was a United Irishmen whose family originated in Scotland but had land in County Down. FitzGerald had attended the Volunteer convention in Dungannon with him, had been drawn to Rowan by his address to the Volunteers. In Paris, FitzGerald had also met John and Henry Sheares, members of the Jacobin Club and ardent republicans. John Sheares had watched Louis XVI being guillotined and was said to have a handkerchief stained with the King's blood.

It was some time before O'Connor was drawn into the Society. FitzGerald was far more impulsive. The young Lord was excited by America, by France and by his previous military experience. He believed when he returned to Ireland that the Volunteers would provide the basis for a republican revolution. Seeing them divided, losing momentum, he went off in search of more energetic radicals. He quickly discovered the United Irishmen. FitzGerald had neither the education of the young lawyers and graduates who had formed the Society, nor the discipline of the professional members. He offered energetic commitment. His mother had educated him on Rousseau. His step-father had eighteen step-children and five young ones of his own. He had not been able to teach Lord Edward discretion. Lord Edward made up for it with warm-hearted enthusiasm which few people could resist.

It was astonishing to the United Irishmen to find the Duke of Leinster's brother knocking on their doors, a green kerchief round his neck, his hair cropped in the republican fashion. Of course they wanted to attract the Protestant gentry into their midst; theirs was to be a Union of all the Irish men. But the Duke was a man of high position and his brother an unexpected convert. This 'enfant terrible' of the Dublin parliament was clearly sincere. While he was in France, he had already spoken to Paine about the Volunteers, how they might underpin an Irish revolution. Before the parliamentary session of 1793 was over, the first French agent, an American named Oswald, had made his way to Ireland and to FitzGerald.

The United Irishmen were a visible and open Society. In Dublin they held meetings in Tailor's Hall, and committee meetings in member's houses. The leading United men in the capital were Simon Butler, Thomas Addis Emmet, Drennan and Tone. Lord Edward took Oswald to visit some of them but they were cautious. Ireland was not looking for a revolution. The United Irishmen were focused on the twin goals of reform and Catholic emancipation. Lord Edward, disconsolate, retired to the country.

Arthur O'Connor went to England when the parliamentary session ended. He had become very close to Francis Burdett who was well connected in London society. In August of that year Burdett married Sophia, daughter of Thomas Coutts, the banker. Burdett knew the Prince of Wales and his mistress Mrs Fitzherbert, the Duchess of York and the Duchess of Devonshire.[3] Georgiana Cavendish was the daughter of the Earl Spencer and had married the Duke of Devonshire in 1775. Her sister, Harriet was married to John Ponsonby, Viscount Duncannon. Harriet had been the lover of Sheridan. These two sisters were the focal point for Whig society in London. The older woman, Elizabeth, Viscountess Melbourne, had also played this role and kept up a warm friendship with Georgiana when the young Duchess became the star of the Whig salons. In Georgiana's household lived her friend Lady Elizabeth Foster, the Duke's lover. These interlocking families had supported the Hanoverian succession and considered themselves as guarantors of the liberal constitution. Into their drawing rooms came Sheridan, orator and theatre-owner, Charles James Fox, gambler, fortune-spender, charmer and intellectual, Grey, a mild and reasonable man, Lord Moira with an estate in Ulster, Lord Suffolk, Lord Holland, the Ponsonbys and the FitzGeralds. These were the Prince's party. Sheridan had been the Prince of Wales' most intimate political friend and adviser during the Regency crisis. The King, George III, despised the loose-living friends of his eldest son, removed Fox from office at the first opportunity.

They were fashionable, powerful, glittering and allowed themselves considerable licence. But while the Duchess and her sister pursued love affairs and visited the theatre with the politicians and peers who surrounded them, serious politics were brought forward in their town houses, around their dining-room tables. They lived in St James; the men could leave their dinners and return to the House by a brief walk. The palace was close by. Fox, however, had his home in the pleasant countryside of Surrey at St Anne's Hill. Since his liaison with Elizabeth Armistead, he led a more sober life. He loved to escape the Commons and the drawing-rooms, to return to the quiet lanes, listen to the birds in the nearby woods and to read the finest European literature.

Whether they had aptitude or not, these gentlemen were born with places ready for them in the Houses of Parliament. They filled them with more or less competence. Sheridan was quite different. His ancestors were Gaelic Irish, his father a theatre-owner and Sheridan had talked and acted his way into the drama of eighteenth-century London politics. Edmund Burke came from a not dissimilar background. He was in the London parliament because he was a man of deep and impressive intellect.

His family connections, his friend Burdett, later Lord Edward, gave Arthur O'Connor easy access to this circle. He had hovered around the edges of the Whig opposition when he was in London in his twenties and had briefly met the Duchess of Leinster there in 1787. Now he was 30, a member of parliament and more self-assured. His uncle Richard Longfield had introduced him in London society some years before but Longfield's associates were more conservative. O'Connor was moving away from the Irish Ascendancy, was despondent about the patriot Opposition and wholly against the war, as were the Whigs.

With Francis Burdett,

... neither had a secret from the other nor a thought good or bad we did not communicate. As to ourselves to such a degree had our friendship grown that he entreated me to ask his sister-in-law Miss Coutts, afterwards Lady Gilford, in marriage and he would give me half his fortune. The vow I made to devote my life to the relieving Ireland had forbid me to involve any woman in a Union with a man whose life was already disposed of, rendered marriage impossible.[4]

This noble dedication allowed him to escape the advances of aristocratic ladies with an eye to marriage. It was also a cover. In Ireland there was a woman with whom he was already deeply involved. Some time during 1793, O'Connor's lover gave birth to a son.[5] There was no question of marriage and the young woman remained in the shadows of O'Connor's life until she met the FitzGeralds some years later. Burdett knew of her but did not know her. Despite her affair with O'Connor, she does not seem to have come to England but to have stayed with, or near her family in Ireland. O'Connor's close friends knew this lover who bore his child but it was a liaison he never wrote about. Mistresses were not uncommon. Richard Longfield had two children by Mary Donelly of Nassau Street in Dublin who later received bequests in his will.[6]

O'Connor could be very gallant in the fashion of the times but was by nature intense and deep. He had not the temperament to marry for money. He commented on women's characters as much as their looks, talked to them of current issues. It was not typical drawing-room behaviour. O'Connor had made a liaison in Ireland which was sufficiently important and long standing for Burdett to take an interest. There may have been others. Women were not closely chaperoned. O'Connor was good-looking, had explosive passions. He could be jovial and charming, but could also brood, sink into introspection. His intellect seemed to annoy men more than women. In his intimacies with women, he was discreet, almost secretive. It was an age when sensibility was fashionable. Although affairs were acceptable, honour was important.

Women either loved or loathed Arthur. Lord Edward's sister was entranced, Drennan's sister was unimpressed. She at one time thought him noble, later that he had a bad countenance. Lady Elizabeth Foster was disgusted. O'Connor was handsome but his intensity and unwillingness to compromise made him threatening to some, devastating to others.

During the autumn of 1793, he was in Bath where he met Edmund Burke. 'The interest we both took in freeing our country-men from their religious persecution was the bond of this friend-ship.'[7] The two men differed completely over the French Revolution, 'of which I took special care never to utter a syllable leaving our Irish bond entire. He passed his evening tête à tête at my lodging where he stretched full length on my sopha. He enjoyed his ease, he was then 73 and yet his legs were as fine and neat as a young man of twenty which he attributed to his taking an horizon-tal position as often as he could take that liberty. He was convinced that George III never had, nor ever would have, while they lived any real Minister than Bute for the first two years and Jenkinson ever after'.[8] Burke believed that no British Minister was appointed with-out the agreement of this confidante and policies were altered at his command. The Whigs left spies near Buckingham House and dis-covered a humble carriage often stopped after midnight at the palace and waited several hours. These visits seemed to coincide with changes in ministerial appointments.

This was a particular grievance of Burke's. Jenkinson was cer-tainly the King's political agent and intermediary with the East India Company. Burke was infuriated by the position of this Court favourite. Asked by O'Connor who were the most talented men in parliament, Burke expressed his distress at his own rift with Fox and Sheridan over the French Revolution, but said Fox was very gifted; also Chatham, Townsend, Barre and Pitt. Others classed him, Burke, with them. However, 'we are but children to Sheridan, he has more genius than us all together'.[9]

Because his young friend supported Catholic emancipation, Burke assumed he was sympathetic to the religion. O'Connor made it clear that he had a strong aversion to it and ardently wished for emancipation because of its benefit to Ireland, because it was the right of men and because political and commercial freedom might allow Roman Catholics to shake off what he considered priestly superstition. Burke went silent.[10] His father had conformed to the Established Church but his mother was a Catholic, as was his wife. Burke may have received a Catholic education. He was careful in his political career but O'Connor saw that the older man 'had retained the prejudice of his early education. He imagined I, like himself, had a hankering after popery'.[11]

Burke had no interest in economics. 'In all my most intimate conversations with Edmund Burke I perceived his disdain of this indispensible science. It was always *your* Economical Science with a sneer.' Burke, who liked ornamental eloquence, 'should not bear the shackles of positive, unflinching principles of science.'[12]

The 1794 parliamentary session in Ireland was a pivotal one. O'Connor was in Dublin. He spent little time in Cork now. His elder brother Daniel was still in London, married to the sister of his first wife, who had died. Arthur's father had gone to live with Robert in his new house, while brother Roger's growing family filled Connerville. No longer close to Richard Longfield, O'Connor began to take his own course.

Parliament was much influenced by the war. Grattan believed that Ireland's best interests lay in the connection with Britain and that his country should support the sister kingdom in the conflict. This disappointed the United Irishmen. Ponsonby re-introduced his reform Bill which Grattan supported. Parliament was concerned that partial reform might lead, as in France, to anarchic revolution. The Bill failed.

During this session a second French agent arrived in Dublin, the Rev Jackson. He confided in Cockayne who introduced him to Tone and got access to Rowan, then in prison for sedition. Cockayne then betrayed Jackson to the Castle. Jackson was imprisoned, the United Irishmen alarmed. Rowan escaped from prison and fled to France. The government seized the papers of the United Irishmen and arrested Drennan. John Philpot Curran MP, a gifted lawyer and staunch member of the opposition, defended Drennan as he had Rowan. He would later represent Jackson. For a time the Society of United Irishmen became dormant. In Belfast the United men saw that reform might well elude them and began to consider establishing an independent Irish Republic, with the help of France.

In June 1794 Lord Edward moved into a small house in Kildare. His wife Pamela was pregnant. She was well and cheerful but her husband's republican fervour frightened her. Her supposed father, the Duc d'Orleans had been guillotined and Madame de Genlis, her mother, had left France. Pamela's nation was in the worst throes of the Terror. As she spoke to Edward in French or her pretty broken English, she tried to dissuade him from his revolutionary enthusiasm. 'She had seen too much of the French Revolution. She was married just as they [her family] were emigrating, flying in fear and leaving their friends in danger of being guillotined, all their property gone. She had a perfect horror of the Revolution and of republican ideas', her daughter said of her.[13]

O'Connor came often to visit the FitzGeralds in Kildare. Lord Edward 'was one and thirty before he discovered what he ever after called the twin of his soul. When at the time when he was self-elected to free his country or die for Her, he met a soul, "twin to his own" was his expression, because each breathed and loved alike, and their object Ireland', wrote Lord Edward's sister Lady Lucy.[14] This twin was Arthur O'Connor. Lord Edward was the sun to O'Connor's moon.

Lord Edward was supposedly recruiting militia men for his brother but actually was advertising his republican views and sounding out the local men for the United Irish cause. Dissatisfaction was growing, both in response to the *Northern Star* and because the military presence in Ireland was increasing. France spread ideas of men's rights. France was at war with Britain. In Ireland the Catholics paid tithes to the Protestant church. There were no Catholics in parliament The simplest farmer could recognise injustice and instability.

During that summer O'Connor was in London. According to Lady Elizabeth Foster, 'he supped at Devonshire House and I have seen him in our box at the opera'.[15] This was the first time she had seen him and she did not like him as 'his countenance appeared to me gloomy and designing ... I disliked a vulgar familiarity in his manner and a want of openness in his countenance, and I begged of my dear G [Georgiana] not to see him often'.[16] Lady Elizabeth didn't care for Henry Grattan either, she thought him coxcombical. Perhaps she didn't care for the Irish manner. She was very distrustful of Sheridan and his influence on the Prince of Wales.

In December 1794, Pitt appointed Earl Fitzwilliam as Lord Lieutenant. To all but a few, this was welcome news in Dublin where Fitzwilliam was considered liberal, honest and a friend of Catholic emancipation. He arrived on 4 January 1795. Arthur O'Connor was in Dublin for the new parliamentary session, with great expectations. The United Irishmen were dormant but the leaders had hopes that their aims would be met. Agrarian violence was increasing. Fitzwilliam recognised the weakness of the government, the seething rural discontent and the unrepresentative nature of parliament. He immediately changed the Administration, bringing in Ponsonby and Curran, removing Cooke, Wolfe and Toler. Most importantly and with the agreement of Pitt, he sacked John Beresford. There would be a high price to pay.

Beresford was the symbol of corruption, said to own one quarter of public appointments in Ireland. It seemed corruption was to be rooted out, reform might follow. Fitzwilliam was raising funds for the navy and militia, there was a dynamism in parliament. If the country was to remain loyal, Fitzwilliam saw that Catholic emancipation could not be delayed. With the Lord Lieutenant's consent, Grattan put forward a bill. Cautiously, the Dublin parliament prepared itself to take the big step.

On 14 February, a letter from London warned Fitzwilliam of problems. On 25 February William Drennan reported the gossip, 'it is said the Marquis of Buckingham groped his way a second time up the backstairs and told the King he would violate his Coronation oath by granting a total emancipation to the Catholics – upon which the King who is very pious and religious, altered his opinion on the subject entirely – all is again topsy turvy'.[17]

The tide, on which the young reformers moved so triumphantly, began to turn. Only later did stories arrive from London. O'Connor heard,

... the facts have come to light to show that it was not the

Catholic question which made Pitt break the engagement he had taken with the Duke of Portland and Lord Fitzwilliam, these facts are that the dismissal of the Beresfords, Wolfe and Toler was the real cause. When Beresford received his dismissal he posted off to London, saw his patron Jenkinson, and when this Minister of Ministers, this maker and breaker of Ministers saw the King, Pitt got his orders and was forced to yield.[18]

As a man of honour Pitt was bound not to expose the character of Lord Fitzwilliam with the Irish nation by making him break his promise, but I am not estimating the honour of Pitt, I have had too much to do with the break of his and his agents of their most solemn engagements with me.[19]

The reforms afoot in Dublin alarmed the King. The Opposition were being given positions of power, Whigs and Reformers were in the Cabinet. Parliament was poised to admit Roman Catholics. The King made a clear decision.

On 10 March 1795 George III wrote to Pitt,

I am much pleased with Mr Pitt's account that both the Earl Camden and Mr Pelham are willing to accept the offices of Ld Lt and Secretary for the kingdom which have been rendered more difficult by the strange conduct of Earl Fitzwilliam. I approve of Earl Camden being nominated in the Great Council Room tomorrow and I trust he will understand that he is to reinstate and to support the old English interest as well as the Protestant religion.

George R.[20]

Fitzwilliam was recalled. He left Ireland on 25 March 1795 and with him went much of Ireland's hope. In Dublin, people wore mourning. The Whigs were furious, the young radicals felt rage and impotence surge in them once more. Lord Edward paced. Inside Arthur O'Connor the tide turned. He had played his part as a young gentleman of the Ascendancy, but a man must be true to his principles. The vigour of the nation was being wasted. Men of ability were powerless. How could Ireland develop under this corrupt and partial leadership? All her energy, her resources, her people must be engaged. For O'Connor, no further compromise was possible.

Fitzgibbon advised Beresford to sue. In fact Beresford soon would get back all his old offices and patronage. The radicals later expressed their rage and bitterness by a corruption of the Anglican liturgy:

CREAD

I believe in John Beresford, the Father Almighty of the Revenue, Creator of the North Wall, the OTTIWELL Jobb and the Coal Tax, and in his true son JOHN CLAUDIUS, who was conceived in the spirit of the Chancellor, born of the Virgin Custom-House, suffered under Earl Fitzwilliam, was stigmatised, spurned at and dismissed.

The third week he arose again, ascended into the cabinet and sitteth on the right hand of his Father, from whence he shall come to Judge by Court Martial both the Quick and the Dead, those who are to be Hanged and those whose Fortunes are to be Confiscated, I believe in the Holy Earl of Clare, in the Holy Orange Lodges, in the Communion of Commissioners, in the forgiveness of Sins by Acts of Indemnity, in the Resurrection of the protestant Ascendancy and Jobbing everlasting.   Amen.[21]

On 14 April 1795, Lord Shannon wrote to his son,

I yesterday waited on His X [the new Lord Lieutenant, Earl Camden] – his business was to talk over the Question that was first to come on upon the meeting of the House – it is decidedly the opinion of the Cabinet, as well as his own that the Representative Franchise should be resisted and Mr G's [Grattan] Bill thrown out. He is not afraid of Mobs or newspapers, sure how much the Question involves the interests of both England and Ireland, considers the Protestant Establishment as being at stake and in short, if supported, is ready to stand the Brunt.[22]

Did the Grandees of the Ascendancy have any conception of how horrible the Brunt would be? Thus braced, they went back into parliament.

On 23 April Jackson was tried, found guilty and took poison. He died in the dock awaiting sentence. Fearful, McNally of the United Irishmen turned informer. From then on, his reports arrived regularly in the Castle. At court and in Dublin Castle the reforming tendency had reached its limit. Now it would recede, an anxious hold would tighten in place of liberal reform. Yet, despite the heavy hand now descending on Irish political life, Grattan introduced his Catholic Bill.

O'Connor left his home in Merrion Square, paced along the streets of Dublin. At the entrance to the Parliament House, tense faces and unquiet hands expressed the pent-up state of Members. It was a critical moment. 'It was in face of this wanton sporting with every feeling of the Irish nation, that I resolved to make one last appeal to reason, common sense and justice; and if these failed, to have recourse to that resistance to such flagrant acknowledged oppression, which the laws of my country gave me.'[23] O'Connor had set his course.

'One of the most remarkable speeches in this debate was delivered by Arthur O'Connor,' wrote Lecky. 'Like Emmet, McNevin and FitzGerald, he had not yet joined the United Irishmen; but he was already at heart a rebel; his speech is in a different key from the others ... and it shows clearly both the influence of the new French ideas, and the process by which so many were now passing rapidly into rebellion.'[24]

O'Connor's political view reached maturity on 4 May 1795 when he spoke in the House of Commons.

What do the whole of the arguments which have been advanced on this night, against the emancipation of our Catholic countrymen, by the gentlemen of the opposite side of the House amount to? To a mere unsupported assertion, that it would destroy our constitution in church and state.

O'Connor says Ireland never enjoyed the liberties of the British constitution. The country, he said, was run by a small aristocratical monopoly.

> Here is a system by which our national character would be degraded in the eyes of surrounding nations ... The men who usurp the whole political power of the country, the men who have converted the whole representation of Ireland into family patrimony; to the poverty, to the oppression, and to the disgrace of the nation, and to the monstrous aggrandizement of themselves, their relatives, and their servile adherents; these are the men who oppose Catholic emancipation, and why? – Because Catholic emancipation would be incompatible with their accursed monopoly.
>
> On this night, your adoption or rejection of this bill must determine in the eyes of the Irish nation, which you represent, the Minister of England, or the people of Ireland ... If you shall have convinced them that instead of rising or falling with England, they are never to rise ... it is human nature, that you shall have driven the people of this country to court the alliance of any nation able and willing to break the chains of a bondage not more galling to their feelings than restrictive of their prosperity.

He warned those on the government benches, who spoke against the bill,

> Do not depend on the bayonet for the support of your measure; believe me that in proportion as your measures require force to support them, in an exact proportion, are they radically and mischievously bad. Is it not enough that you live in the age and in the midst of the horrors of revolution, to deter you from acting in contempt of public opinion. You must be blind not to perceive that the whole European mind has undergone a revolution.
>
> The cause of freedom is the cause of God.[25]

The Bill was thrown out. There would not be Catholic members of parliament. Emancipation seemed impossible to achieve. From this point on, Irish political life became polarised.

Short-hand was a well-established skill and speeches, debates and trials were published verbatim. Soon, O'Connor's speech was widely discussed. Wolfe Tone described it as 'the ablest and honestest speech, to my mind, that ever was made in that house'.[26] The absolute declaration of his position caused comment among radicals in Ireland and Britain, among the government supporters and among independents.

Edmund Burke wrote to Fitzwilliam:

It should seem as if young O'Connor gave himself his full swing. I am sorry for it. He has good parts; and on his Uncle Longfield's death he will have a large fortune. I saw him at Bath about three years ago. He was then an enthusiast, an admirer of Rousseau and the French writers, but, as I thought, very tractable; and had taken, on the whole, a very proper direction. What became of him after that time I never knew: I saw he had a mind of great energy, and was capable of much good or of much evil.[27]

To Thomas Hussey, Burke wrote: 'That one speech, though full of fire and animation, was not warmed with the fire of heaven. I am sorry for it. I have seen that gentleman but once. He is certainly a man of parts, but one who has dealt too much in the philosophy of France.'[28]

John Knox wrote to Arthur O'Connor at Merrion Square: 'I congratulate you very heartily on your late speech which I understand contained more political boldness than any ever delivered in a House of Commons. What says Lord Longueville upon the occasion?'[29]

Richard Longfield had been made a Baron that year in reward for his loyalty and service to the state and he was very displeased with his nephew's speech. Arthur had slipped from independence and republicanism to radical vehemence and challenge to the parliamentary system on which the landed interest depended. Arthur's eloquence made this alarming. The bitterness and anger of his nephew's speech sent a chill through the uncle. This was rather more than the customary speeches of Grattan and the patriots; here was a growing rage and contempt for the system. The split between the newly created Lord Longueville and Arthur O'Connor became unbridgeable. Longueville disinherited his nephew and took away his patronage. O'Connor lost his parliamentary seat.

This long and impassioned speech was his last attempt to influence through parliament. When the Bill was defeated, he lost trust in that body. The speech was also a threat. Lord Edward had been flirting with French agents, Tone had worked with Jackson. O'Connor had held back, but no longer.

> The more I examined the state of things the firmer the conviction I acquired, that every right, every principle of law and Justice sanctioned the most rigorous resistance to this state of misery and oppression. I studied the state of the public mind in the capital, in the south, in the west and I went to the north to seek it ... here I found an ardour for liberty, a love of independence accompanied with an intelligence that was not to be found in any population of Europe except that of the lowlands of Scotland. This decided me to fix my hopes of being able to establish a republic in Ireland in the north among the Presbyterians. I found no difficulty in gaining the entire confidence of the men who composed the Northern Executive.[30]

After the arrests of Rowan and Drennan, the seizing of papers, the Society of United Irishmen had been dormant. Gradually through 1794 they re-established themselves in Belfast. They were now a secret and more radical group.

'The system for uniting classes of Irishmen had been discontinued since the beginning of 1793,' wrote O'Connor,

> ... when persecution raged with such violence throughout all Ireland. It was in 1795 after Pitt's breach of faith with Lord Fitzwilliam and the Irish nation that the Union was pushed with the greatest vigour. Then it was that it was agreed between me and the Northern Executive that they should continue their

most strenuous efforts and that Lord Edward FitzGerald and I should propagate the Union in the other three provinces and particularly in Leinster.[31]

From the north I went to London at the end of 1795, where the part I had taken in Ireland procured me the most cordial reception from the Opposition ... With these highly honourable independent men I found myself in an atmosphere congenial to my soul.[32]

On 13 June 1795 Wolfe Tone left Ireland for America. Implicated with Jackson, he was a marked man. His talent as a writer, his work for the Catholic Committee and emancipation had made him famous, but his memorial for Jackson had endangered him. He fled to Philadelphia. He had already agreed with Emmet, Russell, Simms, Neilson and Teeling that he would act as agent to the French, seeking aid in a bid for Ireland's independence. In fact America was congenial and Tone was considering settling there when news reached him that republican activity was increasing in Ireland. He was pressed back into action. On 1 January 1796, he left his wife, children and sister in America and sailed for France.

The United Irish movement was active again. Now members took an oath 'to obtain an equal, full and adequate representation of all the people of Ireland'.[33] Members undertook to work for a Union of all the Irish people. The Defenders were drawn in. Continuous efforts were required to teach all Irishmen to work together within the Union. Prejudice ran deep. The oath did not mention republican government nor separation from England but several of its leaders had these goals. Others were more circumspect. It was this divergence of opinion about their ultimate ends that was to be one of their principal weaknesses.

The other was spies and informers. Among the Castle papers and the correspondence of the Dublin government with London are the reports, memorials, requests for payment and accounts paid, of the men who betrayed the United Irishmen to government. From the first letter of Wolfe Tone in 1791 until the rising of 1798, and after, almost every move on the part of the United men was known to the government. Occasionally, the informers embroidered to make their reports fatter and more valuable. Sometimes they used them to settle old scores with rivals and enemies, sometimes they surmised and were wrong. But vital information was fed to government continuously and fatally for the Union of Irishmen.

Arthur O'Connor was discreet and secretive. He alarmed Dublin Castle by the faintness of the trail he left behind him. The Castle received few reports of him, almost none of his letters. The government saw well enough what the man did in public but his private actions were hard for them to find. The sunlight of Lord Edward's activities was visible and clear. The moonlight movement of O'Connor's shadow was difficult to discern. Bold in oratory and pamphlet, he was taciturn in correspondence, secretive, almost indiscernible in conspiracy.

Chapter 8

EMISSARY OF THE UNITED IRISHMEN

I will represent myself as the man who united the minds and forces of the North and the South of Ireland to join in separation and that formed the treaty with France.[1]

After the suppression of the Dublin Society of United Irishmen in May 1794, the movement had broken down. Emmet was debating reform with Grattan. Drennan was careful. Lord Edward spent most of his time in Kildare with his wife and new baby. Romantic, he turned to the native culture as he had in America. He enjoyed the local music, danced jigs, drank whiskey and tended his garden. But his contacts among the radicals had grown, become firm.

In Belfast, the Society of United Irishmen persisted. The *Northern Star* propagated their ideas despite two failed prosecutions by the government. The *Star* printed extracts from the works of the philosopher John Locke and of Thomas Paine. But the Society went underground and was re-structured. The meetings became secret and a pyramidal system was created based on local societies of no more than 35 people. Each of these sent three delegates to a barony committee which sent delegates to the county committee. When two or more county committees had been formed, delegates created a provincial committee. This was to lead to a National Directory. Names were never to be reported from one meeting to another. Delegates to the barony did not mention their comrades, nor the barony members when they came home. This structure protected the members' identity and could be adapted for military purposes.

After his speech on Catholic emancipation, O'Connor's career took a new direction. Lord Edward had been talking revolution ever since they met but Arthur had hoped that parliamentary reform was still possible. Lord Fitzwilliam's appointment had raised his hopes, his recall blasted those hopes like frost in June. The defeat of Grattan's bill turned disappointment to rage. But in Dublin, the United leaders were inactive; in the countryside of Munster, Leinster and Connaught, United activity hardly existed. O'Connor travelled north.

In Belfast he met the leaders, 'Robert and William Simms, Samuel Neilson, William Tennent, Dr White and two others'.[2] For the first four of these men, O'Connor had great respect and admiration. Presbyterians, free-thinking and well-educated, there was a strong resonance with his own rationalist views. In Belfast the ideas of the Enlightenment had penetrated, commercial prosperity bred confidence, energy and courage. It had a different atmosphere altogether from Ascendancy Dublin's wealth and terrors, from the conservative and superstitious mood of the rural south. Belfast had an understanding of liberty; it was clear air that O'Connor breathed with joy.

Tall, well dressed and well spoken, the power of O'Connor's personality was obvious. His intellectual ability, the direction of his ideas must have impressed the Belfast republicans. They accepted him as one of their own. Arthur O'Connor was an impressive man. He had Irish grace and ease of manner but was equally familiar with high society in London. He was highly educated. Once engaged by an idea or course of action, he could not be deflected and his speech had arrived before him as his credentials.

Arms were being smuggled into Ireland. Government raids in the north brought in some arms, but they also antagonised the population who were arrested or harassed. At night, Defenders and United men broke into country houses to steal weapons, despite the prohibitions of their leaders. The country was restive, the government anxious. Lord Camden was installed as Lord Lieutenant in Dublin Castle, Mr Pelham his Secretary was ailing and unwell. The war with France was proving expensive, Mr Pitt had been forced to raise new taxes and take out heavy loans. But in France the Terror began to subside. Robespierre fell in July 1794, a new constitution was adopted in 1795 and a Directory of five men took office. With real government, France posed a greater threat to Britain, while Ireland became increasingly disturbed and violent. The country was passing away from civil government towards martial law. It was not difficult to recruit United Irishmen.

Arthur O'Connor joined the Ulster provincial committee. While the Dublin society remained inactive, vacillated, he, the Belfast committee and Lord Edward moved their plans forward. It was important to build the organisation from the ground up. Societies were proliferating in Ulster and Lord Edward was recruiting in Kildare.

Lord Longueville had rejected Arthur in disgust. New elections were due in 1797. The seat for Philipstown would be given to a more loyal associate. As for Longueville's land and fortune, he had other relatives who would show more regard for conservative values. If Arthur was taking up French radicalism, Lord Longueville would certainly not entrust him with the family estates. O'Connor was disappointed in his expectations, wounded by the rejection, and bitter. Wealth meant a great deal to him. But he must follow his own ideals. Lord Lansdowne said it was unfair since Longueville had known Arthur's views from the start.[3] But his uncle had sat through the speech in which O'Connor castigated the political establishment of Ireland and threatened them with foreign intervention. Longueville would not soften and O'Connor would not change his views.

He must have been vacillating about how to act. Towards the end of 1795 O'Connor travelled from Belfast to London where he took rooms at No. 13 Grafton Street, Fitzroy Square.[4] He quickly became an intimate of Fox, Sheridan and their circle.

> It was delicious to me to live with and to hear men imbued with the genuine love of their country, discussing her interests with the warmth and truth which conviction furnishes the mind. Fox and the opposition saw in me a man of unshaken principles who spoke as he thought and this mutual openness of each other created mutual confidence and mutual esteem.[5]

Though I lived with all the Opposition in perfect confidence those with whom I was most particularly linked and to whom I was most intimately attached was Fox and Sheridan. It was impossible to live and converse intimately and confidentially with men so highly gifted, with men whose noble frankness made the basis of all they said and did, without loving them. Fox with the reserved and serious manner of an Englishman was as freely communicative as man could be. After three years intimate knowledge of this great and good man, I declare ... that he was incapable of deceit or of swerving an iota from the impression the subject matter made upon his senses, he appeared to me a human chronomettre which marks time with unerring exactitude.[6]

In my intimacy with these distinguished men I had occasion to observe the immense impression profound scientific discussions of the French Constituent Assembly had made on every European.[7]

Man was taken with his strong propensity to seize on the produce of the labour of others and invert it to his own enjoyment leaving the producer nothing for his pains ... The Whigs as the Tories owed their pre-eminence to the monopoly feudal law of primogeniture. Hence the French revolution that placed its government on the Eternal principle of Equality was as averse to the Whig as to the Tory.[8]

The difference between Whig and Tory was the liberal attitudes of the former. O'Connor felt their ideas were not wholly consistent. He wanted government based on a real scientific understanding of man's nature, on the principle of equality, the whole enshrined in law. 'The grounds for the great and generous minds of Fox and Sheridan for preferring them [the French principles] was the progress they offered for the human race.'[9] The problems which France had in establishing a system on these principles did not, in O'Connor's view, make the principles wrong. Fox was more concerned about the war.

How often have I heard my beloved Fox give vent to the poignant grief he felt at seeing his country threw away the inestimable blessings of a peace she could have so greatly turned to her prosperity, for that war which he saw must in the end be her ruin. What a heart piercing thought to see himself the but and object of the fanatical enmity of his country while the man who employed such vile deception to draw them to their ruin was their idol.[10]

Pitt was, indeed, very popular. Fox was seen as a francophile, a lover of Jacobins, as unpatriotic. He had never had a good public image. A decade earlier William Drennan's sister had referred to Pitt as 'that angelic youth' and North and Fox as 'those dangerous monsters'.[11] As the intimate of two founding United Irishmen, she shared many of their values. Pitt was upright and clean-living in her eyes. Fox was too intellectual for the popular press, too international in his perspective; he was fascinating company for O'Connor.

'With what delight I look back on those delicious conversations tête à tête with this great and good man at his villa at Anne's Hill when till midnight we walked amidst the warblings of his nightingales he so delighted to hear. It was here away from the bustle and the littleness of the world we sought in what possible way England could be saved.'[12] O'Connor had always believed that Britain's mismanagement of her relationship with Ireland was to the enormous detriment of both. If Britain ruled Ireland, it must be on the basis of absolute equality, with Ireland as much a part of the whole as the shires of England. Dublin could not affect government in London so the relationship was never balanced. Now Ireland suffered Pitt, with war, debt and loss of civil rights. In one year Pitt had raised £17m in taxes and £51m from loans for the ruinous cost of the war. All this would weaken the country and bear down on the people while still the question of reform was not solved.

One day we dined with Lord Robert Spencer. Grey and Lauderdale were maintaining the great solidity a thorough reform would give to the monarchy. I maintained that no thorough reform could ever be effected (but) by the destruction of the feudal laws of primogenture and as an extension, in the participation in the Lords. Then reform and republic, in exclusion of hereditary privilege, would be synonomous. At this, Grey and Lauderdale took fire and accused me of giving an argument which was the strongest against reform. I answered it was not a question of furnishing an argument for or against reform, but a question of fact. I appealed to Fox, who said to Grey and Lauderdale, 'you are children to deny what O'Connor advances. Do you not perceive that a Minister of the Monarchy who from the vast patronage of the craven and the imperfect state of the representation can count on a majority, and a Minister who from the perfect representatives could not count on any majority, are in directly opposite situations, that in the first case the monarchy leads and governs, and in the other is led and governed'.[13]

These men were very occupied by the balance of power between the monarch, the government and parliament. History had shown that the monarch could be controlled, even removed or replaced; far harder to control or replace the government. For this reason, the role and membership of parliament was a question of absolute priority. It alone could act, on behalf of the nation, in controlling the government.[14]

I proposed a dinner at the famous beef-steak chop house – Dolly's, in the city. We were a dozen. Lauderdale and I walked together. In passing through New Gate Street he quitted my arm suddenly and ran into a Book-seller's shop – it was the famous Eatons! I followed him some short time after and found him filling his pocket with pamphlets. On coming out he said, 'I have found here a pamphlet which when it came out puzzled Fox and all of us to define who could be the author. It is a most extraordinary work.' In saying this he gave me one. On looking at it, I found it was the pamphlet I had written years before when at Ryde at the house of my friend General Knox. We found Fox, Grey and Sheridan arrived and sitting round the dinner table, awaiting the arrival of the others. Lauderdale threw one of the pamphlets to Grey who, on reading the title page, said he had heard of it, that it was a most wicked pamphlet, to which Lauderdale replied 'it was O'Connor who wrote it'. Now of all men Grey was the most serious and would not offend anyone on any account, he was very angry with Lauderdale and accused him of saying things to put friends at variance. He declared to me he had never read the pamphlet. I requested he would read it and if he found anything reprehensible or that he thought unfounded to communicate it to me. In two or three days after I met Mrs Grey who told me Grey desired much to see me, she believed it was about a pamphlet, if I would dine with them that day we should be alone and free to discuss it. The first word Grey said to me when we met was, 'well I have read your little work with the greatest attention and I declare that I subscribe to every tittle of it'. As it was not a little republican, I had frequent occasion to perceive that Grey's mind was expanding out of the old routine and some time after, at a little supper party with the Duchess of Devonshire, I learnt I was not the only one to perceive it for the Duchess, on hearing Grey express him with great warmth on the state to which Pitt was bringing the nation, observed that since his intimacy with me he was becoming a republican, to which Grey replied that he had the strongest conviction that to serve his country he should be a Jacobin but he acknowledged to his shame, he had not the resolution to do what he ought.[15]

What was a Jacobin? A member of the French political club which struggled for the principles of extreme democracy and absolute equality, in which there was no hereditary rank or privilege, and all had equal rights.[16] Arguments still raged over how this could be achieved but universal male suffrage was the common idea and abolition of hereditary political power important. Votes for women were hardly discussed, in France, Britain or Ireland. There is some suggestion that Lord Edward had picked up the idea of female suffrage in France where radical circles included women of education and influence. O'Connor may have considered this idea but does not specifically discuss it. It was raised by Mary McCracken, sister of a Presbyterian Ulster United man.[17]

My intimacy with Fox and Sheridan augmented every day until it arrived on a most entire mutual confidence. Fox was constrained with the Whigs who still adhered to him and with me the conversation was free as air; what gained me confidence with Fox was my never advancing anything without giving the principle that governed my opinion.[18]

My intimacy with Sheridan was equally confidential, but of a different shade from the difference of the two men. Though Sheridan had not been in Ireland after the age of eleven, he was essentially an Irishman with the heart and affectionate feelings of that country. On arriving at London in 1795 I did not seek an introduction but wrote to Sheridan to know when I could find him at home. My first words were to express I had long felt to know the countryman I had heard with such admiration and delight in 1787. He received me with the warmest expression of his desire to cultivate my friendship. Never did a warmer nor a more sincere friendship unite two hearts together.[19]

They spent a great deal of time discussing Edmund Burke and agreed that he had an extraordinary intellect but a heart which was unclear and prejudiced. Although Burke believed in the laws of nature and seemed a man of reason, yet both Sheridan and O'Connor agreed that Burke loved aristocracy and hankered after popery.[20] In any case there had been an irreparable rift between the Opposition and Burke over his *Reflections on the Revolution in France*. They were all wounded by the split but could not heal it.

In the constant society of those inestimable men my time passed in a state of happiness given to few to enjoy. I remarked in Sheridan a kind of instinct I myself inherited from my adored mother ... which enabled me to distinguish the sentiments those I was in contact with entertained towards me. I had a most extraordinary proof of this sense in Sheridan. At a supper at his house of at least fifty persons, he rose from the bottom of the long table to come to the top where Mrs Grey and I were conversing, to whisper in my ear, 'don't be making comparisons between my wife and my former one'. The fact is it was the subject of our conversation, though in a low whisper for we were quite close to Mrs Sheridan and he was at the other extremity. I assured him we neither said [nor] thought anything that was [not] what his heart could wish. He pressed my hand affectionately. This made an astonishing impression on Mrs Grey, so strong that she assured me we durst not even think of anything which could be displeasing to Sheridan.[21]

This life of dining-room politics could not continue. In Ireland, the state of the country was becoming ever more volatile. Britain was scarcely better. Bad harvests had pushed up the price of grain. The cost of the war was soaring and Pitt was sufficiently worried about rural discontent to draw up new plans for poor relief and apprenticeships. Britain was very over-extended in military terms and her allies capitulating. A great deal depended on the British navy.

Radical discontent was pervasive. The London Corresponding Society, set up in 1792, read works by Paine and other radicals. A similar movement grew up in Scotland. They exchanged greetings with the French Assembly until war made this seditious. Pressing for reform, they also became divided among themselves. Severe sentences for sedition in Scotland made the London Society more defiant. Three leaders, Hardy, Tooke and Thelwall, were charged with high treason in late 1794. They were discharged. The Society went into suspension.

Ireland was in a far more drastic condition. Rural sectarian violence was on the increase as the Peep O'Days Boys, Defenders and the newly created Orange Order all took vengeance. In the political classes, there was polarisation. The commercial life of the nation was disrupted because trade was increasingly difficult with war at sea. The Catholic leaders were disaffected from government over emancipation. Poor harvests, high rents, tithes and new taxes bore down on the common man while the militia grew in numbers and was scattered through the country in small undisciplined units. Lord Camden was nervous. His letters from Dublin Castle to the Secretary of State in London, the Duke of Portland, became more irascible, the grammar more uncertain, his handwriting ever more indecipherable. Luckily his secretaries were capable and official letters could be transcribed by clerks. But the secret correspondence could only be written by his closest associates. The packets, the ships which sailed across the Irish Sea almost daily, brought letters which crossed each other, worried and fumed. When one such letter took six days, the recipient complained how slow the mail was becoming.

In Ulster, the Orange Order had begun in 1794 after the sectarian Battle of the Diamond. In two years the Order had spread through Ulster and caused fear in the south. Wherever United Irish Societies sprang up, Orange lodges followed. The early ideas of cultural equality, as envisaged by the United Irishmen, held no attraction for Orangemen, who swore an oath 'to support the King and his heirs as long as he or they support the Protestant Ascendancy'.[22]

'The information I received from the north, from Dublin and from the south was alarming',[23] wrote O'Connor. Recalling Fitzwilliam had been a catastrophe for Pitt's policy in Ireland but he had the orders of the King to contend with. George III was quite clear in his own mind that he had the right to appoint his Ministers, even if he had occasionally to take note of majorities in parliament. The last British monarch to try to re-establish powers lost during the Civil War and Glorious Revolution, George III imagined the nation was his inherited estate. His children were liberal and self-indulgent. Under Queen Victoria the terms of British constitutional monarchy established firm precedents from which it continued to develop. George III failed in re-taking power, but irreparable harm resulted.

Letters from Ireland shook O'Connor. The United Irish Societies had grown rapidly in the north, 'spread like fire through all Ulster'[24] and the same spirit pervaded east, south and west. United societies began to penetrate the strongly Gaelic province of Connaught though here they were more a Defender and Catholic movement. As a political club, it had allowed Irishmen of many backgrounds to identify themselves as a single nation through debate. This function faded. The Societies became practical, hurried into military preparation.

The reports which reached Arthur in London became increasingly urgent and he returned to Ireland. They were not exaggerated. The state of the country was deteriorating and every action of the government made it worse. Ministers seemed astonished that their methods for quieting discontent had increased the fever. They thought they were dealing with ignorant people who could be led or crushed but men who know their rights are harder to control. 'What a lesson this for a statesman.' In Belfast, O'Connor was quickly reunited with the leaders of the United Irishmen. 'The Executive informed me they had made me the President of the Union and Commander in Chief and that, resolved to avoid every rash movement, they would arm themselves with patience, that if the Volunteers had not been disarmed, things would be soon settled but as they were, we must find means to repair them. It was not difficult for me to comprehend that of all necessity we should be drawn to seek for foreign aid.'[25]

First he went south to see the public mood in Dublin, settle his affairs and investigate the state of the country. A new urgency had entered the reform movement as it was driven inexorably towards the mental state of revolution. O'Connor wasted no time in making his decisions. In Dublin he put his house up for sale, along with his horses, carriage and furniture. He went down to Cork.[26] His brother Roger had all the wild spirit necessary for rebellion. He had charm and local contacts. Roger began enlisting United men throughout the county. Arthur spent considerable time organising the agents of the United Irishmen, for organisation was paramount for recruiting and for building a structure of command.[27]

The Leinster provincial committee had been organised but O'Connor did not feel constrained by it. Although he had a great regard for Oliver Bond and Henry Jackson, he was impatient with Thomas Addis Emmet.[28] Emmet was O'Connor's only rival for the intellectual leadership of the movement. The son of Dr Robert Emmet MD, State Physician, Thomas had learnt medicine in Edinburgh, but after his elder brother died, changed to law and took an outstanding degree at Trinity. He was a thoughtful man of integrity, who had grown up in the city of Cork and then lived and worked in Dublin. He married in 1792 and had children. Cautious and legalistic, he had none of the fire of O'Connor nor the spontaneity of FitzGerald.[29]

The structure of the United Irishmen had never been fully rebuilt after 1794. In O'Connor's perception the National

Executive was composed of the Ulster provincial committee, himself and Lord Edward. Of this executive he had just been appointed President and Commander-in-Chief.[30] That the constitution of the Union provided for a National Executive elected by four provincial committees was not something he could wait for. Every day the situation became more unstable. The war escalated. Britain was hard-pressed, financially and militarily. If ever she was to receive a final blow from Ireland supported by continental allies, a blow which would make her leave go, now was the moment. If Thomas Addis Emmet wanted to spend his time talking reform with Henry Grattan, he could be overruled. O'Connor was among the tradesmen of Dublin and Cork, out in the countryside, talking to men who might be asked to fight for the independence of their country, trying to show them how to see beyond the local religious rivalries and perceive one Ireland, the Union of Irishmen. This was Ireland to him, this was the world in which he had been raised, where he had hunted, learned soldiering.

He arrived in Kildare in February, to spend time with his 'beloved Lord Edward'.[31] FitzGerald had not abandoned parliament. He spoke out there against the Insurrection Bill in February 1796, a Bill which gave sweeping powers to local magistrates and made oath-administration a capital offence. But parliament seemed less and less relevant. Bills were being passed quickly to reduce rights and increase arbitrary power for those in authority.

Pamela FitzGerald, known as Lady Edward, was pregnant again. Little Eddy, 'avec des grands yeux blues', was a healthy child and beginning to run about. Pamela was an adoring and capable mother but her life in rural Kildare was neither peaceful nor safe. Her husband's visitors were radicals. He spent most of his time out in the countryside talking to farmers and inviting them into the movement. Like O'Connor, Lord Edward had spent most of his childhood in the country, learning to ride and shoot. Now his brother's tenants were his potential converts. He propagated reform, emancipation and a brotherhood of the sects. When O'Connor wrote to Charles Fox, these were the terms in which he described the country.[32] Alone together, O'Connor and FitzGerald discussed other possibilities.

O'Connor returned to London.

The account I gave to Fox, Sheridan, Grey and the opposition caused them the greatest sorrow and made them loud in the execration of Pitt's wantoness and bad faith that had brought the Empire to such jeopardy. My excellent friends sympathised with me and it seems as I afterwards discovered they perceived I had become thoughtful and lost much of my usual gaiety.[33]

Philosophy and science might illuminate the decision. When he acted, it would be irrevocable. In London he could talk to Francis Burdett of Ireland's problems, to Fox and Sheridan of Irish politics but he no longer spoke freely. He moved too in increasingly radical circles. On 3 March 1796, he met William Godwin and over the next two months they met frequently, at dinner, for coffee, once at the opera, where they discussed radical politics.[34] Godwin was seven years older than O'Connor, born at Wisbech, East Anglia where his father was a dissenting Minister. Godwin had made his name writing *An Enquiry concerning Political Justice*. He knew Paine whose *Rights of Man* had been published with his direction. The poet, Samuel Taylor Coleridge, was a political disciple of his, later a close friend. At this time, Godwin was embarking on a love affair with Mary Wollstonecraft the feminist author, whose Irish mother was a friend of Archibald Hamilton Rowan. Their daughter would later marry the poet Percy Bysshe Shelley.

Godwin was a dry, clever and earnest man. An example of his dinner invitation to a friend reads: 'Mr Kennedy and Mr Curran ... dine with me tomorrow. Will you make one; I love anything that resembles the Trinity. To represent the unity, which is the soul of all religion, I shall put nothing but one marrow-bone on the table. We starve at the vulgar hour of four.'[35]

Godwin was at the centre of a radical circle which included Burdett, O'Connor, Horne Tooke, Coleridge and Paine. He made lists of people he wished to meet, then got introductions to them. He read their work carefully, noted and discussed it. O'Connor's pamphlet *Measures of Ministry* ... was noted in Godwin's journal during the period when they met frequently.[36] Fox, Sheridan,

Curran and many leading free-thinkers were among his acquaintances.

O'Connor explored this new group of radicals. In London, different prejudices lodged in men's minds from those which Ireland
clung to. The English had a surprising attachment to primogeniture.

> In my youth I passed a day with Horne Tooke at his house at
> Wimbledon. The French laws of succession was the subject of
> discussion; in the midst of it, Tooke drew a long poniard-knife
> from his pocket, opened the blade, and presenting it towards
> me with a furious look: 'This,' said he, 'is the argument I
> employ with men who take the side of the question that you
> do.' I took an early moment to quit the room, and was followed
> by Sir Francis Burdett, who was so shocked with this action of
> Tooke's, that he expressed his sorrow and astonishment so
> superior a man should, in his own house, break off a discussion
> in so brutal a manner.[37]

On 28 March 1796, Charles Fox wrote to Arthur O'Connor at
Grafton Street to say that Mr Lambert might be willing to sell him a
parliamentary seat for £3,000 Irish. 'I owe you my apologies for not
having sooner acquainted you with these particulars. I am with great
truth and regard, sir, your obedient humble servant, C.J. Fox.'[38]

It is not clear whether the seat was for the British or Irish parliament, though it is unlikely a British seat would be sold for Irish
pounds. O'Connor was still vacillating between parliament and
rebellion. The mental strain was intense. He, the philosopher who
studied so carefully modern theories of law, economics and constitution must wrestle with himself, the Irishman, proud, passionate
with deep racial memory who desired only that Ireland be a free
nation. It was now becoming impossible to reconcile the two.

O'Connor made up his mind. 'From the beginning of May
1796, my determination was firmly taken to take the decided step
of negotiating foreign alliance.'[39] He got the necessary letters for a
visit to Switzerland.

Two 'United Scotchmen' called on him, one by the name of

Kennedy, who had heard he was President of the Irish Union and wanted him to take command of the United Scots. O'Connor refused, on the grounds that he could not well perform the two offices, let the Scots go without taking their addresses and later regretted the loss of contact.[40]

Tone was in Paris. He had made contact with Carnot, a member of the Directory and was trying to negotiate for French military support for Ireland. O'Connor received decisive letters from Belfast.

Early in May, Lord Edward arrived in London with Pamela, seven months pregnant, and their baby son.

> Edward entered with a serious look quite unusual and without embracing me asked me if we were without the hearing of anyone, for that he had something of the highest importance to communicate. Here I stopped him, 'I see by your face you are come to tell me that you have seen the Northern Executive and that they have sent you to tell me the time is come for me to negotiate alliance with France.' 'In the name of God,' says Edward, 'who could have told you, on my sacred honor not one letter of it has ever escaped my lips.' I told him it was impossible for me not to see that at the rate the Irish government were goading the people the same idea of the necessity of resistance must strike everyone, that I had so anticipated the idea of the executive that all my preparations were made and I shewed him my letters etc. We then immediately settled that he and Pamela should set out for Hamburg to see her mother Madame de Genlis, that I would follow him immediately.[41]

Arthur was now introduced to Lord Edward's sister. Lady Lucy FitzGerald had a similar temperament to her brother. In her diary she recorded: 'we went to the exhibition: we had company to dinner – Mr O'Connor, the man who made the famous speech. He is Edward's great friend, of course a great Democrat. There was a great dinner at our house ...' and 'The Edwards set off for Hamburg. They leave their child here.'[42]

Charles James Fox, Lord Edward's cousin was a francophile,

keen to see representative government set up in France, but he also abhorred violence and was devoted to his own country, England. He knew well enough the kind of government which ruled Ireland. It is a difficult question just how much he knew of FitzGerald's motives for the trip to France. O'Connor was exceptionally discreet and talked in terms of political science. Lord Edward was less cautious. Lewins, a senior United Irishman later wrote that Fox did not know of the plans but asked Lord Edward if they concerned Irish independence. FitzGerald replied that they did. At which, Fox exclaimed, 'Good God, do nothing without being certain.'[43]

Before they left London, the FitzGeralds visited Devonshire House. Pamela's daughter later wrote:

... my mother told me she supped at Devonshire House, and the Duke of York took her in to supper, and speaking kindly about my father and regretting the course of politics, he at last said: 'Allow me to advise you as a friend most seriously, use your influence, your whole influence, to deter Lord Edward from going abroad. More is known of the plans of those he thinks his friends than you can imagine, in short,' he added, 'all is known.' She tried on returning home to persuade him to give up Hamburg, but she did not succeed.[44]

Lord Edward left his tiny son with his mother, the Duchess of Leinster and took Pamela to Hamburg. It was the only northern European port open to the British because of the war and French control of the Dutch fleet. Madame de Genlis was in Hamburg for the wedding of her niece Henriette to Mr Mathiessen. This was the pretext for the FitzGerald's visit, Pamela and Henriette had grown up together.

The government had numberless informers, whose motives ranged from desire for payment and advancement, to loyalty to the government and the crown, to fear of revolution. In Dublin, the most prominent was the barrister Leonard McNally, but there were many more. Information, too, reached Dublin Castle and the London government from overseas merchants, spies in the French diplomatic service and gentlemen travelling abroad. They also opened letters and read them, before sending them on.

In Paris, Tone had already done all the preliminary work. He had opened communications with the Directory and got access to Carnot. By April he had received an outline offer of assistance from the Directory. Drafting a concrete proposal took time. He had spent weeks on drafting and re-drafting his memorial on the state of Ireland. He had had tedious, almost daily meetings with Henri Clarke, a second generation Irishman in the French Ministry of War, working in French, a language he found difficult. But Tone had been away from Ireland for a year. The Directory had not committed themselves. A descent on Ireland was attractive; separating her from England might prove a fatal blow to their enemy. But Tone alone could not convince the French. British naval power was a reality and France could not afford unsuccessful naval expeditions. The French fleets must be used with economy and precision. France was now more confident on land. Her armies in Europe had had a number of important victories over the Austrians. Bonaparte was already in Italy, had entered papal territory and agreed an armistice with Pope Pius VI. The philosophical revolution moved on. Benjamin Constant, a young Swiss in the circle of Madame de Staël published a pamphlet, *De la force du gouvernement actuel et de la necessite de s'y vallier*, (On the strength of the present government and the need to support it). He was arguing, as Burke had, that effective government was essential in France where liberty had unleashed terror. He was arguing, as O'Connor did, that the French Revolution was an historical necessity, was bound to happen.

In fact the French government was not strong. It needed all the support it could get. It could not afford any defeats, naval, military or civic. Tone was put to the test through the long lonely months he spent in Paris in 1796, trying to convince the Directory that the Irish would rise in significant numbers and that the government forces were weak. Finding a courier to take a message to Ireland also proved difficult. It was not until mid-June that O'Shee arrived in Hamburg on this mission. He got no further, never reached Ireland. By August he had become unnecessary.

Ireland's emissaries were already on their way towards France.

Lord Edward and Pamela arrived in Hamburg on 10 May in time for Henriette's marriage. Madame de Genlis was already in town. Lord Edward immediately approached Reinhard, the French Minister in Hamburg. Reinhard appraised him and reported to his superiors that the young Irishman was sincere and highly motivated but not suitable to take any command. O'Connor arrived on 5 June. Reinhard took a different view of him. He listened to all O'Connor said and advised his superiors to take this new emissary seriously. O'Connor relates that on his arrival he was very disturbed to find that FitzGerald had allowed Reinhard to bring a third person to their meetings and hear all his confidential reports. O'Connor was sure this man was sold to the British. When O'Connor attended such a meeting and met the third party, his suspicions were confirmed and he broke off negotiations.[45]

Reinhard had already filed two reports, on 6 and 19 June, to Delacroix in Paris. Carefully and in cipher, he set out all the information which the Irishmen gave. It largely confirmed what Tone had already told them. O'Connor and FitzGerald did not know that Tone was in France, believed only that he was on his way. Tone, likewise, had not heard that O'Connor and FitzGerald were in Europe as official emissaries of the United Irishmen. Nor were O'Connor and FitzGerald given French access to O'Shee when he arrived in Hamburg.

Hamburg was alive with spies. The Irishmen were too conspicuous. O'Connor was worried about the possible leakage of information, either through informers in the town, or through the third person at their meetings with Reinhard. The two men left for Basle, leaving Pamela, who had given birth to a daughter, in the care of Madame de Genlis and Henriette Mathiessen. Basle is in Switzerland, on the border with France and Germany, high in the Alps. Here, they immediately called on the French Ambassador Barthelemey.[46] O'Connor's French was poor, but FitzGerald had spent much of his adolescence in France and was married to a Frenchwoman. His command of the language was good. O'Connor's information on Ireland, the social groups, political condition, United Irish numbers and military potential was convincing. He believed much of the militia was disaffected. Only 10-

12,000 troops would be effective for the crown. The memorial sent to the Directory from Basle and prepared by O'Connor and FitzGerald stated that the Irish could not rise prior to the arrival of a French force, as they lacked arms, and by the Gunpowder and Insurrection Acts it had become impossible to get them.[47] Anyone could be searched at any time and seized if they were outdoors at night. If the French were concerned over the British navy, they should remember that half the sailors were Irish. The militia was split between the Protestant officers who would support the government and the Catholic men who would aid the Revolution. O'Connor's parliamentary speech had won him notoriety as an orator among the politically aware in Europe, as well as in Britain and Ireland. He was clear in information and bold in argument. He requested a more senior meeting.

FitzGerald pointed out that France had already sent agents to offer support to the republicans in Ireland; they were now taking up the offer. O'Connor was clear about militia and rebel numbers. They said that the fourteen northern counties were organised for rebellion and they were recruiting quickly in the other eighteen. What the United Irishmen needed was arms.

The emissaries from Ireland were both gentlemen, they came from the most powerful sections of society in Dublin and London. FitzGerald's family was one of the foremost in Ireland. O'Connor too had status, was clear, incisive and a man of weight. They carried the names of paramount Irish clans. They had the credentials of the Irish republican leadership; O'Connor had been appointed to deal for the United Irishmen. The French Directory recognised their standing.

The memorials of O'Connor and FitzGerald added weight to Tone's arguments. They came directly from Ireland and reported on the current state of disaffection. The French had warned Tone they would not launch an expedition on his authority alone and when O'Connor's memorial arrived in Paris, Clarke showed it to him, asking if he knew the handwriting. He did not. He mused in his diary: 'It is curious the coincidence between the paper he read to me and those I have given here, though upon second thoughts, as truth is uniform, it would be still more extraordinary if they should vary.'[48]

O'Connor and FitzGerald could not stay long in Basle. Under a Swiss order, no foreigner could remain there for more than three days, lest Basle should become a centre of information trafficking. So they made a walking tour to Berne, Friebourg, Lausanne and Lake Geneva, returning by Lake Neuchatel. This was a brief and joyful interlude for the two young men. High in the mountains, in a democratic state where they could walk and talk freely, they revelled in the clear air and exercise. Edward loved outdoor life, it reminded him of his long, wild journey through America years before. They swam in the cold water, ate their lunch lying on the mountainsides.

While they were walking in the mountains, Ireland's future was being settled in Paris. The Directory had decided to try for a descent on Ireland and, at the end of June, gave General Lazare Hoche command of the expedition. On 12 July, Tone met Hoche.[49] The son of a royal groom who had become a General at the age of 25, Hoche was still young. In 1794 he had been given command of the western armies of France. Another General, Napoleon Bonaparte, had been put in command of the army in Italy in March of that year. Hoche immediately cross-questioned Tone about military preparations, supplies for his troops and discussed the ports of embarkation for the fleet. On 16 July, Hoche requested advice from the Directory on how to act once in Ireland. The reply was that he should remain in command, so long as he was in the country at the head of his forces. Tone's recommendation for a provisional government was accepted but if the Irish had a real desire for monarchy, as was often reported, France had no objection. It might be possible to give the crown to one of their native chiefs, Hoche told Tone. Ireland would be expected to form an alliance against England and give to France special status in commerce.

On 22 July, Hoche's aide de camp was sent to Switzerland to meet O'Connor. On 23 July Hoche asked Tone about FitzGerald and O'Connor. Tone wrote in his diary:

Hoche then asked me, did I know one Arthur O'Connor? I

replied, I did, and that I entertained the highest opinion of his talents, principles and patriotism. He asked me, 'Did he not some time ago make *"an explosion"* in the Irish parliament?' I replied he made the ablest and honestest speech, to my mind, that ever was made in that house. Well, said he, will he join us? I answered, I hoped as he was *'foncierement Irlandais'*, that he undoubtedly would. So it seems O'Connor's speech is well known here. If ever I meet him, as I hope I may, I will tell him what Hoche said, and the character he bears in France. It must be highly gratifying to his feelings. Hoche then went on to say, 'There is a lord in your country (I was a little surprised at this beginning, knowing as I do what stuff our Irish peers are made of), he is son to a duke; is he not a patriot?' I immediately smoked my lover, Lord Edward FitzGerald, and gave Hoche a very good account of him.[50]

Hoche went on to ask about the Duke of Leinster and Fitzgibbon and the conversation passed, as always, to the quantity of arms that France must provide to liberate Ireland.

On returning to Basle, O'Connor and FitzGerald received their answer from M. Barthelemey. The Directory would negotiate with the aim of a treaty. General Hoche had been appointed to negotiate. Lord Edward could not enter France because of Pamela's connection to the Duc d'Orleans. Arthur O'Connor was to be sole negotiator. A senior French officer was to take O'Connor to his rendez-vous with Hoche.

Edward returned to Hamburg where Pamela and his daughter awaited him. She had been used as the excuse for their journey to the continent but it was poor cover. Hamburg buzzed with speculation. Lord Edward said O'Connor was still walking in Switzerland. That too was weak, since on the journey to Hamburg Lord Edward had gossiped freely with a fellow passenger in the coach. The lady was intimate with a friend of Pitt and immediately wrote to her confidante, telling him all she had just heard from the charming young Irish lord.[51] Pamela was only relieved to see him safely returned. It was 10 August.

Tone had several meetings with Hoche. He was to be adjutant-general in Hoche's Etat-Major. As security for Ireland's affiliation to France, Tone offered 'our honour as gentlemen'. Hoche offered the same on behalf of France. The General had already experienced France during the Terror. He knew well enough about honour in time of revolution. 'Who are these Orangeboys?' he asked. Tone tried to explain. Were there great plains in Ireland? Tone said not, described the nature of an Irish ditch and hedge to him.[52]

In Switzerland, O'Connor was introduced to General Cribleur, who was to be his escort.[53] On 12 August Hoche left Paris for his headquarters at Rennes.

O'Connor set out across France to meet him.

Chapter 9

THE TREATY WITH FRANCE

Wolfe Tone's journal for 23 February 1796 reads: 'Looked over Paine's *Age of Reason*, second part. Damned trash! His wit is, without exception, the very worst I ever saw.'[1]

On 20 June he wrote: 'Today is my birthday – I am 33 years old. At that age Alexander had conquered the world; at that age Wolfe had completed his reputation, and expired in the arms of victory. Well, it is not my fault if I am not as great a man as Alexander or Wolfe. I have as good dispositions for glory as either of them.'[2]

Tone remained in Paris, waiting through the stuffy summer days while O'Connor set off to meet Hoche and finalise terms with revolutionary France. By then Tone was far more cheerful, his mission was succeeding although he was not informed of the negotiations with O'Connor. All he knew was that another channel had been opened between France and Ireland. O'Connor now knew about Tone and had recommended him to the Directory, requested that he attend the meeting.[3] The French had decided otherwise.

The expedition would sail from Brittany. Hoche had his headquarters at Rennes. O'Connor was travelling across France to meet him, giving his identity as an American.[4] Tone was left in Paris with nothing to do.

Of Tone, O'Connor had a high opinion.

Speaking of this distinguished hero, noble and highly talented man Tone, though a distinguished writer he had not the talent of public speaking. To the Catholics he rendered most essential service by his admirable pen. He has been erroneously made the father of the United Irish Society. This was really begun in

Belfast and the real fathers were the editors of the *Northern Star* in Belfast. But Tone in September 1791 wrote an admirable pamphlet entitled the northern Whig. This was circulated in the greatest profusion and had immediate success in promoting the cause of Union. The patriotic men of Belfast who have taken the lead in promoting Ireland's liberty and independence published large editions of this excellent pamphlet of Tone's.[5]

From Basle, 'I had requested of Carnot most earnestly that Tone should accompany the person that should be named to treat with me'. When O'Connor arrived at Rennes he was greatly disappointed to find that they had sent 'a presumptuous blackguard of the name of Ducket'. He insisted to General Hedoville that he could not deal with this man 'that with such mistakes it was impossible any expedition could succeed. Hedoville assured me I should never see this fellow more and that the mistake was inexplicable to him.'[6]

After waiting for Hoche at Rennes nearly a fortnight, 'I received a letter which informed me it was at Angers I should meet him, a distance of nearly 60 English miles, the roads were very bad'. He saw Hoche briefly that night, the following day they sat down in an atmosphere of frankness and goodwill, to negotiate the liberation of Ireland. 'I perceived he had gathered the idea that Ireland was a second La Vendée for the ignorance and the servility of the Irish to their priests and nobles.'[7]

Hoche began the next day by telling me, he had it in orders from the Directory to discuss with me the nature of the expedition and the places they should be directed to. I was aware of this from some hints I received at Hoche's headquarters at Rennes, that before my arrival the plan was to invade England. He then said an invasion of England had been resolved on of 25,000 and that at the same time a smaller one of 5,000 might be sent to Ireland where it was presumed very few troops would be left from the necessity of sending all against the invasion of England.[8]

There had certainly been a French plan to land revolutionaries in Wales and Cornwall to stir up discontent while an expedition landed in Ireland. Tone had been asked to write propaganda for them but refused on the grounds that he didn't know the English grievances. There had certainly been plans to send fleets from both Holland and Brittany, though these had been abandoned during July. In fact, plans had been evolving all summer.

O'Connor gives his account of his response to Hoche:

> As I had had time to turn the subject in my thoughts, I answered him at some length by exposing that never were two countries more diametrically different in every particular than Ireland and England, that the latter was an independent nation, proud of the immense domination she exercised over her extensive possessions all over the Globe, that not a man in all the country who would not risk his life and his last shilling to repell the invaders, Whig or Tory, aristocrat or democrat, Protestant, Presbyterian or Catholic, all would unite to repel the enemy. That an invasion consisted of two parts, the probability of affecting a landing, the second the probability of conquering the country. I shewed him on the map Falmouth, Plymouth, Dartmouth, Weymouth, Yarmouth, Portsmouth and asked, if with the signal passing from all these places enough of English ships should not come in time to attack the invading fleet before she could disembark her troops, her horses, artillery and ammunition.[9]

O'Connor argued that if the French got ashore in Cornwall they would have a long journey and extended supply lines if their object was London. 'Every inch of ground would be contested with the most desperate valor, the roads broken up, the bridges destroyed ...' The English army would come at them from the flanks and the rear. The population of London was 1.2 million and there was also the rest of England and the whole of Scotland to conquer.[10]

Now Ireland, argued O'Connor, was another question. The French fleet could put out into the ocean and use the strong west wind to bring her ashore on Ireland's west coast. The same wind would keep the English fleet in the Channel. They should choose a moment after an equinoctial gale when the British ships would be driven up into their ports. In Ireland 'every man would support you'.

> I ended by assuring him that I had passed several years in England, that I knew the people perfectly well and would assure him the most vigorous and determined resistance a French invasion would meet, would be from those who were most averse to the war against France, that Fox, Sheridan, Grey, Whitbread and all the Opposition would be found amongst the most undaunted antagonists to the invader of their country. After many other arguments, Hoche avowed that he was the most ardently bent on the plan of the two expeditions but from the unanswerable reasons I had given he was perfectly satisfied, that against England presented too little chance to be hazarded.[11]

Next day they discussed the state of Ireland.

> I began by making him understand that the men of Ireland on whom we could depend to join us were divided into two populations dramatically opposed in mental qualities, the one the Presbyterians of Ulster, the other the Catholics of Leinster, Munster and Connaught. The first is a population of the best informed people in Europe and of the best public spirit and independence ... not a parish that has not a little library and all instruct and regale themselves with the reading of the excellent Journal the *Northern Star*. This population lives at ease in small farms of 20-25 acres and by the loom for weaving linen, raising the flax they weave; it was in Ulster the greatest mass of the Volunteers was formed.[12]
>
> The other three provinces are most Catholics generally uneducated without any manufacturing industry and entirely restricted to seek their living in cultivating lands. They have not the twentieth part of the capital indispensible to extract the greatest produce from their farms.[13]

However, said O'Connor, Ireland was not like the Vendée,

'even the Irish papists have a considerable advantage over the very best part of the French population in fitness for liberal institutions'. Before 1789 the French had no experience of representative government nor in civil liberty nor in all classes paying tax. For centuries even the Irish Catholics had experience of all those institutions. They have representative government, they see how it is abused and want it reformed. 'Not a man of those papists could be arrested without a formal charge on oath before a magistrate.' Bail must be accepted and he cannot be tried unless a grand jury of 24 local men consider the proofs worthy of a trial. He must be tried before 'an Enlightened Judge' and a jury who must be unanimous in their verdict. He has the right to a defence lawyer. In the Vendée the priests were an anti-Revolutionary force, in Ireland they would have less of that kind of influence said O'Connor, since the American and French revolutions.[14]

'In the Presbyterians I found men whose religious ideas gave an independence to everything they did and said, but with the Catholics I found the as yet indelible mark of the long and cruel tyranny they had endured, this made them timorous.' If the Representation of Ireland was given to the Papists there was no doubt they would exclude the Protestants and Presbyterians. For this reason, O'Connor told Hoche, he had fixed his Etat-Major at Belfast, in the midst of the old Volunteers who could still furnish him with 50,000 men trained to marching in line and passing into column. In the Societies of United Irishmen in the North was sound good sense on political institutions.

'The progress of Ireland in establishing her liberty must depend on the influence given to the Presbyterians. I did not conceal from Hoche that if Ireland contained but the Papist population I never could have attempted separation from England.' O'Connor thought the Catholic aristocracy too few and too timid to rely on, the Catholic commercial men 'very much superior but on either I had little reliance for their bearing the brunt of the first attack while I placed the greatest reliance on the bravery of the Papist peasant in which there was the making of the best troops in Europe.'

Ireland was hilly and folded, intersected with small enclosures of banks topped with furze. It was impossible to march in line or use cavalry but the Irish peasant was agile, swift, entirely adapted to his terrain.[15]

Hoche listened carefully and said he felt very well informed on Ireland. O'Connor says, 'I never conversed with any man who had a clearer comprehension or one that made more pertinent remarks.' They went over every detail relevant to the expedition.[16]

'The next day we discussed the terms of the treaty. [Hoche] began by saying he took it for granted we would give France the monopoly of our commerce. I observed it would be usurping an immense power not a particle of which belonged to me.' The first thing was to elect a representative body and an executive. They alone could regulate her commerce. O'Connor's own opinion was for free trade. Hoche looked mistrustful. O'Connor suggested that, since Hoche was a dedicated soldier, he could not have studied economics. He should understand, however, that the primary reason for Ireland seeking independence, was the way in which England monopolised Irish commerce. As an island with magnificent ports, Ireland's prosperity depended on maximising the number of foreign vessels using them. 'Nothing was so abhorrent to my nature than the entertaining hatred of any kind and most of all hatred to my fellow man because they were of a different nation.' Equally, France and Britain might become friends, so might England and Ireland. It was the system England was using in Ireland that O'Connor was averse to. 'To found our own system on national hatred would be, not only the most anti-social, anti-scientific but the most ruinous.' He told Hoche about the Fitzwilliam affair. Hoche was apparently satisfied with this explanation and took the point about free trade.[17]

They discussed the place for landing. O'Connor pulled out his map of Ireland. He assumed Galway Bay the best position, central, minimising the march to Dublin and among people who would support it. Hoche wanted O'Connor to mobilise a corps to take positions ahead of him, so that his own advance would be swift. O'Connor's plan was to march 30,000 Volunteers from Belfast to Dublin, then to advance to the Shannon, driving 'the enemy' between Hoche and himself.[18]

Between O'Connor and the Directory 'the express stipulation' was that 'we should make the treaty that had been made between the French and the Americans the basis of ours', as if Hoche was Rochembeau and O'Connor Washington. In battle Hoche should have complete command but in administration and civil government O'Connor should 'exercise the chief command'.[19]

Hoche was unable to pay O'Connor's expenses. The Irishman was obliged also to pay for the officer who accompanied him to the border. Hoche would get the expedition under way as soon as possible, O'Connor should return immediately to Ireland to prepare for it. His return journey was through Pays Bas, Holland, Westphalia and Luxembourg to Hamburg where he met Edward. They sailed for England.[20]

In London he visited his friends, gave a gift to the Duchess of Devonshire and set out for Belfast via Port Patrick and Donaghadee, accompanied by Sir Francis Burdett.[21] This friend was the only one who knew that Arthur had been in France. He had told Fox nothing, in order not to compromise his friend. O'Connor believed that Fox would agree that oppression in Ireland justified the right to resist. He later had an opportunity to discover if this was true.

In Belfast, O'Connor reported to the Northern Executive and began arrangements for the arrival of the French.[22] Next, he went to Dublin and talked to Henry Jackson 'one of the frankest and bravest men I ever knew'. When he heard of the treaty, Jackson said 'I am with you to the last drop of my blood'. Jackson said that his son-in-law, Bond, would be with them too.[23]

> I wished to find some Catholics in whose courage and discretion I could confide. This required time and I was pressed to prepare the south. I therefore deferred it until the coming of Edward who had not, as yet, left London. After visiting the country of Cork and activating the propagation of the Union I returned to the capital where with Edward I sought to complete the number and here Burdett left me to return to England.[24]

In Cork, they visited Connerville. Burdett met Arthur's brother, Roger with Wilhamena and the six children. Roger had by now recruited several agents for the United Irishmen; they in turn were bringing in more men. Edward O'Finn in Cork city, John Swiney and Micheál Óg Ó Longáin were all leading men in the Munster Society.[25] At Connerville, the men could sit by the wide fireplace and lean together earnestly, calculating the numbers of men who had joined, who were staunch, if necessary who had arms. If Burdett did not know about the negotiations in France, or the expected descent, he certainly experienced the nature of the meetings that Arthur and Roger held in Cork that autumn. Arthur was very close regarding his French journey. He told no one the exact details of his treaty with Hoche, very few United Irishmen knew that a French invasion was planned, only that they must create a military structure and prepare.

The key men in Dublin had to be warned. At Edward's suggestion, they informed McNeven, a doctor and Richard McCormick, secretary to the Catholic Committee, both Catholics themselves. These two gave as their opinion that none of the 400 Catholic members who had taken the test in 1792 and 1793 would join this new venture. Edward was outraged. He was risking his life and fortune for the emancipation of Catholics and none of them would take the risk himself, said he.[26] Arthur approached Emmet.

I then addressed myself to Thomas Emmet, but from knowing the extreme timidity of his character, I addressed him with reserve. I told him things were so far advanced, that a rising was unavoidable, desired to know if he felt sufficient firmness in taking part. He frankly told me that neither his disposition nor his habits led him to think he would have the firmness to engage in a revolution, that he imagined he could speak his opinions at a public assembly but that he was not a man of action. With applauding his frankness I told him we should make use of his talents later.[27]

The two conspirators returned to Edward's cottage in Kildare. Edward had left his small son with his mother, as a sort of gift to placate her while he risked his own life. Pamela and her baby daughter were in Kildare. She was brave about the loss of her child but it wounded her. She was brave too, about the urgent and secretive activities of her husband and 'dear Arthur'. Her strategy now was not to ask too many questions, lest knowledge might weaken her position if she were cross-questioned.[28]

In the North, the Orange Order was becoming more militant. Despite the Insurrection and Indemnity Acts which gave the authorities sweeping powers, little was done to curb their militancy. The more aggressive the Orange Order became, the faster United Irishmen were recruited, either directly or by amalgamation with the Defenders. Those suspected of being government informers, and their relatives, were murdered by the Defender network.

In Dublin, Mr Secretary Pelham's health deteriorated and he sailed for convalescence in England. The Earl of Shannon was in the Cabinet, busy in Dublin, his son Henry in charge of the family estates at Castlemartyr in East Cork. On 15 August 1796 Lord Shannon wrote 'if you don't suffer the rabbits to be thinned, for they can never be entirpated, they will overrun the whole paddock'.[29] Further west, at Connerville, Roger O'Connor prepared his house to welcome French invaders. Wilhamena, his wife and the six children must have noticed their father's busy consultations with local men, but then all the county gentry were earnest and anxious. At next door Fort Robert, Roger's brother Robert Conner was quite as earnestly consulting with men of the Orange persuasion, beating his riding crop against the highly-polished leather of his long hunting boots. Out in the fields the people laboured to bring in the harvest and murmured.

In France on 17 September, Tone wrote in his journal, 'at three o'clock in the afternoon left Paris! I certainly did not expect, on my arrival to have succeeded as well as I have done ... Allons! I am now afloat again; Let us see what will come of this voyage!'[30]

He still did not know that Hoche and O'Connor had made terms. Tone and O'Connor never met. But the treaty had been made, Hoche was preparing the expedition, 'the Northern Whig' had his command and a military uniform which made him ecstatic. Tone, the irrepressible, took his merry spirits off to military headquarters in Brittany.

In September, Samuel Neilson was arrested, the brothers Simms took over the *Northern Star*. Also arrested were Russell,

McCracken and Charles Teeling.

Parliament met briefly in Dublin during October and November, to partially suspend Habeas Corpus. Grattan opposed vehemently. Outrages had been committed in Armagh, when Catholics had been attacked and driven from their homes. Grattan accused the government of 'supineness and impartiality'. Meanwhile Lord Camden informed the Duke of Portland that the gentry wanted to establish a Yeomanry corps, 'for their own and the protection of the country'. They had little faith in the militia. This was agreed and Conolly, the husband of Lord Edward's aunt Louisa, together with Lord Charlemont, erstwhile leader of the Volunteers, eagerly supported the formation of the new force. In Ulster, harvesting became a way for the disaffected to meet, on the pretext of digging potatoes. 6,000 men marching through the fields with spades on their shoulders filled the government with alarm.

Arthur O'Connor knew his task. He had to rouse the disaffected, primarily in the North, then keep them in readiness until the moment of the French landing. The British troops would then march west and his men must form up into a military body and march on Dublin.[31]

Arthur spent much time at Kildare with Edward, in his cottage on the edge of the Curragh. Here, riding out one morning, they met a group of twenty cavalry officers who blocked their way and demanded that Lord Edward take off his green silk cravat, his republican badge. O'Connor told them they were neither officers nor gentlemen to contest with two, when they were twenty. If they sent only two of their group, 'we would speak to them'. No answer came. O'Connor complained to General Dundas. His own brother William, commander of the Cork militia in that camp, said however much he differed with Arthur over politics, this was no behaviour for senior enlisted men. At a ball soon after, none of the ladies would dance with these officers.[32]

Soon after this, a message arrived for O'Connor from Hoche to say that the French fleet would sail in six weeks to two months.[33]

In October, Edward's sister, Lady Lucy FitzGerald, arrived in Ireland to visit her relations, Aunt Louisa Conolly at Castletown and her brother the Duke of Leinster. On 21 November 1796, Lady Lucy wrote in her diary, 'I went to town. Mr Ogilvie gave us a snack at Leinster House. Lady Edward came to town too. Mr O'Connor came to see her, but we did not see him, as Mr Ogilvie would not invite him in.' On 27 November she records, 'Lady Edward and I left Carton and came to Kildare, where we found Mr O'Connor and Edward. Nothing can be more comfortable than this little habitation. Mr O'Connor read us the play of *Julius Caesar*.'[34]

Arthur made a great impression on Lady Lucy. She was 25, auburn haired and full of life. She was warm and spontaneous, with a temperament much like her brother's. Her short diary entries reveal her character, vivid and clear. She fought with her stepfather, enjoyed parties, adored her brother and had never met a man like O'Connor. Democracy was heady, in Ireland the air seemed charged with it. Lady Lucy had danced quadrilles in London ballrooms; jigs with the apothecary were new. She took it all in her stride, enjoyed everything but Arthur O'Connor she found disturbing, fascinating. He was wonderful to look at, exciting to dance with, but his ideas shocked her. He did not disguise them. At a dinner with the FitzGeralds, O'Connor held forth vehemently against hypocricy and superstition in Christianity. After Pamela left the room, he was criticised sternly by a preacher for speaking in such a way before ladies.[35]

Arthur's religious views were too radical for Lady Lucy.

3 December 1796: Arthur, Pamela and I had a conversation I <u>never</u> shall forget. I never heard anything of the kind before. I was very much amused and interested, lost in admiration of such superior talents but not <u>convinced</u>, and grieved to tears at such a mind supposing itself perishable. December 4, Ed v. angry with us for sitting up; he and Mr O'Connor set off on a Tour.[36]

To prepare for the arrival of 'our allies', Edward and Arthur went to Connaught to check the line of operation from Galway Bay. On horseback, they rode to Athlone, then Banaher with two bridges over the Shannon, where they examined passes over the river.[37]

In passing through Roscommon we overtook six peasants, all fine stout athletic men, one in particular was a model for strength and activity. His countenance was most expressive. I asked him if the people were happy and content in the country. He looked at me to see if I was serious. 'Oh yes, they are as happy as misery can make them.' 'Have they the courage to fight to get better?' Here, looking on his companions he answered, 'Gentlemen, we do not know you, do not expect we should answer you but look at these wretched styes built in the bog on your right and see those flocks of bullocks on your left in fine grass up to their knees and ask yourself if we men can value life, not to risk, when they are treated worse than the brute beasts.' He said this with an energy and a determined look that left no doubt of what must be his feelings of the inhabitants of this country. I asked him if he had ever heard that anyone took interest in their misery and was doing anything to relieve them, for instance if they had heard of Grattan, or Flood or Ponsonby. He said he never had heard of such men. 'See you sir, all these men are for themselves, they have all we pay between them; and for this they wrangle with one another.' 'Have not heard within this year there was something doing for Ireland?' 'Oh yes, we have heard it. It goes that we are all to be one, protestant and papist, and join against the Saxons. The story is rife that the old chiefs are stirring again.' 'And who are they?' 'Why they talk of an O'Connor and a FitzGerald, and that the French will be with Ireland, for see you, we have an old prophecy that as Ireland was lost under an O'Connor it can never be gained but by the same. This is all the tattle in Connaught these months past.'[38]

As they reined in their horses, bridles jangling, O'Connor asked about the Catholic gentry. The Connaught man, after a glance at his companions, answered they had not the spunk to venture, were middle men who lived off 'our misery'. He quoted Latin and

O'Connor commented 'you are a scholar'. 'I was the master of scholars but the people are too poor to pay for the education of their children and I was forced to abandon my school.'

'We parted telling him to have courage and left them some money to drink to the freedom of Ireland.'[39]

'We went to O'Conor of Belenagare, where I was received as a child of the family.'[40]

Charles O'Conor, son of Arthur's childhood acquaintance, had written the memoirs of his family and Dr McDermott, his son-in-law was a United Irishman.[41] Charles had taken the test and told Charles Fox by letter it was nothing dangerous.[42] To McDermott, Arthur and Edward confided the forthcoming arrival of a French expedition. While McDermott sounded out his people, FitzGerald and O'Connor visited Protestant gentry of their acquaintance who treated them with generous Irish kindness. It was their servants, however, who were United men and, having travelled with their masters to Dublin, knew O'Connor and FitzGerald as leaders of the movement. In their reception of these two, were loaded gestures of recognition and affection. The servants spread news of their presence to the local men around. But McDermott had no success with the Catholic gentry. He said only that at best 'they won't be against you'. 'Such,' says O'Connor, 'are the vile fruits of long and cruel oppression that renders the slave incapable of breaking the chains that bind him.'[43]

On 11 December Lady Lucy wrote in her diary:

> At 3 o'clock they came home to our great joy: gave us an account of their reception at the <u>King of Connaught</u>. His name is O'Connor also, so he addressed them: Arthur O'Connor, you are welcome. House of Leinster, I am proud to see you within my doors.[44]

> December 13: We had a dance in the evening. Our company was Cummins [the Apothecary] and the Butcher's daughters. I danced with Arthur. We danced a great many Irish jigs. Ed is a famous hand at them. December 14: We read Volny's *Ruins*. Arthur shocked me by a thing he said; he is so odd one must not judge him by other people.[45]

The following day, Lord and Lady Castlereagh arrived to take Lady Lucy back to Dublin. Robert Stewart, so popular when he was elected to parliament for an Ulster seat in 1790, was now becoming an important figure in the administration. He was related to the FitzGeralds and came from a family with estates in Ulster, where they were considered good landlords and neighbours. In 1791 William Drennan had written to Sam McTeir, 'I saw Robert Stewart once in the House and once out of it – He is certainly a most promising young man, and one of the handsomest in the house, perhaps to become, one day the most able'.[46]

As the guests sat in the parlour of the cottage in Kildare, waiting for Lady Lucy to prepare for the drive to Dublin, Stewart and O'Connor had time to measure each other. They were moving into their final positions before the drama climaxed. By the time they met again, they would be fixed in the spotlight by which history would record them. By then it would be too late to change their roles. In the small room in Kildare, they sat, both tall men of high intellect, an immovable concept of honour in both. But deep down, they were different, living on utterly different urges. Castlereagh was an aspiring servant of Empire but O'Connor had discovered his role as Celtic Chieftain of the Enlightenment. It was a difficult part to play.

Chapter 10

ARRIVAL OF THE FRENCH

The Duke of Portland, principal Secretary of State to the government in London, had persuaded the King to sign the Irish Insurrection Act in the early summer of 1796. But he was not happy about it. 'I thought it my duty to call the peculiar attention of all the King's confidential servants to so uncommon an act of legislation ...'[1] he wrote to Lord Camden. 'We concluded the measure to be necessary because it had your Exec's sanction ...' To Mr Pelham he wrote of his astonishment that a country using the same system of government as Britain should require it.

Under the Insurrection Act, a death sentence could be imposed for administering, and transportation for life for taking, a seditious oath. All arms had to be registered. If any district was proclaimed as disturbed under the Act, a curfew began at dusk until dawn. During curfew, JPs could go through houses to check on the whereabouts of inhabitants and search for arms. JPs could demand the surrender even of registered arms. There were clauses against 'tumultuous assemblies', night-time meetings in public houses and against seditious papers. JPs could send men untried to the fleets. This Act was a powerful reversal of long established rights. In the conditions of Ireland in 1796, it was also open to violent abuse.

In July, Camden received intelligence that Ambassadors for the United Irishmen were in France negotiating with the Directory for aid. After harvest, it was said, the people intended to throw off the English yoke.[2] In August, Camden, wanting to seize those he most suspected, decided he must suspend habeas corpus. In this too, London acquiesced.

Arthur O'Connor was active and visible as an antagonist to government. Only he and Hoche knew the exact details of the planned French invasion. It was part of their agreement that the plans should be secret, to avoid the constant leakage of information through spies, informers and loose tongues.[3] O'Connor had little time in which to prepare the north. Elections for parliament were due in 1797 and he put himself forward as a candidate for County Antrim.[4] This gave him a pretext for public speaking and printed addresses. In October the *Northern Star* printed his address *To the Free Electors of County Antrim* and reprinted it twice more. It was an inflammatory and challenging document. If the monopoly of parliamentary seats by a few and the sale of that parliament 'to another country' is all that Irish politics offers, 'I pledge myself to you and to my country, to use every means in my power to affect its destruction'.[5]

In November, a National Executive of the United Irishmen was officially set up with O'Connor as President. He told Charles James Fox he had taken the Test.[6] In evidence later, he said he never took it, since he was a founder of the new, reconstituted movement. The National Executive drew from those of Ulster and Leinster. The other two provinces had not then been organised. O'Connor names the Leinster Executive as Oliver Bond, Henry Jackson, William McNeven, himself and Lord Edward. These five directed the southern United Irishmen towards the French-led rising. Emmet, O'Connor says, was not a member of this group.[7]

A messenger called MacSheehy was sent by Hoche in November to liaise with the United men and to report to Hoche on conditions in Ireland. The General was concerned over delays to the expedition; he had given O'Connor to understand that the French would already be underway. MacSheehy reached Ireland and met McCormick, McNeven, Lewins and Bond.[8] He did not see O'Connor which the latter believed was the deliberate work of McCormick and McNeven.[9] O'Connor perceived the Catholic United Irishmen as a separate cabal who did not discuss openly or vote individually, but had their own agenda. He did, however, get the information that Hoche was sailing in six weeks' time. He expected the French in January or February of the new year.

In England, Sir Francis Burdett had just bought a parliamentary seat from the Duke of Newcastle for £4,000. In the autumn he was preparing himself for the Commons. Despite the parlous state of Britain in her war with France, and given his at least partial knowledge of his friend's position, Burdett's letters to O'Connor in October 1796 seem very calm. Doubtless at Arthur's instigation he was careful what he wrote and he does not seem to have known exactly what O'Connor had been doing in France. He knew enough though, to see that his friend's political opposition to government was becoming more radical and more militant.

On 29 October, Burdett wrote from England: 'I wish you would send me some subject for composition, and some thoughts upon composition in general, and particularly, of that sort in which you excel so much, I mean political composition. This at your leisure moments as matter of amusements.'[10]

Despite organising an armed rebellion, O'Connor did have leisure; to read to Lady Lucy and Pamela, to participate in FitzGerald's dances. Burdett goes on, 'I follow your advice – read less and take more exercise, and go in the water every other morning so that I hope my physic will at least be equal to my moral.' Regarding England, he does add, 'All over the country one meets nothing but soldiers and every village almost has a barrack – such a system surely cannot last.'[11]

In late November, Burdett's tone was still mild. 'Everything concerning Ireland is extremely interesting – in what way is it that the trade of Ireland is oppressed by this country? Do not the merchants and manufacturers trade upon equal advantages with our own? Has she anything more to complain of besides the oppression of the Catholics and the corrupt system of government?'[12]

Burdett enquires for O'Connor's lover: 'How goes on your poor friend, is she still in the enchanted castle and do the Brother Giants still defend it from all approach?'[13]

Burdett had been married for three years but was not faithful. Despite living in the house of his father-in-law, he had several affairs, one famous. But Burdett was living in radical and Whig circles in London where liaisons were public, sophisticated and fashionable. O'Connor's only known intimacy was in Ireland and had been extremely discreet. It seems the woman's family had now closed around her but she had O'Connor's child, a son of about two and a half.

On 3 November, Arthur received a letter begging him to hurry to send money as the writer's income was very limited and 'so great a part of it as your interest, must be a great loss to me'.[14] The name was then heavily scribbled over to obliterate it, then the letter was scrumpled up but the scrumpler changed his mind and smoothed the letter out, preserved it among the very few papers he kept.

Early the following year, O'Connor received an unsigned letter. The writer knew Edward, had been alone and was about to move on, had received a letter and knew that Arthur was well, 'may you be ever so my best of friends'.[15]

In January 1797 Burdett complains, 'you never tell me a word about your poor friend for whose situation I feel a most lively interest'.[16] Arthur had other concerns over the winter of 1796-97. But Burdett seems not to have known or understood the extremity of his friend's situation.

O'Connor's friend General John Knox knew how much he was risking. On 26 December, he wrote to Arthur from Dungannon in County Tyrone where he was training Yeomanry:

> In the name of God what put it into your head to propose yourself as a candidate for Antrim, and with that mad address? Take my advice – postpone politics till sober times of peace. The present times are dangerous. It often makes me melancholy to think of the prospects of the north of Ireland. The people seem inclined to rush upon their own destruction. I wish you were in Grafton Street, the Isle of Wight or anywhere else than in the neighbourhood of Belfast.[17]

Lord Camden could not think of any acts of parliament which might quieten the country.[18] He had concentrated on organising the military, defending the coast and trying to get inside information on the United Irish rebels. Lord Carhampton was Commander-in-Chief in Ireland and General Lake was Commander of the northern district, but the former did not inspire Camden with confidence and the latter relied solely on force.

The British government was in peace negotiations with France which broke down on 15 December. On the same day, the French expedition finally sailed from Brest. Tone was aboard the flagship *Indomptable*. General Hoche and the Admiral in charge, Morad de Galles, together with the treasury for the expedition, were on *Fraternité*. Tone had been composing the flyer which they would give out to the people when they landed in Ireland. The catch phrase was:

Maintenant ou Jamais, Maintenant pour Toujours
Now or Never, Now and Forever

The address reads:

Friends and Irishmen, The soldiers of Liberty do not appear in vain on the shores you inhabit – They bring to you Freedom and Independence; and these blessings belong to you in all their plenitude. From an English colony you arise an Irish nation, from colonists you become a people.[19]

There had been several drafts for this, the final one agreed in both French and English. It was then printed in the English version. It was essential that Tone be among the first to land and that the Irish receive the French with the correct interpretation. The address was not printed in Gaelic, the large majority of the Gaelic speaking population did not read.

Bonaparte was having great success in Italy and one of the delays was the redeployment of part of Hoche's troops to the Italian campaign. Nevertheless on 15 December 1796, 43 ships sailed with 13,975 soldiers aboard and considerable arms and ammunition. Tone's long wait was over. 'The signal is now flying to get under way, so one way or other the affair will be at last brought to a decision, and God knows how sincerely I rejoice at it. The wind is right aft, Huzza! At one we got under way.'[20] It was late in the year to sail north-west. They took a route which might avoid the enemy ships in the Channel. Their passage through the Raz was treacherous. They did escape the British blockade, but one French ship sank and

25 were scattered. Hoche and the Admiral on *Fraternité* were separated from the group and blown further out into the Atlantic. General Grouchy, second in command, was still with the main fleet.

Lord Edward was in Dublin. Arthur O'Connor was in Ulster.

As the time approached when the French were to arrive I left Edward in Leinster and took up my quarters at a country house Magee, the printer of the *Evening Post* lent me within a half a mile of Belfast, where I solicited votes for the County of Antrim ... Nothing could exceed the public spirit of the north, never was time better employed in preparing the minds of the people for the arrival of our allies. The Executive took the lead and all followed ...[21]

Everything was arranged for all the old Volunteers marching on Dublin the instant the English troops should be marched off to the western coast, when every one was to provide himself with the best arms he could until we got to Dublin, when I could find all the means for a perfect organisation and equipment of my army and then march to the Shannon, putting the English army between us and our allies.[22]

O'Connor exaggerated. The North was extremely restive but the Volunteers had been disbanded. His own fledgling military organisation was wholly untried. The huge gatherings for potato digging continued. Arms were plundered and ash trees cut down to make pike handles. In the forges of village blacksmiths the hammering went on, pike heads being beaten into shape, with their long blade and side head, tall weapons that could be used both to pierce and to chop.

Meanwhile at sea General Grouchy and Admiral Bouvet had assumed command until Hoche and the *Fraternité* should re-join the fleet. Hoche had kept his plans very secret. Although British agents knew the fleet had sailed, they believed it was going south to Portugal. The French encountered no English ships. But evasion through the Raz was their undoing. Hoche could not regain the fleet. Bouvet relied on written instructions in case of separation;

these he now opened. He was to sail to Mizen Head at the south-west tip of Ireland and wait five days for the separated ships. If none came, they should proceed to the mouth of the Shannon and wait a further three days. If the fleet was not there reunited, they must return to Brest. Bouvet set his course for Mizen Head.

The weather was fine when they sighted Ireland. Mizen Head being very exposed, they tucked themselves into the entrance to Bantry Bay and on 22 December, fifteen ships of the French navy anchored off Bear Island. Others, trying to re-join the fleet, approached the entrance to the Bay.[23]

O'Connor was working on the plan he had made with Hoche in August. 'Bantry Bay was the rallying point, Galway Bay was that of debarcation. The fact is the sailing was hurried.'[24] O'Connor, poised in Belfast, was not the first to hear the news.

Mr White of Seafield Park, near Bantry, was Lord Longueville's brother-in-law. He and Mrs White had heard reports from seamen of a French fleet off the southern coast. On the morning of 23 December, they could see them quite clearly. The country people were flustered. 'The French are in the Bay', they told each other excitedly, expecting an immediate landing or military engagement. It was not forthcoming. Mrs White set off towards Cork city and on the road met an English officer who raced back to Cork with the news.[25]

Dalrymple, Commander of the southern forces based at Cork, immediately sent off a despatch to Pelham. 'Captain Cotter reports that on his road he met with Mrs White, who had quitted Bantry, she informed him there were 25 sail of French men of War, beating to windward in Bantry Bay.'[26] Dalrymple had some artillery at Bandon but the weather, having been fine, now deteriorated, camping troops out would be 'inconvenient' and it would be several days before he could get 2,000 men to west Cork.

Mr White acted with decision. He had his cattle driven inland, he called up his Yeomanry and organised his positions. Two local men named McCarthy undertook to supply the English troops with potatoes but there were no troops to hand.[27]

The night on which the French anchored was the night on which the weather changed. An off shore gale with snow scattered twenty ships working their way towards the Bay and played havoc with the fifteen already at anchor. Grouchy and Bouvet knew only that they were to wait five days then sail north to the Shannon. They had no information on landing. With half the fleet and less than 7,000 troops they were in a quandary. Meanwhile the gale increased in ferocity.

O'Connor was not expecting the French for some weeks. The plan was to marshal his troops and wait until the army in Dublin marched west.[28] None of O'Connor's men were ready for action. FitzGerald was in Kildare, where United organisation was strong. But he too was caught unprepared. It was Christmas. Lady Lucy was at Aunt Louisa's mansion of Castletown but kept up her diary: 'Christmas Day. Alarm of the French being off the coast of Ireland. Troops marching, all in consternation about the French. They have been trying to work into Bantry Bay.'[29]

The troops did not leave Dublin, they mobilised to defend the capital. In rural Cork, the people showed no sign of rising in support of a French invasion, but either remained calm, or assisted the crown troops, albeit mainly verbally. General Smith at Limerick heard that in every cabin the people were boiling potatoes for his men. The gentry and clergy, both Catholic and Protestant, made loyal speeches, the Yeomanry followed their gentry and funds were certainly collected to support the soldiers.[30]

O'Connor was in the midst of public agitation in Ulster.

'When the arrival of the French was known at Belfast the High Sheriff called a meeting of all the inhabitants in and about Belfast ... the object was to get the people to take an oath to fight against the French'. The United Irish Executive 'pressed me to oppose it'.[31] O'Connor was a striking figure, tall and dark, his strong features and intense eyes showing prominently among the pressing mass of restive citizens at the meeting. He pushed his way to the front and insisted on speaking. He pointed out that if the High Sheriff was calling for order, he should name the places where there was disorder since it was his job to keep the peace. The Sheriff was not, said O'Connor, a recruiting sergeant and the people had already been disarmed by law. Now, rather than being defended by 100,000 Volunteers they had 20,000 English mercenaries who instead of defending the Irish, 'disarmed us like slaves.' 'Let them do the fighting while we await the issue,' he said and here the meeting went into uproar. Afraid of violence, O'Connor now calmed the people. The Sheriff hastily dissolved the meeting.[32]

The French meanwhile had decided to hazard a landing but by Christmas Day the weather made it impossible. Then fog descended. The French leaders disagreed. The wind was still strong and off shore. They were close to a rocky coast. Several ships dragged their anchors. On 27 December the last French ships, tearing at their anchor lines, gave in to the wind and set out to sea. The heavy ships rode up on the high waves, plunged through spume, but despite the screaming wind and treacherous rocks, the last of the French fleet set their course, as ordered, for the mouth of the Shannon. There was no sign of their commander. The long lines of the winter fields of western Ireland were barely visible against the spray and heavy sky. They were only a quarter of the fleet that had sailed from Brittany and they had no clear orders for landing. Shouting over the roar and thud of the sea, new orders were given, the helmsmen took them up and the fleet turned south for France.

O'Connor was with the Northern Executive of the United Irishmen when news reached them that the French had gone.[33]

Under pressure of the emergency in west Cork, Dalrymple had a fit and fell off his chair. Many were sorry he recovered. His orders were to burn Bantry in case of a French landing. Lord Longueville was incensed; 'he would have given up Bantry and all my deeds, leases and valuables would have been destroyed.' His nephews were prime movers in this fomentation.

> I wish to God that some means was found to put a stop to Mr Arthur O'Connor's treasonable proceedings at Belfast. He has a brother here who is his twin in all species of treason, but he was closely watched. Whatever he was hatching was of a most dangerous and diabolical tendency. As to Arthur I wish he was confined and also his brother here until the war is over. I cannot help them being my relation, but Arthur O'Connor has never been my acquaintance since he abused and voted against Mr Pelham.[34]

The Irish authorities breathed a sigh of relief and remarked warmly on the co-operation and loyalty of the people. O'Connor believed they were only biding their time.

> The fact is that when I went to the South with Burdett in September 1796, I took particular care that all the people of this coast should be well organised and I acquired the certitude that this great zeal after the departure of the fleet was but a veil to cover themselves from suspicion and that in no part of Ireland were the people more resolute to second the expedition than those at Bantry and all along the coast.[35]
>
> At the moment the French fleet had sailed for France the Government circulated through the post office the most virulent diatribe filled with the most unfounded calumnies with the view to blast my character.[36]

O'Connor was in an appalling predicament. He had exposed himself dangerously with the expectation of a quick climax when the French expedition arrived. The French had neither aborted the mission nor carried it out. They had appeared like a chimera to taunt and tempt, then floated away in the foam of the December sea. O'Connor would have enormous difficulties making contact with Hoche again. Even to get messages to France was impeded by war, spies and the tight control of government over passports and shipping. The rebels used Pamela and her cousin in Hamburg, Mrs Mathiessen as a way to send letters to the continent. It was a slow route and not above the intelligence of the authorities to investigate.

Ireland, particularly Ulster, was in a dangerous condition. The increasing militancy of the United Irishmen, drilling at night, manufacturing pikes, plundering arms and the recruiting of both farmers and soldiers, were clearly all in preparation for an armed rebellion. The poor people's grievances over taxes, tithes and rent became a ground swell of rising discontent and lawlessness. The mass of people outside the system, already living by crime and chance, would quickly be sucked into the vortex of revolution.

Under the Insurrection Act, parts of County Down and Armagh were proclaimed, also Newry, Armagh city and

Dungannon in Tyrone. As 1797 began Derry, Donegal and north-west County Tyrone were also proclaimed. Lord Camden saw that soon the border counties, parts of Leinster and even County Cork would reach the same highly militant condition.

It was O'Connor's business to make sure they did. The greater his army, the more disciplined, well armed and co-ordinated his revolutionary force was, the quicker it would achieve its aims, the less loss of life would be involved in the final denouement. But he had to get the French back to Irish shores. They would bring heavy artillery, arms and ammunition, military expertise and confidence. It was important that the goaded people should not rise too soon. The quickest and surest way of getting a message to Hoche was to send it publicly, through the Press.[37] O'Connor knew the law and he tested it to its limits. He wrote another address, *To the Free Electors of the County of Antrim* and published it, through the press-es of the *Northern Star*, on 27 January 1797. [See appendix for full address]

O'Connor was ill with a fever which he says he caught at the meeting at Belfast during the Bantry Bay alarm.[38] He was under supreme mental, emotional and physical pressure. The moral dilemma was acute, for O'Connor was a man who knew and loved the intricacies of the law. It was for the rights which he believed the law guaranteed that he was fighting. His friends in England, who he revered, were in significant public positions and he could not know if they would forgive rebellion in time of war. His family, with the brilliant exception of Roger, were MPs and soldiers, firm in the establishment. He was risking his liberty, his life, his fortune, his good name and the lives of his countrymen for what he believed were inalienable rights. Only success could justify his actions.

If he had fever in January, he had in fact been ill in the autumn. In November 1796, Matty McTier wrote to William Drennan,

> O'Connor I suppose will now try to support the *Star* and the *Star* him. He wears a black silk hankerchief tied on his head so as to resemble a black crop having lost his hair in a fever and disclaiming a wig. He is an odd figure, tall, dark and penetrat-ing with that native vulgarity of face you observe in the Irish –

his manner is plain – he is silent and no way attractive, his oper-ations are not yet commenced whatever they are to be, and he has made few acquaintances – the Election apathy is very appar-ent – yet it may be blown up, by such a spark as this, who I imagine is not only combustible but deep.[39]

He had been a spark right enough. The fever which attacked him more than once that winter may have been caused by the extreme tensions racking him, or the rage which seemed to burn up uncontrollably within him. Now, with the new year beginning and parliament returned to its last session before the election, O'Connor lit a political fire through the public prints of Ulster and blew hard on it.

Lord Edward visited him in January. Pamela's letters arrived at Arthur's house for her husband. 'My heart is in Belfast,' she said, 'Bon soir, my dearest beloved friend,' she signed herself 'ta fidele'.[40] Edward returned to Kildare. O'Connor published his paper.

The address *To the Free Electors of the County of Antrim* was print-ed as a single sheet article for easy distribution. It opens reasonably enough:

> Fellow citizens,
> The Post Office is so immediately dependent on the Government, that any anonymous production issuing from thence, must be looked on as coming from the Administration itself; in this light I have viewed the anonymous paper which has been so industriously distributed through the Post Offices of the North, avowedly to deprive me of whatever share of your confidence I might have gained ...

He says he will vindicate himself against an Administration which has lost the whole confidence of the nation. He says he accepted a seat from Lord Longueville hoping to improve the con-dition of Ireland, but saw that without a proper National Government, an annihilation of factions and abolition of Religious Distinctions Ireland could not have her Rights and Liberties. He says he voted for total Catholic emancipation in 1793. It is a lie that he turned against the government when refused a Commissioner's place, he had actually refused it himself and been disinherited by Lord Longueville for his principles.

Having created a momentum of grievance in the rhythm and language of the paper, O'Connor changes tempo as he goes into the attack:

> Abandoned Administration! who have trampled on the liberties of my country, do you presume to accuse me of dissuading my countrymen from arming to oppose an invasion, which your's and your accomplices have provoked? Is it that the inalienable rights of free-born men to make the laws by delegates of their choice, should be bartered and sold by usurpers and traitors, that I should persuade them to arm? Is it that our markets, our manufactures and commerce, should be sold to that nation which appoints our Government, and distributes our patronage, that I should persuade them to arm? ... is it to support the suspension of the habeas corpus Bill, which has destroyed the bulwark of liberty by withholding the Trial by Jury, that I should persuade them to arm? Is it to rivet the bolts, or to guard the dungeons of their fellow-citizens, who, torn from their homes and their families by Administration, vainly demand that Trial by Jury, which by proving their innocence must establish its guilt, that I should persuade them to arm? ... Go, Impotents, to the Catholics, whose elevated hopes of all glorious freedom, you have been appointed to tauntingly blast, and if they should charge you with the crimes of your mission, although you cannot plead the having raised them to equal rights with their fellow-citizens, you can at least boast that you have levelled those rights to the standard of Catholic thraldom!

The address then catalogues the corruption of the system, suggests that the Administration itself is an invader, that it has brought foreign troops from England and Scotland to suppress constitutional liberties and it challenges Britain. 'Too long her slaves, we must shew her we are resolved to be FREE!'

'I will neither be conquered by England or France; nor are we any more bound to a disadvantageous alliance to one than we are to the other;' and O'Connor catalogues Ireland's grievances against Britain. The address ends with a pledge:

Think it not presumptuous, my countrymen, that one who loves liberty, should seek her in the only asylum she has left; – think it not presumptuous, my fellow-citizens, that one who will never out-live the threatened liberties of his country, should seek an advanced post where he may triumph in her cause, or fall in her defence. In contempt of calumny, UNITED with you in brotherly love and affection, and in the glorious cause of Reform, I will ever remain your faithful friend and fellow-citizen,

Arthur O'Connor.

Whether Hoche ever heard of this publication is not clear but Lord Camden read it all right. He knew O'Connor had been in Hamburg with Lord Edward. He had watched the ever bolder style of campaign. But he was unwilling to arrest a popular and aristocratic man if he could not bring him to trial. Camden was irresolute. The address came like a grenade under his feet.

Lady Lucy was in Dublin. Her relatives had warned her that Edward was in too deep.

Jan 2. Aunt Sarah took me apart to talk of very unpleasant subjects: made me low, indeed I am wretchedly so. Jan 6. Had a letter from Eddy. He is going to Belfast to Arthur, who is ill. He desires me to be ready for the Giant's Causeway [in Antrim] in all the *horrors of Winter*. Pamela is for prudence and no Giant's Causeway. I don't exactly make out why.

Her elder brother spelled it out for her.

Jan 19. Charles came to see me, and frightened me about Edward, saying that Lord Camden had information against him, and that he must leave the country. I am constantly agitated with these kind of things, which quite distract me. Edward is at Belfast which is the cause of all this. Jan 31. Eddy came to see me and cheered me by his presence. We read Arthur O'Connor's address to the County of Antrim. It is glorious, but I think Government won't let it pass.[41]

Lady Lucy had been ill a good deal in January. Her brother wrote to her, 'you are a goose, but too dear a one, come here and let us have you comfortably. I hate your being ill, the fact is you are tormented and that is what sets your bile to work.'[42] But whether it was O'Connor, Edward's intrigues or anxiety which tormented Lucy is not clear.

Matty McTier suspected that O'Connor had other motives for his paper than simply stating his position. In a letter to William Drennan she speculated:

> Do you think O'Connor would ever have written that paper but from a desire of being taken up, or, rather, an impatience to bring on some work which the disappointment of the French retarded. He is now said to be mad. There is too much method. I heard several government people say if the French had boldly landed, even without their artillery, they would have been successful. This may be a step of that nature. It is not a rash paper that is written in a hurry. It has been the result both of thought and consultation, and I think the present effect must either be a King's messenger or the avowed cowardice of government.[43]

General Lake already had instructions to watch O'Connor. At the beginning of February the government decided to act. On 3 February the two Simms brothers were arrested, the offices of the *Northern Star* raided, papers, typeface and books confiscated. In a simultaneous raid on O'Connor's house, his papers were taken, sealed and sent to Dublin.[44] O'Connor, who had left on the boat, was arrested in Dublin on a charge of seditious libel.

There was little to incriminate him among his personal papers; polite letters from Charles Fox and General Knox, a letter from his agent in Cork dated 17 January telling him 'There is upwards of seven or eight thousand soldiers from Bandon to Bantry, the French landed on Whiddy island upwards of six hundred, God blew a storm on them and sent them to the rout but still the people are in dread, I have secured every shilling belonging to your honour.'[45]

There was a letter from Burdett of 15 January, 'I really know not how to live without you – you are really the only man I ever knew who made me really better for living with – all other men make me worse ... What a fortunate storm you have been delivered by, from an invasion.'[46]

These were not seditious documents, as the Castle officials could easily see. Sick with fever, O'Connor was taken to the Council Chamber, to face Lord Camden, Fitzgibbon the Chancellor and the Council. Here he was informed he was accused of High Treason. O'Connor answered that it was a pretence to deprive him of his liberty, that they knew he 'lived but for the liberty of his country' and to assert that liberty was not High Treason. Since 1782 Ireland had been free to make treaties with any country she chose. It was treason, said O'Connor, to deny this right.[47] The Lord Lieutenant could not allow this sort of speech to go on in front of the Privy Council. He dismissed O'Connor.

'Hence I was imprisoned in an ancient Tower which had not been inhabited for centuries. The walls were twelve feet thick and so full of fleas that the moment I got into bed I was devoured and tortured by them. Not a soul but my jailer was suffered to approach me for the six months I was incarcerated in this dungeon.' He was a strong man and recovered from the fever. Immediately he set about converting his jailer to the United Irish cause.

The United leaders had to re-establish contact with France. In February they chose Edward Lewins, a lawyer fluent in French. He was carefully briefed and arrived in Hamburg at the end of March where Mrs Mathiessen introduced him to Reinhard.

Early in March, Camden decided that Ulster could only be controlled by decisive action. As Lord Lieutenant, he was nominally at the head of the military forces in Ireland. He ordered General Lake to disarm all those districts in which outrages had occurred. This was most of Ulster and Lake had a very free hand. He used it. While parliament debated the illegality of this order, Lake issued a proclamation in Belfast on 13 March 1797 and set to work. It was impossible to send senior officers out with all the parties of soldiers searching for arms. Their methods were soon being reported to government, to magistrates, to landlords who might be just and offer some protection. Cabins were burnt, men and boys killed, men tortured until they gave information on arms. Lady Moira in County Down received pitiful letters from local people,[48] her husband spoke in the British parliament that November, protesting at the evils of the army in Ulster. A Welsh regiment, the Ancient Britons, was stationed in Newry. Their name became a byword for savagery.

While the troops disarmed the North, the United men continued to recruit and where possible, continued to arm. In parallel, the Orange Order became an increasingly powerful force in Ulster, militant, violent and loyal to the crown. The violence of Orangemen against Catholics escalated. The government began to see these extreme loyalists as allies in their struggle to hold the country.

In March, Fox spoke in the British parliament on conciliation for Ireland and Burdett made his maiden speech in support. In May, Grattan seceded from the Irish parliament in protest. In July the Prince of Wales protested that 'I have repeatedly recommended conciliatory measures as best suited to the generous temper of the Irish nation, most consonant to the British constitution and best calculated to regain the confidence and affection of all ranks of people.'[49]

The Northern Star had been revived under the management of Thomas Corbett but in May the Monaghan militia attacked the offices, smashed the presses and silenced the paper.

O'Connor was in solitary confinement in the old tower of Dublin Castle. No charge had been brought and summer was advancing. The government had to make up its mind.

---- *Chapter 11* ----

IMPRISONMENT AND AGITATION

'It is by their affections alone that the Irish people will be governed,'[1] Mary Anne McCracken told Dr Madden much later.
As 1797 began, their affections were divided. Despite the aims of
the United Irishmen to draw all religious and racial groups into one
political movement, there were factions in the Union and in the
country there were symptoms of civil war. Arthur O'Connor's family was divided, as were many others. United men had friends and
relatives in the British army, fighting against France or stationed in
Ireland. Ulster Protestants might be United Irishmen or
Orangemen. Catholic peasants might be forging pikes or loyal to
government for fear of any kind of war.

In symbolism, mottoes, songs and verse, the factions forged
their identities. ERIN GO BRAH – Ireland for Ever – was on the
flags of the United Irishmen. Symbols awoke old cultural memories, everywhere the harp stood for Ireland. The United Irishmen
added the motto: *She is new-strung and will be Played.* They published republican ballads in *Paddy's Resource* and learnt French
democratic songs. The United Irish catechism went:

> What have you got in your hand?
> A green bough.
> Where did it first grow?
> In America.
> Where did it bud?
> In France.
> Where are you going to plant it?
> In the crown of Great Britain.

Meanwhile the cost of war mounted. Early in 1797 Britain abandoned the gold standard. The following winter income tax was introduced. In April, British naval mutinies at Spithead and the Nore created a crisis. Sailors' pay was increased and they went back to work. Pitt kept his nerve.

While tension mounted, Arthur O'Connor was locked in the Bermingham Tower. Edward FitzGerald immediately applied to visit him and was refused.[2] Francis Burdett was deeply disturbed by his friend's imprisonment, applied unsuccessfully to visit and wrote constantly to the FitzGeralds for news.[3]

Lady Lucy went down to the Castle. She could see Arthur at the window of his prison, 'we kissed our hands to each other'.[4] The other State Prisoners were in the new goal at Kilmainham, a model prison built outside Dublin on a small rise for air and designed to avoid the fevers which ravaged the old city prisons. Gentlemen prisoners were given a room each with a fireplace. Eight State Prisoners were arrested in the autumn of 1796. The gaoler at Kilmainham was instructed to give them the best apartments, best beds, a separate table for each and 'by no means to let any of them want for any particular'. In six months his account totalled £1091 for food, beer, claret, port, cleaning rooms, washing clothes, fuel and candles. The Treasury paid these items for State Prisoners.[5] O'Connor was kept on the same terms.[6] He was waited on by his servant, his dog lived with him. He could supplement his diet if he wished.

But O'Connor was held apart. He had made himself a formidable enemy to government. His connections meant they would keep him to a certain standard, but his skills as an inflammatory orator and his galvanising influence alarmed them. They kept him in solitary confinement and well away from the other prisoners. Within the Castle, their own headquarters, they had him where they wanted him.

He had the attendance of a doctor over a period of three weeks.[7] Visitors he was not allowed. Having befriended the jailer, he was able to get books from Lord Edward, in which they scribbled messages, passed back and forth. O'Connor had never been confined before. A big man who lived in opulent circles, he was now alone in a small, stone room.

1. *Anne Conner, mother of Arthur O'Connor.*

2. *Richard Longfield, Lord Longueville.*

3. *Roger O'Connor, brother of Arthur O'Connor.*

4. *Daniel Conner, brother of Arthur O'Connor.*

5. Charles James Fox.

6. Richard Brinsley Sheridan.

7. Sir Francis Burdett,
5th Baronet.

8. Edmund Burke.

9. Theobald Wolfe Tone (1763-1798).

10. *The Dublin Volunteers, College Green, 4 November 1779.*

11. *Lady Pamela Fitzgerald and her daughter.*

12. Arthur O'Connor introducing Charles James Fox to Napoleon.
Cartoon by Gillray.

13. Fort George, Inverness, Scotland.

14. Lord Edward FitzGerald.

15. Henry Grattan, statesman.

16. Robert Stewart,
Viscount Castlereagh.

17. John Jeffreys Pratt, Marquess of
Camden (1759-1840).

18. William Pitt the younger, MP, British Prime Minister.

19. *Eliza Condorcet O'Connor.*   20. *Arthur Condorcet O'Connor.*

21. *Château de Bignon-Mirabeau.*

Tormented with violent headaches for want of air I went on the top of the tower. This was perceived by the spies that surrounded the Tower and the next day when the jailer went up on the top, he was fired at by one of the sentries, whose ball grazed his cheek. On the jailer accusing him of firing at him he answered he had imagined it was the prisoner he fired at. This was repeated when I was reading at the window.[8]

The notes which O'Connor wrote to the FitzGeralds vary between extravagant emotion in the romantic fashion and reminders on United organisation. To Pamela and Lucy:

ten thousand thanks to my ever dearest Pa for her little purse and to the dear good-hearted Lucy for her Royal Unction. I saw my dear beloved friend from my grated prison: alas! she looked pale, she grieves for her friend. Do not then, dear friends, add to his misery by letting it prey upon your warm generous hearts. I can bear my own sufferings without a sigh, but the sight of you, my ever dear, dear friends, brings torrents from my eyes![9]

He finds the 'monotonous, lonesome, ever-reigning solitude' very difficult and remembers with nostalgia 'the dear song, and the old dance, the conversation, the humble meal and the jug of native punch'. The days in Kildare had been happy ones. But physical confinement was the real problem for so vigorous a man. 'I am becoming weaker and weaker every day from want of exercise, and am now busy inventing some way of taking much exercise in a small space. My poor faithful dog is in want of exercise: it watches every stir I take and sympathises with its master. What a work I shall have to get Lucy's ointment [the Royal Unction] to the root of my thick hair.'[10] If Matty McTeir was right and he had lost it through fever last autumn, it had quickly grown again.

But he also writes about the comparative salaries of Catholic and Presbyterian clergy, advises discretion to a United colleague since little law now protects the citizens if they speak without caution. He writes about the comparative boundaries of Protestant and Catholic parishes.

Lady Lucy was impressed by Burdett's loyalty to O'Connor. 'There never was such a friend as Mr Burdett seems in all his conduct towards Arthur. We get letters every day. Edward is called *Faithful* in them, Pamela *Violette*, and I *Good Heart*.'[11] In the same month, Lady Lucy saw Arthur's son who came to Lord Edward's house. The boy was now four.[12] She may have known of O'Connor's lover and child before but she had not encountered them. Edward already knew them and could reassure the lady about Arthur. Only his closest friends ever mentioned the liaison. The secretiveness of Arthur's nature had thrown a cloak over the woman and child.

In England, O'Connor's address had caused great excitement. Sarah Napier, Lord Edward's Aunt was in the country 'but even here the public talk is so great about O'Connor's letter and confinement that one hears of nothing else'.[13] It was considered a fine composition, plain, forcible and well written, 'for what is good writing meant for, but to be well understood and to make an impression?' Lawyers said there was no High Treason in it, that government only increased O'Connor's influence by arresting him for a clever sedition. Sarah Napier thought its intentions bad. Separation for Ireland would mean greater impoverishment. France and Britain would fight over her.

> I really do think that to try to promote our shaking off the yoke of England, by means of the French, and at this moment of danger, is cruel to poor Ireland, in the most barbarous degree – for it is egging on the poor deluded people of Ireland to dash into certain misery and destruction during the lives of the present race – and upon all these considerations, I do most sincerely from my heart condemn O'Connor, who is vain and arrogant enough to think his judgement ought to lead his country into a revolution.[14]

The FitzGerald family to some extent blamed O'Connor for Edward's revolutionary activities. They, and Dublin society even more, suspected Pamela whose background was among French radicals.[15] In fact, Edward's rebellious fervour was his own. He 'had got his republican ideas in America, and on his return they were fostered by Charles Fox and Mr Sheridan'[16] his daughter later concluded. His heart was in revolution and O'Connor, who was analytical and deep, must have been swayed by Edward's spontaneous responses. Pamela was terrified of their schemes, cautious, yet even Burdett referred to her as 'his dangerous little wife'.

O'Connor, from both pride and a sense of honour, would never have admitted that Lord Edward had influenced him towards rebellion. Yet, at many critical moments when O'Connor seemed likely to compromise, to pursue a political career, to move to England, to lose the momentum, Edward FitzGerald appeared and O'Connor once more took up the banner. FitzGerald alone had not the skills. He had what the age demanded, emotional spontaneity and O'Connor, an introvert, had not. FitzGerald touched chords in O'Connor who spoke out, wrote, took action, planned, organised and executed at a level FitzGerald could not achieve. Both of them were bound by their particular conception of honour to their commitments, to Ireland, to a path already chosen. This was in some ways admirable and in some ways a restriction to clear thought. Honour was a high priority. They had a very developed concept of what it was and judged others by it. Lord Edward also moved O'Connor. Burdett adored him.

In March, Burdett sent a Mr Mansell to enquire about Arthur and in his maiden speech, Burdett proclaimed his affection for O'Connor. 'Good God,' said Burdett, 'that treason to Ireland and the name of O'Connor should be preposterously linked together as he is capable of everything that is great, generous and noble for his country's good.'[17] Burdett rejoiced at Ireland's resistance to tyranny. Should not tyranny be everywhere resisted?

Honour might be paramount, but friendship was sacred and expressed in romantic terms. The tender feelings were those which mattered, regardless of gender, overshadowing desire and passion. Lord Edward fitted this era perfectly, O'Connor not so naturally. His romanticism reads awkwardly, his rationality cuts in, incisive, demanding. Under the words is a simmering energy, independent, arrogant and fiery which has not made its peace with history or with the culture in which he lives. What Irishman had made that peace?

The Union of Irishmen had been set up to reconcile the divided nation as well as reform it. Now they were plotting war.

From prison, O'Connor could do little. He heard a rising was imminent. Arms, a uniform and horses were ready for him at the house of a friend.[18] But while the government delayed charging O'Connor, while Lake disarmed Ulster, the United Irish Executive debated and did not act. While a French descent was imminent, O'Connor had had a commanding role. A second French landing seemed uncertain. Those who argued caution gained ground. Of these, Thomas Addis Emmet was prominent. He became a member of the Leinster Executive in January amidst violent divisions.[19] Lewins in Hamburg was negotiating French military aid and a loan from either France or Spain for £500,000.[20] Sent on to Frankfurt, Lewins met Hoche and Tone. Here he learnt that France was preparing a naval attack on England, possibly through Ireland. It was to sail from Holland. In June, Hoche, Tone and Lewins moved to the Hague in preparation. Tone could join the Dutch fleet but they wanted no French Generals on board.[21] Lewins left for Paris with Hoche who was almost immediately implicated in a military coup.

Lord Edward was still dedicated to urgent military action. The French sent an agent who could not proceed beyond London. Lord Edward suggested Lucy return to England and, under cover of escorting her, brother and sister travelled to London in May where FitzGerald gave Jagerhorn an impressive account of United Irish numbers at 100,000 but emphasised their shortage of arms.[22]

In June, the United Irish Executive sent McNeven to Hamburg where he negotiated with Reinhard.[23] By August, he was in Paris where Lewins introduced him to the Directory.[24] It was Hoche who encouraged McNeven to believe that the French planned an imminent descent upon Ireland.

O'Connor was informed of none of these dealings. By June the Irish Attorney General gave his view that regarding the address *To the Free Electors of the County of Antrim*, O'Connor should be prosecuted for a misdemeanour. It could not be High Treason as it in no way attacked the King.[25] This was bad news for Camden who had taken the advice of Fitzgibbon to press the capital charge. Camden told the Duke of Portland that 'much obloquy must ensue' if, after five months close confinement, the charge was to be so slight.[26] Perhaps they should charge him with High Treason and be prepared to lose the case. The chief law officers of the two kingdoms strongly disagreed. What should Camden do?

O'Connor, who in July had finally been allowed pen and paper, demanded either trial or freedom, 'having suffered during this period of solitary exclusion from every species of intercourse with the world, and every enjoyment which makes life worth possessing, the rack and injury of my fortune, the loss of my health and the ruin of my constitution from a total deprivation of air and exercise, entitle me to my liberty on giving bail for my appearance to answer the charge when government may think fit to bring it to trial'.[27]

By the end of July, they had decided to free O'Connor. He was allowed visitors and told to offer bail.[28] Camden, curiously, considered it 'more liberal' to let him out in time for O'Connor to stand in the Antrim election.[29] Most of the elections were over or had been uncontested, Lord Edward had stood down from Kildare. Many leading citizens had lost confidence in parliament.

In fact O'Connor was freed the day after the Antrim election. Drennan called on him at the Hotel where he found O'Connor in good spirits and 'tolerably healthy'.

His paleness was pathetic from the idea of his confinement – He is certainly a singular looking man as Grattan also is, but the ladies might, and I believe many do think O'Connor singularly handsome. He twice repeated the name of some lady who had been already to see him but I could not catch the name, which showed somewhat of the character of Don Mathias in Gilblas. I believe he goes into the country immediately to drink the spirit of the Mountain Breeze.[30]

As soon as he had ridden in the mountains, stretched his cramped muscles walking on the hillsides and felt the free passage of the wind, O'Connor was quick to reunite with the Executive. Emmet had again been attempting a pact for reform with Grattan, while also taking a lead in the Union of Irishmen. Grattan, however, would not deal with the United Irishmen, whom he considered dangerous and extreme. Had there been a real hope of reform, Emmet said he planned to send a message to France to cancel the invasion.[31] He was sure that insurrection would fail without invasion and was insistent that nothing should be tried without the French. As to France taking over Ireland, the Irish once roused could see off the French, thought he. In any case, the Executive had the new idea that it would raise a loan and buy invasion. Once free and with improved trade, they would have no problem paying off the £500,000.[32]

Emmet drove O'Connor demented.

One of the first persons I met was Thomas Addis Emmet who told me he had become one of the Executive where there had been violent divisions between those who desired an insurrection and those who opposed it, that he was one of the latter and succeeded only by threatening the others to go to the Castle and discover all. It is not possible to express the indignation I felt at hearing this account from Emmet. I reminded him of the confession he made me of his want of nerve to engage in a rising. Why then had he in despite of his acknowledged timidity, engaged in a situation he knew he was incapable of discharging the duties. The fruits of this were sapping the roots of the confidence that formed the existence of the association, to cover his want of resolution ... This was the first consequence of this man's engaging in what he had not the courage to execute and this led to several others.[33]

Emmet and Drennan had been in the Dublin Union early on, but the active leaders had fled or were in prison. The northern leaders were more militant. There had been a long lapse into which O'Connor had strode, taken over. Now, as Emmet steered a quasi-political course, he found the United Irishmen had changed into a military and revolutionary movement, much as Tone had envisaged. Emmet had been close to Tone but this was not his milieu. Now that Ireland was arming, he found himself in a movement very different from the debating forum he had joined early in the decade and he attempted to re-direct it.

O'Connor found that little had been done for 'the progress of the Union'[34] while he was jailed. *The Northern Star* had been silenced. A man named Walter Cox had started the *Union Star*, a paper of violent attitudes advocating assassination. Watty Cox was a gunsmith turned journalist and a United Irishman. When O'Connor was released, he persuaded Cox not to print the *Union Star*.[35] Meanwhile, a reward was offered by the government for the name of the author. To take the place of the *Union Star*, O'Connor with others from the Executive now put their money into a new paper. The majority of the capital for the *Press* seems to have been put up by Valentine Lawless, son of the Catholic Lord Cloncurry, both of whom were members of the Union in Dublin.[36] On 28 September 1797 the first issue appeared in Dublin. The *Press* had a more literary style than the *Northern Star*. Like the Belfast paper its object was 'to extinguish party animosity and introduce a cordial union of all the people' and 'to produce a reform in the abuses of government'.[37] It would also 'assert and claim her commercial rights, inculcate maxims of economy and liberty' and 'class Ireland on the scale of nations'. It tested to the limit the famous British right to freedom of the press.

Every paper had to register its name, proprietor and printer with the authorities. Peter Finnerty was registered as owner,[38] Charles Brennan was printer[39] and O'Connor was in fact the editor. Brennan had been apprenticed to William Corbet, a young printer on the *Northern Star*. Later, when the rebellion was over, William Corbet wrote to John Pollock, Crown Prosecutor for Leinster, that at the end of 1797, 'you wanted full information on the *Press* and at great risk, I got it.'[40] It was Corbet who provided information on Brennan who was imprisoned for debt.

John Stockdale then became printer. He had printed the proceedings of the United Irish Societies in 1794. Stockdale had already fallen foul of the government in 1796 by printing the works of Thomas Paine on his press at 62 Abbey Street, Dublin now the registered office of the *Press*.[41] The printers were important men, the newspapers and pamphlets they produced a great weapon in the development of democratic consciousness. They knew each other and worked together in offices behind the old houses of Belfast and Dublin, with heavy brass letterheads, wooden blocks, thick paper and the smell of warm ink. Walter Cox turned informer late in 1797, so did Corbet.[42] Stockdale remained a man of integrity, a man who printed Paine and Volney, imprisoned several times for his stubborn determination to print a free press.

'No liberty can survive the liberty of the *Press*'[43] the paper contended and they appealed

> TO THE KING – To the throne itself your scourged people are now driven to look for a mitigation of oppressions which are become intolerable. On ordinary occasions, it would look like a saucy affectation of familiarity with greatness, to address a Sovereign; but in the moment of such terrible omen as the present ... it is the bounden duty of every citizen to speak, and of every King to hear.[44]

The *Press* received anonymous articles in its box, from which some were chosen for publication.[45] O'Connor wrote for it, they published extracts from Volney's *Natural Law*, scandalous versions of the ideas of the Orange Order designed to ignite the old Defenders and bring them into the Union[46] and an Ode to the Memory of William Orr for which Finnerty was prosecuted and imprisoned.[47] Orr was a Presbyterian farmer and United Irishman of good character who was executed for administering oaths. The government used the Insurrection Act to press this charge for the first time and there were irregularities in the trial – but Orr was hanged. The outcry was fierce. *Remember Orr*, cried the people as they went into rebellion and the battlecry rang on down the ages.

Finnerty was arrested in November. There were threats of a public whipping. Found guilty of libel, he was sentenced to two years imprisonment and one hour in the pillory. On 30 December, he was fastened to the wooden pillory opposite the Session House in Green Street. This drew a great crowd. Arthur O'Connor stood beside him during the hour. Finnerty spoke a few brave words. The presence of his friends prevented molestation. Some highly respectable citizens were there. The tall figure of

O'Connor, challenging, like the physical symbol of honour, stood for the right to free speech. The people cheered Finnerty's words and the Armagh militia treated them roughly.

O'Connor now publicly declared himself proprietor.[48] They had been paying spies to tell them, he asserted, 'Had they sent to me ... I would have told them what I now tell you; I did set up the *Press*, though in a legal sense I was not the proprietor.'[49] Now, he was taking the position officially. At this news, the circulation doubled to 6,000. He maintained constant vigilance as compositors slipped in 'discreditable articles to satisfy their passions'. When one such appeared saying that Lady Fitzgibbon was bald and wore a wig, O'Connor 'waited on the lady' to put the matter right.[50] He wanted no scandal and petty gossip, he wanted a free country with a proper economy. Two priests complained to him about the inclusion of Volney, *Natural Law* was not consistent with Catholic doctrine. O'Connor was exasperated, went to their parish and told the local people that their priests were trying to stop them reading the *Press*. Soon, says O'Connor, the priests came back to say that the people would not come to mass. The priests would therefore offer no further objection to the paper.[51] The *Press* was O'Connor's strongest tool for promoting the Union although the government was working hard at provoking the country beyond control.

The effects of General Lake's methods for disarming the North had produced a shocked stillness in the country which could not last. The United Irishmen held the people in check until their plans were completed. In France, Bonaparte had triumphed over the Austrians. Then, after the coup of September in which Hoche was involved, the young General sickened. Before the end of September he was dead. In October the British destroyed the Dutch fleet off the Texel. The ascent of Napoleon Bonaparte in France was based on the ever wider territory he conquered in continental Europe. But on the seas, the British navy was dominant. Ireland, and particularly O'Connor had lost an established ally in Lazare Hoche.

In the British House of Lords, Lord Moira spoke against the army in Ireland, of 'the most absurd as well as the most disgusting tyranny that any nation ever groaned under'.[52]

In November General Sir Ralph Abercromby took over from Carhampton as Commander-in-Chief in Ireland. A distinguished Scots soldier of experience and integrity, Abercromby quickly took stock.

So did the United Irishmen. A five man National Executive directory was appointed in November with one member from each of the four provinces and one director; so Higgins reported to the Castle. In this directory, O'Connor represented Ulster. This situation was critical. The government had played into their hands so often by enraging even the most loyal of citizens, by changes of policy, breaches of faith and blatant corruption. But British naval power would prevent a French descent on Ireland, Ulster seemed beaten into submission and Hoche was gone.

O'Connor and FitzGerald had to deal too with endless intrigues. The Catholic members of the United Irishmen were mainly of the upper class and linked to the old Catholic Committee. O'Connor suspected they leaked information that way. Members of the Catholic Committee tried to dissuade the two leaders from insurrection. They implied that O'Connor and FitzGerald were interlopers, that only Catholics were truly Irishmen, said they brought Catholics into danger, threatened to denounce them to the Castle. This infuriated O'Connor but, ever rational, he asked them how they knew so much if they were not United men. If you betray us, said O'Connor, you risk the vengeance of the people. The Catholics left. 'Edward flew into my arms, "oh my beloved friend how I love you for the sang froid with which you overwhelmed these vile men with your disdain. I should have spoiled it by giving vent to the indignation their dastardly conduct so strongly excited in my mind,"' O'Connor recorded. Edward went on to explain an intrigue designed to make them jealous of each other. O'Connor was cast down.[53] It was impossibly difficult to create Union among this nest of conflicting interest.

'We dined that day with Pamela only and after dining we discussed our situation and the incident of the morning. Edward observed that he could not bring himself to hope for success with such a set of cowardly men.' He might go to Hamburg and live for a time with Madame de Genlis. 'What he would counsel me to do was to save Ireland by getting into the English parliament.'[54] This time Edward clearly advocated retreat. O'Connor listened.

Lord Edward's family had been pressing him to leave Ireland. Their friends in the government had made it plain that all ports were open for him to leave, but if he remained, and remained militant, they had few choices. His sisters had written anxiously from England, the Duke of Leinster had spoken to him. He had been fairly deaf to their pleas until the divisions in the Union began to depress him and 'the twin of his soul'. O'Connor too was undecided. This proposition 'embraced such important interests and was of such an extensive bearing that I requested we should take time to make up our minds'.[55]

Then Arthur received a message from France that the French were preparing another force for Ireland. Once more it became a matter of honour: they could not desert their comrades now, the brave Presbyterians who had worked so hard, so long, the Protestant Union men so staunch and the Catholic peasantry, whom they had spent months organising and whose rights they believed they were fighting for.

Watty Cox was wholly trusted by O'Connor but he was playing a complicated double game.[56] It was O'Connor's idea that Cox should ask for immunity for himself before offering to name the author of the *Union Star*.[57] He presented himself to Secretary Cooke who agreed immunity. Cooke was astonished when Cox named himself. Back came Cox to Frescati, the Duchess of Leinster's villa outside Dublin where O'Connor and the FitzGeralds were staying. Cox woke them at 4am to tell O'Connor of his interview. Also, said Cox, Cooke had offered him a huge reward for testifying against O'Connor but he had turned it down. He also said he had eavesdropped at the Council door and heard Beresford say that O'Connor must not stay at liberty for when he was in the Bermingham Tower, the country had gone quiet.[58]

'On the intelligence of Cox, I went to the Castle where I saw Mr Cooke, the Under-Secretary.' Viscount Castlereagh was now acting Secretary because of the continuing illness of Mr Pelham. To Cooke, 'I communicated the urgent business I had in London'. O'Connor was still on bail. Cooke told him he could go, 'when and for as long as I liked'.[59]

Having informed the Executive, O'Connor went late to join the Packet, going directly to his berth. In the morning, imagine the surprise of the gentlemen on board, leaving the disturbed state of the country and cursing that arch-fiend Arthur O'Connor, when the rebel himself strolled out on deck.[60]

In London, 'I was received with the warmest kindness and affection by my beloved friends.'[61] It was January 1798.

Chapter 12

A FATEFUL JOURNEY

'They may make martyrs and Liberty's roots will be fertilised by the blood of the murdered ...' O'Connor wrote in the *Press* on 1 January 1798.

Since Lake's proclamation of May 1797, every kind of outrage had been perpetrated by troops. Regiments from Britain stationed in Ireland, as well as Irish troops, the largely catholic militia and protestant yeomanry, were all known to behave with horrifying savagery. Where officers had tight control, outrages were not reported but this was the minority of cases. Nor was the brutality of the troops consistently sectarian. Quartered among a restive population, the soldiers drank and had a very free hand. If a soldier was murdered, the troops retaliated with ferocity. Their task was to bring in arms. They burnt houses, half hanged and then revived men to get confessions, half-drowned and revived them, flogged them until arms were given up, shot boys, old men. Women were everywhere at risk. Between dusk and dawn in proclaimed districts, no citizen was safe outdoors.

General Abercromby was as horrified as Lord Moira but for good military reasons. The army were scattered in small groups through the country to keep the people down. To Abercromby, the enemy was external and the army should be in large concentrations to repel invasion. From Bantry, on 28 January the General reported:

I have the pleasure to say I have found the country everywhere quiet, but there exists among the gentlemen the greatest despondency, they believe or effect to believe, that there is a plot in every family, and a conspiracy in every parish, and they would abandon the country, unless the troops were dispersed over the face of it for their protection. I believe the lower ranks heartily hate the gentlemen, because they oppress them, and the gentlemen hate the peasants because they know they deserve to be hated.[1]

What the country needed, in Abercromby's view, was gentlemen with backbone to lead the yeomanry so that he could get some discipline into the regular troops and use them to repel the French. Many landowners were absentees, while even among the most responsible and enlightened there was such total disillusion with parliament and government that they became leaderless and insecure.

Early in February, in France, Bonaparte commanded preparation of a fleet at Dunkirk sufficient for 50,000 men. Ships were to be fitted out in Holland and in all the French Channel ports. Tone and Lewins had reported to Bonaparte. They were optimistic that Ireland was one of his objects. French naval preparations were known in London but not Napoleon's destination. The London government was braced.

The United Irishmen were creating a new nation within the body of the old. By careful organisation of each district into the pyramidal structure, they built the skeleton of both a civic and a military nation. At the vital moment, the new nation must be triggered, for the old nation was putrid with corruption. There was no plan for major reallocation of land, the people would have rent reductions and an abolition of tithes. The trigger would clearly have to be military and for this, arms and expertise were needed. These, the French were to provide. But France was moving from turbulent revolution towards military dictatorship. Making a binding agreement with France was impossible and what had Ireland to offer but a back door into England? Within the Union of Irishmen, important differences arose about how and when to act.

The government, well aware that United organisation was infecting the whole country, wanted to bring about a crisis and eradicate it. Camden told Portland on 8 February:

... although I am convinced that the present tranquillity in the country has proceeded from the measures of coercion government has adopted, yet there are those who conceive it is produced by the influence of the Executive Committee in Dublin, who have given orders that the United Irishmen should now remain perfectly tranquil; and that as they are proceeding to organise the People, steps should be taken to disturb the continuance of this system.[2]

Camden wanted to arrest the leaders even if he could not bring them to trial. If this caused insurrection, so much the better as they could face and quell it. He thought it preferable to choose the moment than be surprised when the enemy were off the coast. He planned to talk to Abercromby and prepare to execute this plan.

Portland was horrified. How could the Chancellor, a man of age and experience, give support to such a rash and violent idea? The government in Ireland was not to act without the permission of the King.[3] But reports from France suggested a second descent on Ireland was imminent. Portland was swayed. By 26 February he conceded to Camden; he could proceed if he felt he must.

Government information on the United Irishmen was detailed. McNally continued on confidential terms with the leaders, and informed. Late in 1797, Lord Edward recruited Thomas Reynolds as United Colonel in Kildare. A Catholic silk merchant connected to the FitzGeralds, Reynolds leased Kilkea Castle from the Duke of Leinster. Highly alarmed by talk from some United faction of assassinating the government, he quickly turned informer. From 'Richardson', the government received details on the Union's negotiations with France. Historians have identified 'Richardson' as Samuel Turner, a member of the Leinster Executive whom Lord Edward had sent to stay with Mrs Mathiessen in Hamburg and in whom he confided. London received information from within the offices of both Reinhard and Bartholomey, including a copy of McNeven's memo to Reinhard.[4] Their information was fairly complete. Gaps and inaccuracies occurred because there were factions within the Union and informers reported only on the meetings they had access to. There was considerable confusion in France.

On Arthur O'Connor the authorities had some information but no evidence. With relief, Dublin heard he had left Ireland early in January, now Whitehall could watch him. On arrival in London, O'Connor stayed with Sir Francis Burdett.[5] A week later he met Lady Lucy who was delighted to see him again. He was frequently in the company of Fox and Sheridan. The latter spoke to Arthur 'most confidentially, because I treated him, and I think he treated me, with a confidence and unreservedness that might have been expected to have arisen alone from a much longer acquaintance'.[6] Neither had any illusions about the political chaos in France. Both men were saddened by the war, illiberal government in England and tyranny in Ireland. O'Connor and Fox were close, Fox later stated that O'Connor was 'very ardent and affectionate in his friendships'.[7]

O'Connor brought his personal papers with him to London. Among them was a long pamphlet of 40,000 words which he finished on 1 February. *The State of Ireland* was published in Dublin, then London, in 1798. It was an unusual and formidable text, in which sophisticated concepts of economics and nationhood drove forward a revolutionary diatribe. *The State of Ireland* was addressed 'To the Irish Nation'. It was based on economic principles and showed the political corruption of Ireland in terms of her natural resources and the plunder of the national capital. It was argued in Adam Smith's terms of wages, rents and profits. This plunder, O'Connor believed, had affected the 'national mind'.

He discussed Ireland's natural resources of land, labour, fisheries and industry. He made clear how under-capitalised her enterprises were, the disadvantages they suffered from export of raw materials, commercial disadvantage, mismanagement and corruption of public finance. The cost of the legal system, of government, of the Established Church increased debt and caused a heavy tax burden, unfairly distributed. Savings were impossible under such a system. He attacked bounties on corn prices with their effect on livestock values. O'Connor's arguments were structured in the language of emerging economic theory but they quickly generated political fire. He was writing in an age when ideas themselves were in revolution.

Trust me, my countrymen, that to explain the political phenomena of our times, to which it is agreed on all sides the history of mankind affords nothing analogous, the primordial principles of *human nature* are the rudder, the compass and the polar star, by which you must steer in the storm, in the new and unexplored regions which human society has so recently entered.

The remedy for Ireland's problems was clear from the rights of man. Monopoly of property had grown up to the detriment of national prosperity and created monopoly of power. It was in the interest of the rich, as well as the poor to abolish monopoly in order to create a healthy prosperous state. In France, this had become essential and brought on revolution. O'Connor believed the British constitution of 1688 established a balance of power and gave rights to the people represented in parliament, including a just use of the public finances and accounts for them. He gave figures for the increasing national debt. In Ireland the balance of power had been corrupted and abused. He gave definitions; 'taking that to be a republic where the public affairs are controlled by the bulk of the people.' He was not concerned whether there should be a King or Peers but they must function within the checks and balances of the constitution.

But the Irish government tried to prevent revolution by suspending rights, by violence, torture and transportation. It ran up crippling debts, destroyed the free press and set spies, man on man. The government could not charge the United People of Ireland with subverting the constitution when they had usurped and corrupted it themselves.

Yes! The People of Ireland have united in a GLORIOUS CONSPIRACY to destroy religious bigotry and national thraldom. [I] have exerted myself by every means in my power to promote that UNION, upon which, in my mind, the salvation of my Country depends, and on which I have staked my life, my name, and all that is dear to me upon earth.

The use of the title 'United People of Ireland' was new. Tone still wrote of United Irishmen. In his memoirs, O'Connor always refers to the movement as 'the Union'. Grattan decried the Union's aim of universal suffrage as madly unrealistic. With 'United People', O'Connor is clearly conscious that both sexes make up the nation. However, nowhere does he state that women should vote.

In London, O'Connor was with dear friends. Losing their company would be 'the greatest sacrifice I have ever made'.[8] He had already lost his uncle, between them once was much love. He had many friends, in Ireland and England, who 'loved me for the gaiety and mirthful turn of my mind'. Despite his cavernous inner world which made him introspective, Arthur was an Irishman, lived in company 'jovially seasoned with true Irish wit'. Now he was among 'some of the choicest spirits that ever animated human frames, that loved me, confided in me and that I loved and confided in. What it cost me to threw myself from this heaven into a gulph so low that it seemed to me another, lower world'.[9]

He knew it would not be long. On 13 February he wrote to his brother Roger that 'I have sold all my property to Burdett yet it may still go on in my name and the rents are to be transmitted to Hugh Bell'.[10] He wrote affectionately to his brother and told him not to expect letters from him for some time. He might get messages to Edward who would 'tell you of me'.[11]

Roger was publishing *The Harp of Erin* in Cork, a United paper on the lines of the *Press*. He had recruited energetically for the Irish Union, going down to the Catholic chapels after mass on Sundays to talk to the people.[12] It was mainly his efforts that made Bandon such a nest of United Irishmen.[13] His brother Robert lived close by and was angrily loyal to the government. Robert kept Pelham at Dublin Castle busy with information on the Union: 'traitors are swearing the people',[14] he wrote. These were his two younger brothers. A Mr Orpen who lived in Cork at the time, relates that in 1797 while walking with a friend in the principal street of that city, Bob Conner of Fort Robert accosted him in a jubilant manner.

'Orpen, my dear fellow' said Bob in a tone of triumph. 'I have got evidence enough that will hang them as round as a hoop,' and so saying Bob passed on.

'Who is Mr Conner so anxious to hang?' asked Orpen's companion.

'His brothers, Arthur and Roger,' replied Orpen, to the great amazement of the inquirer.[15]

Mr Pelham wrote that 'I have received at different times very important information from Mr Robert Conner and indeed he was the first person who gave me information against his brother.'[16] Roger had been tried in Cork in the summer of 1797 but acquitted.

Arthur was still in London. 'Never shall I forget those evenings most of which were spent with Sheridan.' Burdett and Ferguson were often with them. 'It was the failing of this great man to impair his reason by excess of wine as if nature, to satisfy the envy of the world, had sent him this defect to drag him nearer to its level.'[17]

After one such evening of long discussion, Sheridan deep in his cups, O'Connor helped the befuddled genius to his bed. It tore at his heart to see his beloved friend so helpless, yet still so kind and engaging. Mrs Sheridan 'reproached me for being the cause of her husband's excesses'. Arthur felt for her but, said he, Sheridan would always find companions and worse ones, 'for she knew I never drank. Would she find anyone who would take more care of him than I did'. Mrs Sheridan threw herself into O'Connor's arms sobbing, begging to be forgiven. She knew well how much Arthur loved her husband and herself, how Sheridan knew this and stated it, saying 'there was not a man living on whose friendship he counted more than mine or one for whom he had a more sincere and warm affection'.[18]

With Fox, Arthur talked of politics, of Pitt and the war, of the impending ruin of England.

The time arrived when I was to tear myself from the exquisite happiness I enjoyed in the society of men I so loved and esteemed. The whippings, picketings, torturings, burnings, imprisonings so goaded the people I dreaded nothing could restrain them from breaking out, when in a war of pikes against muskets, ball and powder and stones against bullets and grapeshot, victory could not be had but at the price of seas of blood. I saw I had not a moment to lose in ascertaining what we had to expect from French assistance.[19]

There were also moves by the Attorney General to have his bail
estreated. Emmet, one of his bail guarantors, had attended a hearing in Dublin on 12 February, reminding the court that they had
agreed to give warning if O'Connor was required to appear.[20] The
hearing was put off, but for how long? O'Connor had to hurry.

In Ireland, Abercromby spoke his mind. His General Order of
26 February announced that the Irish army was 'in a state of licen-
tiousness which must render it formidable to everyone but the
enemy'.[21] He was horrified by abuses of all kinds by the troops and
gave orders to officers on disciplining their men. The General
Order caused an uproar. Beresford, Fitzgibbon and Foster thought
Abercromby was inviting unrest and determined to get rid of him.
The government in London wanted to know if the abuses were real
and why the army was being publicly undermined. Camden was
harassed.

O'Connor had gone to stay with his friend Hugh Bell in
Charterhouse Square.[22] A merchant in the city of London with
offices in Aldersgate Street, he was an old friend of John Knox, who
had introduced O'Connor.[23] Bell tried to get him passage to
Hamburg but few vessels were crossing, it was believed that even
Hamburg might soon be taken by the French.[24] O'Connor could
not get a passport since he was on bail, and most regular passages
would require one. He then asked John Binns if he could arrange a
crossing. Binns, O'Connor believed, was attached to a merchant
trading house and would have contacts among cross-channel
traders.[25] In fact, Binns was a tradesman, a tailor's apprentice when
he left Dublin in 1794 to settle in London.[26] He and his brother
Benjamin were leading members of the London Corresponding
Society (LCS). They lived at 14 Plough Court in Fetter's Lane, the
house of Evans, Secretary to the Society.[27]

Sheridan had many associates in the London Corresponding
Society, a radical group to which Burdett and Godwin were at one
time affiliated. The LCS was part of the Reform movement of the
British Isles. More militant members, including Irish living in
England, had begun to affiliate the LCS with the United Irishmen.

There were efforts to attach the United Scots. The Irish in Manchester supported republican aims. In these dangerous times, under pressure of war and fear of invasion, the government became ever more repressive. The LCS was now considered seditious. O'Connor's position in Ireland was extreme, he was still on bail. He was careful about associations in London.[28] He moved too, in a different social circle.

Valentine Lawless was in London and spanned these worlds. He reported to the Opposition on the outrages occurring in Ireland.[29] He was involved with the *Courier*, a radical paper from which the *Press* and *The Harp of Erin* borrowed.[30] Through the Catholic network, Lawless met Quigley who was active in United societies throughout the British Isles and was busy trying to link them all to an invasion by France. It was Lawless who introduced Quigley to O'Connor.[31]

> The whole of my plan for getting to France was an egregious foule from first to last, to take a short cut I missed the tide and have passed my life in shoals and misery. Instead of going by Deal I should have gone by Hamburg but it was admitting Quigley to accompany me which principally caused my misfortune.

James Quigley, or O'Quigley, or Fivey, was a Catholic priest who had been in Holland and France, and was an active republican. Both Dublin and London had spies on him. Portland had written to Camden in January that Quigley was in London. 'He last night attended a meeting of the most profligate Jacobins here who assembled at Furnivals Inn.'[32] Early in February he was in Dublin and the government would have taken him up if it had any evidence at all against him. Lord Cloncurry sent a letter to O'Connor begging him to let Quigley, 'a persecuted man', go with him. O'Connor was surprised that Cloncurry knew anything of his plans. To his mind, this showed once again, that the Catholics on the Executive always confided in their co-religionists, without discretion.[33]

He had decided to go to France. Lord Edward had been pressing him to go.[34] O'Connor had sent Edmund O'Finn to Paris in January, pressing Bonaparte for military aid. Since then, Binns had been in Cork and met Roger. The situation was critical. Having set his course, O'Connor pursued it relentlessly. He could have stayed in London but there was no longer a place for him in politics, either in Dublin or London. He might be re-arrested at any time. He identified himself with Ireland in a powerful way. She was now tormented and he felt it personally. His methods had been high-handed but so far he had escaped the law. A strange recklessness invaded his astute mind, took over his driving personality. He packed his fine clothes, asked Hugh Bell to buy him French currency and prepared to leave for France.[35]

In February, a young associate of Lord Edward's, John Allen had left Ireland where was no longer safe. He joined Binns at Plough Court.[36] Quigley had returned from Ireland, heading for France. Stopping in Manchester, he told a meeting of Irish republicans that he was joining O'Connor and would leave to him the business of getting French assistance. With many expectations riding on him, O'Connor agreed to leave immediately for France and to travel with Quigley. He asked Binns to arrange the passage.[37] His young servant, Jeremiah Leary had been with O'Connor since he was a boy. He would travel with them, Allen too. Binns set off for the Kent coast to find a boat.

He enquired in Canterbury, saying he wanted to do a bit of smuggling. He enquired again at Whitstable and Deal. He wanted passage for five men to Calais, Flushing or le Havre. Few boat-owners were willing. The war and new legislation made the crossing very risky. At last Binns found two boat-owners who were willing but they asked £150 and a heavy deposit. Binns went back to London to confer.

Meanwhile, O'Connor, Quigley, Leary and Allen got aboard a hoy, a Thames passage boat, at the Tower steps, brought on board loads of luggage and slipped down the Thames to Whitstable near the mouth of the river. Quigley immediately proved a garrulous and indiscreet travelling companion, fond of liquor and chattering to anyone near him.[38] At Whitstable, O'Connor went ashore to find Binns, now back at Canterbury. The other three travelled to

Margate with the baggage.

All five were reunited in Margate on Monday 27 February. The boat was at Deal but not ready. They put up at the King's Head. O'Connor was travelling as Colonel Morris, Quigley as Captain Jones. O'Connor was apprehensive, Quigley seemed a liability.[39] He was not sure if they had a boat or not, should he return to London and try again for Hamburg – alone?

The next morning, two Bow Street officers came into the Inn with a warrant. Allen, Leary and Binns were downstairs, the officers held them in the parlour. On the first floor, in a private sitting room, they found Quigley drinking tea. They arrested him. O'Connor emerged from the bedroom. Mr Revett, the Bow Street officer, identified himself.

It was too late now for O'Connor to change plans, it was time to think quickly and use what he knew of the law. The officers took them downstairs and while all five were held in the parlour, Revett and Fugion searched the baggage. The prisoners denied ownership. Any papers were sealed and taken for examination before a magistrate at Benson's Hotel. In O'Connor's razor case there was a cypher or code. In a great-coat pocket was Quigley's pocket book containing a paper addressed to the Executive Directory of France. Mr Twopenny, the magistrate, read it, frowned and sent it with the other papers to Bow Street.

The prisoners slept on a mattress in the parlour of an Inn in Canterbury. The following day they were taken to London. Their baggage and papers were opened at the Duke of Portland's office. There was nothing incriminating in O'Connor's luggage. Left alone at Bow Street, the five fellow-travellers took stock. 'When we were alone Quigley told us he hoped these papers may be lost for that if they were produced there was one found in the pocket that would hang us all.'

'From here I was taken to Downing Street to be examined by the Chief of Police and after by Pitt and Dundas. In this interview with Pitt at first glance I could easily perceive a man who was making a strong effort to affect a calm he was very far from possessing and a most malevolent disposition towards me.' O'Connor had written to Bell expressing his concern at having agreed to travel with

Quigley, an indiscreet man he had only just met. This letter had apparently been intercepted and shown to Pitt but the Minister was still determined to prove that Quigley and O'Connor were co-conspirators. O'Connor despised Pitt for this.[40] The interview pleased no one.

'From here I was taken to Cold Bath Fields.'[41] Conditions in this prison were bad, Burdett later mounted a mission to improve them.[42] This was O'Connor's first taste of British prison life. Innocently he asked the jailer's wife for a cup of tea, she drowned him in mockery.[43] The next day he was taken to the Tower of London.

Two halberdiers were posted to guard him and 'to watch if the prisoner be sad or joyous and record every crisis he suffers' but they were civil and the 'wife of the yeoman where I lodged was the kindest of women. I gained her heart by getting her little daughter of six years old to play in the room I was imprisoned in'.[44] O'Connor exerted his Irish charm on his gaolers, talked to them of liberty and extracted a few concessions. In prison, every favour was precious. O'Connor was now being held on a charge of High Treason, a capital offence. Portland instructed the Constable of the Tower, 'you are to keep him safe and close'.[45] None of the prisoners were to have newspapers, O'Connor could take air for half an hour every day. Mr Fugion of Bow Street brought in his clothes.

If he had seen the newspapers, he would have known that further steps had been taken in Ireland. His own paper, the *Press* had been closed. Government officers seized stamped paper, broke the presses and heading blocks. They arrested and imprisoned Stockdale.[46] On 12 March, on Reynolds' information, police broke in on a meeting of the Leinster provincial committee at the house of Oliver Bond in Dublin. They arrested twelve United leaders. They separately arrested Sweetman, Emmet, Jackson and MacNeven. McCormick fled abroad, Lord Edward went into hiding.

Abercromby resigned on 15 March but had not yet left the country. At Camden's insistence he proclaimed martial law on 30 March. The whole country was to be disarmed. Soldiers would live at free quarters until all arms were given up.

Ulster was quiet. Kildare, Tipperary, Limerick, Cork, King's and Queen's counties were particularly volatile. Soldiers descended like locusts. Free quarters gave them licence to live where they liked, to take livestock, produce and whatever else they wanted. To get arms they burnt houses, flogged the peasants without mercy and often to death. Many families were ruined, many men and boys shot dead. A new torture was devised. The pitch-cap imitated the 'croppies', those who cropped their hair in the republican fashion. Linen or thick brown paper was fastened to the head with pitch and set on fire. Pieces of ears were cut off. Rape became common.

On 23 April, Abercromby left Ireland and Lake assumed command. Regiments with good officers behaved with order and some humanity, elsewhere the tyranny of the military became intolerable. Many gentry protested although Lord Shannon seemed unmoved. He told his son, 'in the county of Wicklow, in cases where the man of the house has fled, they whip the children and the ladies on their naked posterior and this <u>mild</u> punishment has produced more pikes than any other expedient yet put in practice'.[47] Perhaps Shannon had not seen the soldiers, young, drunk and vicious, slapping the leather thongs in their hands, laughing with derision while others stripped the women and children.

The people had few leaders and still there was no movement by the French – but they could not bear the level of violence unleashed on them. In hiding, Lord Edward drew up a military strategy. The rebellion was set for the night of 23 May, at the rising of the moon.

On 7 April, O'Connor and his fellow prisoners had been removed from the Tower and taken back to Kent for trial. The Grand Jury was sworn in on 14 April at Maidstone and sent the case forward for trial. Witnesses were to be brought over from Ireland.[48] The five prisoners were indicted for High Treason. Quigley's counsel, Mr Plumer, however, proved that the Jury had been tampered with by the Reverend Arthur Young who had been urging jurors to convict no matter what the evidence. As the trial was for the lives of five men, this was extremely serious.[49]

Burdett applied to the Duke of Portland to see O'Connor 'in order to procure him all those means of defence which justice requires'.[50] He had approached the Privy Council, Mr Wickham and Judge Buller but had been consistently refused. How was

O'Connor to have a fair trial if he could not organise his defence? In fact, O'Connor had a lawyer and witnesses for the defence had been contacted both in England and Ireland.

At last, a fair jury was sworn in on 21 May, the prisoners agreed to be tried together and the trial got under way. Charles Fox had conducted arrangements for O'Connor's defence[51] and Mr Dallas, barrister, defended him.[52] Emerging from the darkness of his dungeon in Maidstone gaol, he found himself in the light of the courtroom and on trial for his life.

Chapter 13

CATASTROPHE

Interviews with his lawyers and the involvement of his friends in his defence meant that news now reached O'Connor. Reports from Ireland were appalling.

> A few days before my trial at Maidstone, I received a note in pencil writing in these terms: 'if you fall, not a drop of your blood that shall not be avenged'. I instantly answered it by these words: 'I conjure you banish from your thoughts all idea of vengeance. Any attempt at this moment without arms, ammunition, officers, discipline of any kind would be madness'.[1]

While O'Connor had been in the Tower, Bonaparte had made a decision. He abandoned the Channel fleet and started building up his army in the south. On 19 May, Bonaparte's Mediterranean fleet sailed from Toulon. London suspected his destination was Ireland. Britain had a fleet under Horatio Nelson close to Toulon with orders to engage the French. 19 May was also the day on which the police broke in to Lord Edward's hiding place in Dublin. But reports had not yet reached England.

Arthur's brother, Roger, was in prison in London. He had been incarcerated during the previous winter in Cork but released. In April he had set out for London to be a witness for Arthur and had written to Portland for permission to see his brother. Having his address was useful, the next day he was arrested. The Duke of Portland had him sent back to Ireland in custody, but Mr Wickham wrote from Whitehall to Viscount Castlereagh asking to have Roger returned to England.[2] He might be a useful witness for the prosecution. Dizzy from arrest and release, disorientated by multiple journeys across the Irish Sea, the effervescent Roger was now firmly imprisoned in London. His distracted wife started out from west Cork for England to get news of him.

The trial of James Quigley, Arthur O'Connor and three others had a weak prosecution case which rested on the paper in Quigley's coat. A multitude of witnesses proved that Binns was looking for a boat to cross the Channel. O'Connor had almost £1,000 in sterling and Louis d'Or. A letter from O'Connor had been found among Lord Edward's papers when search warrants were first issued for FitzGerald in March. This matched the cypher O'Connor carried and showed that he planned to go to France. Despite dangerous items in the cypher such as ships of the line, these were not used in the letter. Although a witness from Ireland identified O'Connor's handwriting, this piece of evidence was not very strong. He told the court he planned to go to France to recover Lady Edward's property for her. The incriminating document was that found on Quigley, the paper addressed to the Executive Directory of France from the Secret Committee of England which invited a French invasion of England in heroic and rousing terms. The paper claimed that British, Irish and Scots societies were in collusion and announced 'we now only wait with impatience to see the hero of Italy, and the brave veterans of the great nation'.[3]

Ireland and England were separate kingdoms and the charge was specific to 'this kingdom'. The prosecution had to prove that Quigley, O'Connor and their associates were inciting rebellion in, and invasion of England. Much court time was taken up in proving that the paper could not have been slipped into Quigley's coat pocket while the prisoners were downstairs. The connection between O'Connor and Quigley then became critical. Hugh Bell was an important witness for O'Connor, stating that he had bought the Louis d'Or for him, had tried to get a cross-channel crossing for him but failed and that he did not believe O'Connor belonged to any English Society or Club. Quigley, Bell said, had visited O'Connor several times at his house but their only connection was that they planned to leave the country together. At this point,

O'Connor cut in to ask questions instead of his counsel.

Did he appear to know Quigley? No, said Bell, many Irishmen came to O'Connor, he tried to avoid making acquaintances, was very guarded in England. Bell agreed that O'Connor did not want to travel with Quigley, he elaborated that this was because Quigley was indiscreet about mentioning his intention of going out of the country. The Judge stopped the questioning. 'Mr O'Connor,' he said, 'do you not see how much this is to the detriment of the other prisoner.'

They had agreed to be tried together but their defence was not a coherent whole. O'Connor's friends had supported him in preparing his case and were in court to give evidence. It was, after all, O'Connor that the government was after: they wanted a conviction. They had gone to great trouble to get witnesses from Ireland and even obscure English ones, like Benjamin Hall. He testified that Sir Francis Burdett had introduced O'Connor to him, so that he could make the gentleman two hunting saddles with holsters for pistols, though not military ones. A hatter testified that he had made a military hat with a black cockade, covered in silk oil cloth.

The evidence which carried most weight was the testimony of the leading figures from the Opposition. They spoke on behalf of O'Connor's character and aims. Charles James Fox said O'Connor lived among them all on confidential terms and that 'I always thought Mr O'Connor to be perfectly well affected to his country; I have always considered him to be a very enlightened man, attached to the principles and the constitution of this country, upon which the present family sit upon the throne, and to which we owe all our liberties'. In this there was a reminder to Fox's hated rival, Mr Pitt, of what the constitution was. The Earl of Suffolk was effusive, talked at length about his first meeting with O'Connor on a passage boat in Ireland in 1787 and what a good impression the defendant had made. Richard Brinsley Sheridan said that he had been 'particularly anxious for his society on account of his character and the recommendation I received respecting him from Ireland'. They were on very confidential terms and he saw that O'Connor 'seemed to be occupied with what he conceived to be the oppressions and injuries inflicted upon Ireland'. Sheridan said he had advised the defendant to go abroad. The Duke of Norfolk had asked to meet O'Connor. Lord Moira said he had only a passing acquaintance. Henry Grattan was asked if he had ever heard any opinion from O'Connor which led him to suppose he could favour an invasion of his country by the French. Grattan said 'no, rather the contrary'. He believed O'Connor's private character a good one. Lord John Russell had a very high opinion of his character, they shared principles of constitutional liberty. The Earl of Thanet gave a similar testimony, as did the Earl of Oxford and Samuel Whitbread.

These were gentlemen whose word was a matter of honour. The court did not consider them capable of perjury. They were professional orators and chose their words with great care, when questioned both by the defence and by the prosecution. There is no reason to believe they lied. O'Connor was certainly devoted to the principles of the constitution and dedicated to his country. He had been immensely discreet. Not long before, O'Connor was passionate about the Volunteers who were to defend Ireland against the French. Perhaps Grattan believed that was still his position. They had seen little of each other since O'Connor left parliament. It was a mute point in all their minds as to who was violating the constitution. One thing O'Connor had never done was to attack the King.

Quigley's defence was weak. He had French and Dutch passports in his pockets, the declarations of the United Irishmen in his papers and the damning paper was his. In less highly charged times, this would not be a capital offence. In 1798 it was. The jury found him Guilty of High Treason. The judge sentenced him to be hanged, drawn and quartered.

The four other prisoners were found 'Not Guilty' and freed.

When I was acquitted, a report was spread that I was to be arrested again in the absence of the habeas corpus law and I was advised to quit the court, but the crowd was so great I could not pass and two bailiffs seized me by the collar. Lord Thanet and Ferguson who aided me in no act but standing in the passage, in the way of the bailiffs, were prosecuted for a rescue and condemned to a year's imprisonment.[4]

Burdett was in court but had not been called as a witness. After the acquittal he was calling urgently to O'Connor who had many supporters in the room. The trial had attracted considerable public attention. The relief his friends felt at the acquittal was immediately followed by fear as Bow Street officers moved to re-arrest him. The published report of the trial states:

> ... a very uncommon and indeed a very unprecedented scene took place in the Court. Two Bow Street officers attempted to seize O'Connor while yet at the bar. This was prevented by the court but some minutes afterwards they attempted it again. Mr O'Connor then got in the body of the court, on which an immense number of peace officers rushed in and the court was thrown into the utmost confusion. Two swords which were lying on the table (part of the prisoners' baggage) were drawn by some persons and several people were struck with them.

Amidst the chaos and shouting, O'Connor was re-arrested on a charge of High Treason, by warrant dated 22 March, signed by the Duke of Portland, to be heard in Ireland. If they could not convict him in one kingdom, they certainly intended to do so in the other. The legalities were highly irregular but O'Connor saw he was not going to be released. He asked to be put in the same prison as his brother.

O'Connor says that Quigley related to visitors that a priest named Griffiths was sent by Pitt to offer him his life if he would inform against O'Connor. Quigley had his conscience to consider and he had no information to give.[5] The King commuted the sentence; Quigley was not drawn and quartered, but hanged until he died.

In prison, the morning after the trial ended, Fox, Sheridan, Grey and Whitbread visited O'Connor. They had offered to pay his legal fees but Roger said he would cover them.[6] Arthur's own finances were heavily depleted by the costs of his work for the Union.

O'Connor was acquitted and re-arrested in Maidstone on 23 May. In London, Lady Lucy was waiting with horrible anxiety for news of her friend.

May 22: I sat all the evening in painful anxiety. I thought the fate of poor O'C was then at the point of being decided. May 23: – Slept little, got up very early and received a note from Burdett from Maidstone with the words, 'Quigley condemned: O'Connor acquitted.' This was at 8 o'clock. Before I had recovered the pleasure this news gave me, Mr O received a letter from the Duke of Portland with the account of Ed. being taken on the 20th. Mr O rushed out of the house and left me in uncertainty as to the particulars, which I did not hear till I dragged myself to Henry's.[7]

News of Lord Edward's arrest reached O'Connor. His beloved friend had been hiding in a house in Dublin. A police officer rushed in. During the ensuing struggle Lord Edward had stabbed the officer to death and had been arrested. He had been shot in the shoulder. The wound was said to be slight. Edward was in Newgate prison in Dublin.

In a separate operation, Henry and John Sheares had been arrested with a damning proclamation. The brothers were head of a faction in the United Irishmen which advocated assassination. O'Connor did not, could not know that John Lawless had fled Ireland, leaving the Union with none of its latest and most violent Executive.

On the night of 23 May, the mail coaches leaving Dublin were to be stopped by United rebels, as a signal for the rising to begin and to paralyse communications. This was partially carried out, the Belfast coach was burnt at Santry, the Munster one at Naas. Three others got through. In Kildare, Queen's County (Laois) and Meath groups of men with pikes gathered in the darkness. By dawn of 24 May, Kildare was up in arms and Dublin was cut off from the south. An attack on the Naas garrison followed. Within days Leinster was contested by frantic groups of militia and yeomen pitched against surging hordes of rebels armed with pikes.

O'Connor was out of touch, imprisoned, powerless. Both governments were determined to get a conviction. Portland wrote to Camden saying he was sending over the trial papers and arranging for the O'Connor brothers to be sent to Dublin.[8] Under no circumstances were they to be freed. Arthur O'Connor had acquired a reputation in England through his speech on Catholic Emancipation, said the Duke, which made it very desirable that he should not have a chance to use his abilities. The brothers would be brought by King's messengers, by Messrs Revett and Fugion of Bow Street and troops.

Instead of obtaining my liberty at the instant the Jury pronounced my acquittal as the law ordained, I was sent to Ireland under a military escort. The first night I was lodged in an Inn, a serjeant placed two dragoons at each side of my bed with pistols loaded and cocked, with orders to blow my brains out if I stirred. I sent for the officer to remonstrate at this order but I found pretty much of the opinion of the serjeant. When I was left alone with my two sentinels, they told me they were not men to murder any man for such fanatics as their officer or their serjeant, that there was not a soldier in the regiment who would not sooner see them dead than touch a hair of my head, it was the Scotch Greys. The next day, four men of the regiment offered to set me at liberty, so well was Scotland disposed towards Ireland.[9]

Perhaps O'Connor is giving a slightly exaggerated report. Probably he was too proud to run as a fugitive, almost certainly he and Roger could not escape. The two brothers had been despatched together from London on 26 May. They made their way across England and into Wales, Roger's red hair blowing, Arthur gazing with fierce intent, the red coats of the soldiers catching the light as the hooves of the horses clattered on stone in the dirt roads. At Holyhead a special packet boat had been arranged with no one else on board. Wind whipped at them, as the two rebel Irishmen were taken aboard. The ropes were cast off.

On arriving at Dublin, I was assailed with every circumstance that could tear the heart, the chosen friend of my soul in the agony of death by the hands of the assassins that attacked him, some seventy of the most active of the Union, called in by one to the Butcher's stake and the people throughout all Ireland beaten after a conflict without arms, ammunition, leaders or discipline.[10]

It was 2 June when Arthur and his brother stepped ashore in Dublin to be taken to cells in Newgate jail. In another part of the prison, Edward's wound had caused septicaemia, he was dying slowly in high fever. Thomas Russell was in Newgate, had been with Edward initially, now no one saw him. News whispered its way incoherently through the stone walls, among the separated men. On 3 June, Lord Edward's Aunt Louisa and his brother Henry were admitted. At 2 o'clock on 4 June, Edward was dead.

Leinster was now in full and open rebellion. The countryside in the south had been in suppressed guerilla warfare all year. On 5 March, Lord Longueville wrote to the Castle of the 'melancholy situation in this part of Ireland. Yesterday at four in the evening, Sir H. Mannix was shot on his return from Castleview to his own house at Richmond'.[11] Shannon and Longueville, now friendly in the hour of crisis, lamented chaos in army orders in April; Shannon admitted 'things look as bad as possible'. But when the two mail coaches were stopped on 23 May and fires lit that would ignite the south-east of Ireland, Shannon kept his nerve. On that day he had written to Harry from Dublin that 'the town is in one uproar, the streets so crowded that one walks with difficulty ... every street is alive with yeomen and one hears no tune but Croppies Lie Down.' The next day he reported 'open rebellion here and the King's troops attacked by the insurgents in several places; martial law proclaimed in the streets by sound of trumpet – we are all now under Lake ... '[12]

The rebellion began in County Kildare with rebel attacks on Clane, Prosperous and Naas in the small hours of 24 May. Michael Reynolds, a Catholic farmer and member of one of Lord Edward's young farmer's groups, led the rebels according to plan. Battle raged in the streets of Naas but the army had cannon and cavalry. The insurgents fought with crazy courage but finally fled, the cavalry chasing them down to kill them.

On the borders of Carlow and Wicklow, the pikemen heard only of early rebel success. Troops were being withdrawn to Naas.

All along the turnpike road where the mail coach to Munster should have run, its absence was noted. Men recognised the signal, heard the messages brought by breathless fellow rebels. They attacked the garrison of Carlow. The coach northwards to Belfast had also been stopped. Meath noted the signal and rose.[13]

By 26 May the rebels in Kildare were routed and those in Meath had been defeated at Tara. Terrible slaughter had occurred in Carlow where fleeing rebels ran into houses, hid in chimneys and fell out in charred heaps when troops burned the house. But on 26 May rebellion broke out in County Wexford.

Without leaders, the rising had become a series of local and rural eruptions. It also became a religious war. As the Catholic peasantry snatched their pikes, the most capable among them assumed command. In the towns under attack, Protestants fled in terror, many were taken prisoner by the rebels. In County Wexford, Father John Murphy led the men with enormous determination and courage. It was in Wexford that pitch-caps had first been invented and here, feeling ran deep. By 28 May the rebels had taken Enniscorthy and were camped at Vinegar Hill. On 30 May they took the city of Wexford.

In Dublin, Castlereagh had heard from London that Bonaparte's fleet had sailed. Dublin was frantically urging London for reinforcements. Then Ulster rose. Henry Joy McCracken's army was near Belfast. An early member of the northern United Irishmen and the only one to lead men in rebellion, McCracken was a 32-year-old Presbyterian and cotton manufacturer. He had a pledge with Tone to free Ireland. Now he acted on it. On 7 June he marched on Antrim. There was fighting at Larne and Randalstown, County Down was poised. McCracken's army was beaten, fleeing rebels hunted down, but the countryside remained in rebel control. Then Down rose. Fighting in Ulster was long and hard; General Nugent, at the head of the army in the north, fought the rebels in a pitched battle on 13 June. The Battle of Ballinahinch, on land owned by Lord Moira, was won decisively by Nugent. The rebellion in Ulster was over.

The Republic of Wexford held out for almost a month. Fighting spread into Wicklow. At Arklow, Father Murphy was killed. Father Philip Roche now took a commanding role. A local gentleman named Bagenal Harvey, Protestant and a United man, was made Commander-in-Chief of the Wexford rebels. But there were abuses which sickened Harvey. After a summary trial, Protestant prisoners were slaughtered at Vinegar Hill and 250 prisoners were burned in a barn at Scullabogue. On 16 June, five English regiments landed at Waterford, followed by 12,000 English militia.

Lord Longueville was dug in at Castle Mary.

June 6, we have fortified Cloyne. I gave timber, bullocks, horses and men. They have taken two companies from Cloyne to Cork, and the same from Middleton – Lord Boyle has fortified Castlemartyr – we are determined not to be surprised. I am satisfied my presence, and my exertions in getting arms and pikes, have prevented a rising here – indeed, the hanging of ten people has been some help to us.[14]

But County Cork, however restive, did not rise. Roger had worked hard at recruiting and the garrison at Bandon was said to have become disaffected.[15] Lord Shannon thought all the country people were in the Union because they were too terrified of the United men not to obey them. John Sheares, however, had been arrested[16] and Cork's two firebrand sons, Arthur and Roger O'Connor were in Newgate prison, Dublin.

At mid-summer, the Wexford rebels were beaten at the battle of Vinegar Hill. They attempted to surrender Wexford city but Lake refused. Prisoners were piked to death by rebels on Wexford Bridge in rage. The army marched in and took the city. Father Roche and Bagenal Harvey were captured and hanged.

Lake gave no quarter. Rebels were hunted down and massacred. Houses were burnt, men and women murdered. Plunder and destruction by soldiers became indiscriminate. Catholic chapels were destroyed. Although rebel vengeance on prisoners and loyalists had occurred throughout, there had not been one report of rape by the insurgents. Once Wexford was re-taken, rape by soldiers became a common occurrence.

Lord Camden had been asking to be replaced for some time. Abercromby had only stayed in Ireland for four months. At last, the London government had found a man who had the qualities necessary to settle Ireland. Lord Cornwallis had been Governor-General of India. On 20 June he arrived to take up two positions, as Lord Lieutenant and as Commander-in-Chief in Ireland.

Prisoners were held in barracks, forts and public buildings. The prisons were full as more men were herded in. In Dublin, they brought stories from the failed rising.

John Philpot Curran visited O'Connor in prison.[17] He confirmed the worst. Lord Edward's body had been taken for burial at St Werburgh's church. Pamela had been ordered out of the country. Rebellion had flared like a straw fire and been extinguished. 'Ireland was made a prey of every species of terror.'[18] 30,000 rebels had been killed and even many in the ruling party were shocked and sickened by the blood-letting and vengeance of the army. The words of Curran fell on Arthur O'Connor with icy finality.

Ruin descended in stone and iron. The small cell, the cold air, the bars, the sound of trapped men, beaten and wounded, closed around him. Out in those lush pastures, gobs of clotted blood, long streaks of dying scarlet scarred the place where cattle grazed, coloured the rivers. It was over. Soldiers' boots trampled the churned earth but the cries were dying away. The rebellion was over, hope was gone. Edward was dead.

O'Connor: 'In those days of stalking butchery, for Edward's precious blood not even the semblance of an inquisition has been held.'[19]

Chapter 14

ANGUISH IN KILMAINHAM

Bonaparte was not heading for Ireland. France was deeply impoverished, she needed a rich prize. Napoleon had set his sights on India and had sailed for Egypt – gateway to the East. Nelson was after him. On the north coast of France, Wolfe Tone kicked his heels and fretted, waiting for a fleet to sail for Ireland. In Paris, Lewins, the accredited agent of the United Irishmen made constant representations to the Directory. Other factions acted independently. Napper Tandy, a populist reformer with a splendid drinker's nose, older than the original United Irishmen but an early member, always disruptive, got the position of Major-General in the French Armée d'Angleterre and was ordered to Dunkirk. With his colleagues, restive Irish dissidents recently arrived in France, Tandy announced that at his appearance, Ireland would rise. The French provided him with a single corsair to try his luck. Another small force was in preparation at Rochefort under General Humbert. Tone recognised Lewins as official negotiator, left him to work in Paris and remained in the north, growing fatalistic.

Britain was stretched to the limit financially. The King carried on as if the kingdom was his private estate. In May Lord Camden had written to Mr Pitt: 'I received yesterday your communication of the Queen's wishes that a pension of £2,000 per an should be granted to the Prince of Mecklenburgh.' Camden was confident that the Irish parliament would vote this sum to the Queen's relative from the public finances.[1]

Two weeks later, the rebellion broke out and costs in Ireland suddenly soared. The British government had to make a loan to Ireland. A voluntary loan scheme began in England through which great proprietors helped to finance the war. Pitt asked the King to contribute. Once the Irish rebellion was crushed, claims for compensation poured into the Castle. Property had been ruined, business destroyed. O'Connor had foretold financial ruin. He had the misery of being proved right.

On matters of policy, King George was clear in his mind. Early in June, while rebellion raged, he wrote to Mr Pitt that 'George R was sorry to send more troops to Ireland', but 'as the Sword is drawn it will not be returned into the sheath until the whole country has submitted without condition, the making any compromise would be perfect destruction'.[2] Ten days later he informed Pitt, 'no further indulgence must be granted to the Roman Catholics, as no Country can be governed where there is more than one Established Religion'.[3]

In Dublin, Lord Cornwallis wasted no time. He was the head of both government and army. The latter was more important in times of martial law. The rebellion had not been completely crushed in Kildare. Pockets of rebels remained at large in the country. Lake was busy hunting them down.

Cornwallis had been sent to settle the country, not extirpate the people. Finding Cooke efficient and Castlereagh very able, he left them to deal with the Castle administration and the parliament. He ignored the Cabinet. The Chancellor, John Fitzgibbon, Earl of Clare had no liking for Catholic emancipation but he was dedicated to Ireland's place in the British Empire and saw that Lake's methods were creating Jacobins, not eliminating them. Cornwallis took note of Clare.

When the realisation of failure broke over him, a grim bitterness seeped through Arthur O'Connor. The death of Edward FitzGerald, the blood-letting during the rebellion, the stupidity of his capture and the annihilation of all his hopes for Ireland seem to have frozen him into a shocked silence. 'The defeat of the rebels was followed by military executions. In a short space of time about two hundred persons were put to death by martial law.'[4]

Rebels in arms were dealt with quickly and ruthlessly. Those taken prisoner were court martialled and many executed. The political prisoners could only be tried under due process of law. Most of the evidence against them came from informers who would not testify. The process of imprisoning, sorting, trying and sentencing all those involved in rebellion became a massive task. Throughout the country, prisons were full, army officers gave and received reports, magistrates heard evidence. The government started looking for prison ships to house the flood of prisoners.

Most hospital admissions in Cork were recorded as due to terror of the rebellion.

Cornwallis determined to turn the tide of slaughter and mass imprisonment. With Clare's support, on 17 July he pushed an act of amnesty through parliament. The Generals were to protect those who surrendered and who took the oath of allegiance.

Now the government turned its attention to the United Irish leaders. Neilson had been arrested and was in Newgate with Russell. O'Connor had been moved to the Marshalsea. His brother Roger was in Bridewell. Bond, Jackson, Byrne, T.A. Emmet, Reynolds and McNevin were in Kilmainham. In June, the government had picked up Robert Simms, William Tennent and Henry Joy McCracken among many others. They were in Belfast gaol. John and Henry Sheares were in Newgate. When they were arrested, a proclamation in John's handwriting was found in Henry's house. It began:

> Irishmen
>
> Your country is free. That vile government which has so long and so cruelly oppressed you is no more. Some of its most atrocious Monsters have already paid the forfeit of their lives and the rest are in our hands.[5]

Both brothers were tried and sentenced to death. Henry panicked and wrote desperate letters to his friend, Sir Jonah Barrington:

> The dreadful die is cast, O Fly I beseech you to the Chancellor and save a man whose fate will kill his family. I have been duped, misled, deceived but with all the good wishes and intentions to do good. Oh my family, my wife, my children, my mother – go to them, let them throw themselves at the

Chancellor's feet. We are to receive sentence at 3 o'clock. Fly I beseech you and save a man who will never cease to pray for you.[6]

It was then 8am on 14 July. Despite the desperate pleas, the two brothers were executed that afternoon. They did not die well. O'Connor was impatient with the independent way the Sheares had acted. He was vexed by the reckless tone of the proclamation.[7] But their cringing deaths were reported throughout the prisons. The Sheares were Cork men, John's passion for bloody revolution and Henry's fear in face of execution, sent further gloom through the prisoners. This was only the beginning of the trials.

Viscount Castlereagh was at the head of the administration in Dublin Castle. He had begun his political career as a liberal reformer but, shocked by the violence of the French Revolution, had become cautious. He married in 1794 and Camden was his brother-in-law. Unlike his Presbyterian ancestors, Castlereagh joined the Established Church. Academically gifted, cool and with-drawn, he had worked long, long hours in the Castle throughout the nerve-wracking months of the rebellion, writing clear and per-tinent letters in his flowery, contorted handwriting.

Reynolds agreed to give evidence. Cornwallis insisted on due process of law. Castlereagh and Cooke obeyed. McCann, Bond and Byrne could probably be convicted on Reynolds' testimony. The trials were held, the three found guilty. McCann was hanged on 19 July. Byrne was to die on 25 July and Bond 26 July. News travelled through Newgate, messages could be sent to other prisons. On 24 July, 64 leading United Irishmen sent a proposal to Lord Castlereagh. Their intermediary was Mr Dobbs, barrister and MP, who called at the Castle with Mr Archer, the Sheriff of Dublin. The State Prisoners offered to make a full disclosure and to accept ban-ishment for life, if their lives were spared, as well as those of Byrne and Bond.[8]

Arthur O'Connor had not signed this paper or lent his weight to it. With sullen rage, he existed in his cell, his strong body caged with all its grief and fury.

The paper was good news for the government. The officials had very little evidence against the remaining State Prisoners. A public confession would be very useful, politically and in print.[9] But the terms were inadequate, released prisoners might conspire with France. Most importantly, the O'Connor brothers and William Sampson had not signed. The Speaker of the House was violently against leniency for any reason. Many loyal citizens would be appalled. It was rejected.

On 25 July, Byrne was executed. The prisoners sent messages of urgent intensity to Arthur O'Connor in the Marshalsea. He must sign, Oliver Bond would be executed next day. Executions were still going on across the country. To his grief and rage was now added moral and intellectual torment. Too many had died by hand of government, did they ask him to negotiate with 'a set of men whose approach taints and whose slightest touch corrupts ... whose hands were reeking with the blood of my beloved countrymen?'[10] He had no interest in his own salvation; 'saving of a life embittered by the most agonising circumstances could have had no share in the part'[11] he now acted. Life had become sour and cruel.

Many lives beside his own were in the balance. The prisoners did not know what evidence there was against them. Curran, their great advocate, had been unable to save the Sheares, Byrne, Bond. 'The men with whom I had acted and whose fidelity to me neither the most profuse offers of government, torture nor death could shake, were led to the mockery of trial before the various tribunals where, like Robespierre's, to be arraigned was to be condemned.'[12] Those who had risked everything to be faithful to the Union had been taken to trial, their comrades saying farewell as if they went to execution. And Bond, 'a man whom I myself had embarked in the business for which his life was to be taken',[13] was to die tomorrow.

But if O'Connor gave a full disclosure, the testimony his Whig friends had given at Maidstone would be open to ridicule. He might do them irreparable political damage, he might undermine their honour and they might look on him in a new light, as a man who had invited foreign invasion. He relied on their view that oppression justified resistance and that 1688 set the principle.

There was no time for prolonged soul-searching. Henry Alexander, a relation of Bond came to the Marshalsea to talk to

O'Connor.[14] Emmet and McNeven were adamant. Later that day, Alexander and Dobbs rushed to the Castle. Castlereagh learnt that O'Connor, and Sampson, were now 'desirous of soliciting the mercy of the crown'. They would give a full disclosure but no names, they would agree to be held until the war ended, they were not to be transported as felons. Those were their terms.[15]

O'Connor requested an interview with Castlereagh. He would bring two colleagues, Emmet and McNeven.[16]

Cornwallis thought the offer advantageous. He wanted confessions, especially from O'Connor and McNeven, 'as the only effectual means of opening the eyes of both countries without disclosing intelligence which could by no means be made public'.[17] He consulted his chief law officers, 'the attractions of the terms of the proposal, but more particularly the offer of O'Connor to disclose his Treason appeared to them to make it highly expedient to entertain the proposition so submitted'.[18] Cornwallis told Castlereagh to accept. The deal was provisional, Bond was respited for five days. Dobbs galloped back to Kilmainham. The news reached Bond twenty minutes before he was to die.[19] He had faced death with calm courage. Suddenly he heard he had five more days of life.

O'Connor, Emmet and McNeven were taken to the Castle for an interview with Lords Clare and Castlereagh.[20] The prisoners emphasised they would give no names, would not incriminate individuals, would agree to remain in custody during the war, not to reside on the continent 'during the contest' or, if sent to the USA, to give security for conforming to terms. They would make no deal that allowed government to send them to Botany Bay or a penal colony.[21]

Reports filtered back from the antipodes that chilled even the bravest. An ex-convict believed 'the usage I have seen men receive in Norfolk Island exceeds in cruelty anything that can be credited. There was, in particular, one poor young man, Michael Cox, from the County of Cork; he was compelled to walk about and work with a chain, weighing twelve pounds on his leg, and while labouring under a dysentery was driven up to his middle in the sea, and obliged to bring heavy packages ashore.' Michael Cox died. The Governor and his men were the law; the penal colonies inspired terror.[22]

O'Connor, Emmet and McNeven were acting on behalf of 79 men. They faced the Chancellor and Castlereagh confident of their own moral position. Clare was firm and dominating, Castlereagh stiff and alert. O'Connor met them with sharp disdain, Emmet as always the lawyer, Dr McNeven was willing to be helpful. Clare told them to prepare a written narrative. He was setting up a Secret Committee of the two Houses of Parliament. The prisoners could be examined by the committees when they had filed their report.[23]

Arthur O'Connor was moved to Kilmainham on 27 July so that the three men could work together.[24] Arthur sent notes to Roger at Bridewell, who had refused to join the negotiations.[25] Roger did not believe there was evidence against him and would not accept banishment.[26] Arthur kept him informed. First, a paper was drafted setting out the terms they had agreed with the government. It was signed by 79 prisoners and delivered to the Castle.[27] Bond was respited for another week.

Kilmainham gaol is built of stone. High windows let in air through bars. Long corridors run beside the rows of cells, chill and shadowy. The gentlemen State Prisoners were given the better rooms, pen and ink. Five days later, a memorial signed by O'Connor, Emmet and McNeven was handed in to the Castle. It bore the unmistakable style of pamphlet writers. Cornwallis read it with a snort. This was not a confession; it was a justification.[28]

The authors had agreed a text among themselves without delay. It owes a great deal to O'Connor's writing style. Emmet was a first class lawyer; the memoir was clear and chronological.[29] It confirmed all the reports of spies and informers. It confirmed the prisoners' treason. Cornwallis received it on 5 August and admitted it was 'ably written'[30] but rejected it. He had not asked for a controversial pamphlet in the modern style. They were to re-write it.

The Memoire begins:

The disunion which had long existed between the Catholics and Protestants of Ireland, particularly those of the Presbyterian religion, was found by experience to be so great an obstacle to the obtaining a Reform in Parliament, on any thing of just and popular principles, that some persons, equally friendly to that measure and to religious toleration, conceived the idea of uniting both sects in pursuit of the same object – a Repeal of the Penal laws, and a reform, including in itself an extension of the Right of Suffrage to the Catholic.

It set out all the obstacles to reform and frankly stated that United Irish societies then turned to revolution. They catalogued the process, explained how the Test was framed to include both reformers and republicans, how the war with France had changed the situation totally. The recall of Fitzwilliam, they said, had in a sense played into their hands by mobilising the Catholics. The Orange lodges had increased United Irish numbers for sad reasons. 'We were none of us members of the United system until September or October 1796.' They believed 500,000 were in the Union. After the Insurrection Bill, the societies began sending in returns which stated their arms and ammunition. The memoir described the United military organisation although they had no general plan of insurrection before 12 March 1798. They stressed their rights under the 1688 constitution. They said their agent had negotiated with France in 1796 and they catalogued all their subsequent relations with that country.

When Cornwallis sent it back,[31] O'Connor had little inclination to re-write it. The three negotiators suggested they be examined if anything was unclear.[32] O'Connor had heard that some of the prisoners were unhappy with the idea of his negotiating for them. He would do nothing until he had consulted with all of them. 'You all know how unwillingly I accepted the having anything to do with this negotiation.' But the others insisted; 'Emmet and McNeven are at my elbow,' he told Roger.[33]

Unknown to Dublin, the French were once more on the high seas. Humbert sailed on 6 August with three frigates and 1,099 men. McNeven was called in to the Lords Committee the next day.[34] He said the Union had extended into Connaught; if the French landed, the people would rise. The Chancellor was more interested in McNeven's memoir to Reinhard, of which he had an extract of a copy. McNeven, who had no copy himself, wondered if he could borrow the Chancellor's.[35]

Before the Commons Committee, McNeven admitted that the people didn't care a jot for Catholic emancipation. They knew all it would do was allow some Catholic Peers into the House of Lords and allow some others to speculate on seats in the Commons.

Thomas Addis Emmet was examined next. He agreed that while he was philosophising, Lord Edward had been arming. He believed there were 300,000 fighting men in the Union. He looked to the destruction of the Establishment of the Church. 'As the human mind grows philosophic, it will I think, wish for the destruction of all religious establishments'[36] and he assumed this would happen to Catholicism. Emmet made a pleasant, equable witness.

O'Connor did not. He was questioned by the Lords first, to whom he stressed there was no connection with societies in England and Scotland. With the Commons he was combative and peremptory. He clearly displayed his contempt of the corruptibility of parliament, its subordination to London. He said the lower orders all knew that members traded seats and sinecures. 'The people,' he said 'are conscious you are self constituted.' One of the Committee responded, 'that we are a parcel of placemen and pensioners?' 'Exactly so,' O'Connor replied. The Committee wanted to know how the people could be settled. 'If you would tranquillise a people, you must cease to oppress them,' he challenged. No, he said, they had not set up a constitution, they would do that when they had an elected government.[37] He would not be drawn on the nature of a republic; he knew better than to talk of deposing Kings.

Castlereagh questioned O'Connor himself. He wanted details of the journey to Switzerland. The two men faced each other.[38] One had power given by government, the other a sense of righteousness drawn from the people. They were the same age, could each have taken the other's path. There was recognition, deep rivalry. O'Connor gave minimal responses, told nothing.

Castlereagh reported to Portland. They had more detail of course from 'Richardson'. At least the examination proved that Hoche's invasion had been solicited. Portland was keen to prove that O'Connor's English friends knew the real object of his journey.[39] How satisfying it would have been for Pitt to prove that Fox had been privy to treason. This they never achieved.

A week later, Humbert's ships anchored in a remote bay in County Mayo. Soon French troops were landing and riding into Killala. Four days later Napper Tandy was afloat, sailing from Dunkirk with 370 men and plenty of arms and proclamations.

In Dublin, there had been a muddle. The paper signed by the 79, agreeing terms, had been sent from the Castle to Belfast, for the information of those conducting trials there. No proper instructions had been enclosed. The paper had mistakenly been published.[40] This was reported to the prisoners in Kilmainham who were enraged. Government were already working to destroy their characters by making out they had betrayed colleagues.

The terms of their imprisonment had been relaxed.[41] It was easy for O'Connor, Emmet and McNeven to get together, compose a riposte, have it taken to the offices of two Dublin newspapers and printed. 'We assure the public,' they said, the report of the Committees is a 'gross and astonishing misrepresentation.'[42] The Castle seethed, the whole point of the confessions was to confirm to the public just how guilty the rebels were. The report was not even out before the prisoners were contradicting it. Buckingham said O'Connor should be hanged, Pitt wrote of 'the very indecent and offensive advertisement of O'Connor and the other traitors'.[43] This would only encourage their friends – and the French were once more ashore.

Troops were converging on Castlebar in Mayo to fight the French and their Irish recruits. Cornwallis was travelling by the Grand Canal to lead the loyal forces. The first engagement, 'The Races of Castlebar' was a victory for the French and occurred on the same day as the advertisement was printed.

O'Connor, Emmet and McNeven were put in strict confinement.[44] They were not to have access to each other. They were to be re-examined. They were shown the drafts of their evidence, ready for the printers. O'Connor agreed they were accurate but stressed there was no connection with English radicals, that the Irish agent had talked the French out of invading Britain.[45] If only he could get that in to the report it would help his position with Fox immeasurably.

The prisoners explained they only wanted to correct the

newspapers, not change their evidence. They signed the drafts. On 11 September, Castlereagh reported to Pitt, 'your wish is accomplished – O'Connor, McNeven and Emmet having this day signed a full acknowledgement of the truth and correctness of the report'.[46] It was sent to the printers for publication.

In London, Burdett's sister-in-law, Fanny Coutts, wrote to her dear friend, Lady Lucy.

> General Knox who is just come over from Ireland and who is a friend of Papa's is a very singularly clever man. I know he said that every one He met here talked of Ireland as a thing quite at an End that it was all quiet and in short that there was an End to the Rebellion ... He said there never was so great a mistake, that it was a little crushed but in the situation to rise at a moment, that the spirit in them was unexampled and unknown their like – this account of it is strange.

She also had news of Lady Lucy's friend.

> Mr Pitt assured a Gentleman last night who told it Papa that both the O'Connors had confessed Everything and claimed Lord Cornwallis Amnesty tis a sort of a thing not to be doubted for Mr Pitt read the letters He had that moment received with the intelligence of it.[47]

The harvest was exceptionally good that year. Despite the continuing arrests, trials, sentences and transportations in provincial towns, out in the fields the people had returned to the rhythm of the seasons. Despite new alarms in Mayo, Lord Shannon's mind returned to his estate. 'I also think,' he told Harry, 'the wheat may be sold for what you mention if no more is offered.' And he remembered something else; 'will you do anything about the rabbits, formerly there were people who were glad to be allowed to catch them.'[48]

On 16 September, government troops beat General Humbert's tiny army at Ballina. The French were taken prisoner and removed to Dublin. On 18 September, Napper Tandy came ashore at

Rutland in Donegal, heard of Humbert's defeat, got back aboard and sailed for France. On 1 October came news of Nelson's victory over the French fleet at Aboukir.

Wolfe Tone had finally sailed from Brest on 6 September. On 12 October an English squadron engaged the French ships in battle. Tone was captured. It was early November when he was brought ashore from Lough Swilly, recognised and jailed in Derry. He was tried by court martial in Dublin. He made no secret of his aims. Realising he would be hanged, not given the dignity of a military execution by shooting, he cut his throat with a penknife. He severed his windpipe, not his artery. Tone died of his wound a week later, on 19 November.

From the time of Lord Edward's death, Lucy FitzGerald's diary ceased. Elizabeth, Lady Holland, her cousin, later recorded:

Lady Lucy is very clever, naturally very lively, but the loss of her late brother has affected her spirits; she is enthusiastic and her affection for him was worked up to a most romantic pitch. She was in his confidence and knew how deeply he was involved in that fatal business in Ireland; any reference to the affair agitates her violently.[49]

Lady Holland recorded how, after Lord Edward's death, when O'Connor was imprisoned, Lady Lucy was at Goodwood.

[O'Connor] being but too intimately connected with Ld E., made her of course anxious about his fate: in short she was ill. Ye Duke of Richmond worked up his imagination, and fancied her grief arose from fear for O'Connor's safety, she being in love with him. He went to her in the most affectionate manner, and proposed if she would confide in him, to obtain O'Connor's release, and assist their marriage. She assured him she only felt the regard due to him as a friend of her own and her brother's.[50]

Lucy wrote to O'Connor, hoping his friends might soon be easy on his account. 'Believe me Arthur I regret your captivity as much and more than I did the first day of it when yet such misfortunes were new to us'[51] and 'It's a sort of melancholy comfort to reflect that nothing so bad can happen again. I cannot again lose Edward.' She tried to cheer him. 'You always were enough of a philosopher be as merry a one as you can be.'[52]

The Report of the Secret Committee was duly published in Dublin and confirmed everything that loyal citizens had suspected. They read out to each other the shocking catalogue of conspiracy, murder, seizure of arms, leading to armed insurrection.

Acts of parliament were drawn up to put the agreement with the State Prisoners into effect. The Banishment Act named 90 men, described them as 'conscious of enormous guilt ... have implored his Majesty's pardon.'[53] Neilson did complain at this text, but was told to keep quiet or the deal was off, they would all be tried.[54] Arthur O'Connor was included in the Act, made no further protest. Roger O'Connor was not named.

Once the reports were complete, a small relaxation of the prisoners' conditions was allowed. This was sufficient for the manuscript of their own report to leave Kilmainham. *Memoire* by O'Connor, Emmet and McNeven was held by their friends but not published until 1802, when they were free. It is a remarkable and candid document. Between the *Report of the Committee of Secrecy* and *Memoire,* all the facts and both sides of the story came out in print.

Everyone blamed someone else. Cornwallis wrote to Portland,

> ... the principal personages here ... are entirely attached and devoted to the British connexion, but they are blinded by their passions and prejudices, talk of nothing but strong measures, and arrogate to themselves the exclusive knowledge of a country, of which from their mode of governing it, they have, in my opinion, proved themselves entirely ignorant.[55]

Pitt was inclined to agree. The Union of Irishmen had been crushed, the British Minister had a different amalgamation in mind. Since the summer he had been discussing the possibility of a legislative Union. The independence achieved by Grattan was a failure,

Pitt believed, for Ireland's parliament was 'radically defective'.

While the Union of the British and Irish parliaments was discussed, O'Connor was locked in his cell in Kilmainham. His father had died not long before. Old Roger had been living with Robert who heartily hated his younger brothers. Robert had been busy with the lawyers. His mother's dowry had come to old Roger after her death and Robert was claiming it.[56] Their father's death left further bequests of land to all five brothers. Arthur did not see his father buried, did not hear the spite of Robert. His affairs were in a terrible state and he applied to Castlereagh to go to England in custody to settle them.[57] He was refused. In November, a rumour reached him and a shaft of bitterness made him write to his uncle. 'It has come to my knowledge from the most unquestionable authority that Mr Edward Cooke the Secretary sent for a Gentleman known to be devoted to your interest and laid your injunction on him to appear as an evidence against me on the late tryal at Maidstone.' Surely, his nephew wrote, Lord Longueville could at least refrain from sending people to testify against him. 'While every other tie has been torn asunder, I still share so large a commonage of blood.'[58] His friends had been wholly loyal to him; not so his blood relations.

Longueville was incensed, sent the letter to Cooke. Regarding O'Connor, he said, 'of all the bad men I was ever acquainted with, he is the worst'.[59] Longueville was grateful to Cooke for not asking him for evidence, although the 'commonage of blood' would not alter his loyalties. He was a staunch friend of the government.

For O'Connor, the most urgent and painful necessity was to make an approach to Fox. He had not admitted negotiating with the French personally, only to being informed of the pact when he officially joined the Union in November 1796. But Fox had seen him and Lord Edward in London, just before their departure for Hamburg that summer. O'Connor had admitted complicity with the enemy and the fact was in print. Fox had testified for his good character only months before the Kilmainham Treaty. Fox would be hounded by the press and public in England. O'Connor was wracked.

The cartoons in the London periodicals made great sport of this treachery.[60] After O'Connor's testimony, Lady Holland, wife of Fox's cousin, noted 'Opposition knocked up by the confession ... in fact too much power thrown into the hands of Government owing to the vile and foolish conduct of Opposition'.[61]

On 11 October, O'Connor wrote to Fox from prison. 'My most dear and most valued friend ... nothing but a conscious integrity of heart ... could enable me to address you with the same confidence and warmth as if I had never been accused of exposing the best and kindest friends to the vilest calumnies to save my own life.'[62] He explained his reasons for treating with government: the continuing and horrifying slaughter, the summary trials and executions, in particular the sentences on Byrne and Bond, and the potential death sentence on the Provincial Committee, men delegated from that organisation 'I myself had created'. He knew what would be said in London, how it would rebound on Fox. He was in terrible agony of mind then, wanted to end it but knew this would not save others. The right to publish his testimony was verbally agreed with government. The terms of the 1688 revolution and the right to resist tyranny were principles he and Fox shared. 'Although I am not conscious of ever shrinking from my duty, I am almost ashamed of life, when so many of my brave and virtuous countrymen have fallen'[63] and 'May God preserve you and those friends so deservedly dear to me, tears start at the remembrances which arise in the gloom of my prison'.[64]

A friend took the letter but only got as far as Manchester. It was brought back, undelivered. At the end of the year, O'Connor sent it again with a second letter. He was more reflective now, calmer. Despite all his regrets 'perhaps there is but one way of passing from one state to another and that, that is a violent one'.[65]

The Society of King's Inns ordered that O'Connor, Emmet and five other United Irish lawyers should be struck off from the Society, as seditious and traitorous. Orders should be posted in the dining hall and in the Courts.

It was winter. Rain fell on the stone walls of Newgate. His fortune was in ruins, his family alienated, FitzGerald and Tone were dead. In his cold cell, O'Connor began writing a long letter to Lord

Castlereagh. It relieved his bitterness, allowed him to summarise what had happened in his own words, in his own mind. To write it to his immediate protagonist made it real, personal. In January, he was searched, the document taken to the Castle, O'Connor separated from the other prisoners. He was kept without exercise in solitary confinement. Nevertheless, his friends were able to print his *Letter to Lord Castlereagh.*

Chapter 15 —————

COLD REFLECTION

It was difficult for the authorities to control communication between the prisoners. Visitors took messages between them but the visitors were also sometimes informers. Secret information to the Castle early in January 1799 said that O'Connor was very anxious to know what the northern leaders had done during the rebellion. Why had the Simms not acted? The same informant visited the prisoners in Belfast and got an answer for O'Connor: the Simms had expected two mail coaches to be stopped, only one had not arrived. The post-mortem went on. The informer told the Castle that McCabe had letters from O'Connor and had gone to London. He had also heard Robert Emmet talking. The younger brother of Thomas Addis Emmet, Robert said a new United Irish Committee and Executive were being formed in Dublin.[1]

O'Connor's wrath was directed at Castlereagh. The United States of America would not take the State Prisoners. Their confinement seemed set to continue.[2] O'Connor saw Castlereagh as the author of infamous breaches of faith. He believed that the State Prisoners had conformed to the terms agreed and should be released. He wanted the *Memoire* written by himself, Emmet and McNeven to be published. Why had government suppressed it? O'Connor also objected in the strongest terms to the wording of the Banishment Act.[3]

Memoire had been smuggled out of prison but not published. The government had published its own report. The paper signed by 73 State Prisoners had, in fact, given no time for their release.[4] Internal government memoirs certainly showed that the authorities believed they had reserved the right to hold the State Prisoners throughout the war if they could not be sent to the USA.[5] The State Prisoners, for their part, believed they had agreed to go to a neutral country and guarantee no complicity with France.[6] Not for the last time, there was disagreement about what had been agreed.

Rufus King, American Ambassador to London, told Castlereagh that he wanted to prevent the Irish State Prisoners being sent to the USA. The American President had the power to deny them, if he had a list of their names 'and their delinquency'.[7] The United States was an independent nation but Mr King explained that 'a portion of our inhabitants have erroneously supposed that our civil and political institutions ... might be improved by a close imitation of France'. French agents pursued this, causing serious divisions in the young American Republic and Mr King was sorry to mention that some recent immigrants from Ireland had acted as malcontents. It would not be helpful to import 'artful leaders'.[8]

There were 90 men named in the Banishment Act. The government considered that fifteen of these posed a real threat and could not be liberated in Europe. The remainder were pardoned, freed and allowed to go to a neutral country.[9]

As early as July 1798 Lord Cornwallis had suggested sending the State Prisoners to Fort George in Scotland. Would it alarm the local people?[10] While government sorted out the evidence, decided which political prisoners it considered the greatest threat and released others, thousands of rebels throughout Ireland were sentenced, often harshly. Large numbers were sent to the penal colonies in Australia where they nurtured their grievances against Britain.[11]

Once the Kilmainham Treaty with the prisoners was agreed, O'Connor was moved to Newgate. He was kept apart from the others as much as possible because he stirred up the more equable men. O'Connor was not intimidated by the government. He was furious at any and every breach of terms. He collected his papers and wrote his long, recriminatory letter to Lord Castlereagh, intended for publication. It catalogued the Chief Secretary's 'dishonourable conduct', for O'Connor had suffered 'insults, injuries and calumnies'. He had never wanted to negotiate and he still challenged the state to bring him to trial. When 'I consented to meet you', he says, 'I expressly stipulated, that some men upon whose honor I could rely, should accompany me. Emmet and McNeven were accordingly joined with me, upon the part of the State Prisoners'. O'Connor details the negotiations and complains at the constant change in terms. He says that Castlereagh has prevented him from seeing Cornwallis, suppressed his writings, defamed and deceived him, 'vilely attempted to furnish grounds for calumny against the Opposition of England'.

'While I live, though it will be within the precincts of the scaffold, I will vindicate my honor,' writes O'Connor, 'I will raise my voice from the depths of my dungeon.'

'Young Lord! I sought you not: you have grappled with my honor upon these troubled waters.' For Castlereagh, O'Connor has only 'pity and contempt'.

The whole document was found in O'Connor's cell and taken to Castlereagh while O'Connor was put in solitary confinement in Newgate.[12] The government were determined to silence O'Connor's literary productions.

Some of the Belfast prisoners had been offered the terms of the Kilmainham Treaty and many had accepted.[13] But Robert Simms, William Tennent and Robert Hunter were not included in the Banishment Act[14] and were held on charges of Treasonable Practices. William Tennent was the son of a Presbyterian minister whose family displayed the industry and growing prosperity of that sect.[15] His letters from prison to his family requested clothes, port, whiskey, vinegar, a razor and strop, the works of Swift. He needed a cravat, white cotton stockings, pantaloons and a tablecloth.[16] O'Connor had no close family to call on for such things. Both his parents were dead. Of his brothers: Daniel was in England, William in the army, Robert trying to get him hanged and Roger was also in prison. Only Roger's wife, Wilhamena, might have helped him but she had problems of her own with a rambling mansion in west Cork, dwindling funds and six children.

Roger was still pressing for release. He sent memorials to the Castle showing there were no grounds for imprisoning him, except that they had 'confounded his case with that of other prisoners'.[17] The 160 soldiers that had moved into Connerville did immeasurable

damage, and he was looking for compensation. He was, he emphasised, second to no man in birth. He would not leave Bridewell
prison until he was set at liberty. But Wilhamena was not allowed
to see him.[18]

Government was far gentler to the Emmets. They told Thomas
Addis he could not leave prison to visit his sick wife as it would
cause too much noise, but she could visit him. Kind letters passed
between Emmet and Mr Marsden at the Castle.[19]

That some prisoners had been released while the principal pro-
tagonists were still held, was a source of grievance and speculation.
O'Connor thought that they would be kept on in Ireland[20] but
before the end of January they were told to prepare to board ships.
They heard they were going to the river Thames but February
passed and nothing happened. Government had to arrange quarters
and get warrants to hold them in another country.[21]

On 18 March, Castlereagh sent a warrant to Major Sirr, head
of the Dublin police, to collect Neilson, Russell, Dowling, Dowdall
and Arthur O'Connor from Newgate and deliver them to an officer
at the Pigeon House.[22] This was at the mouth of the Liffey; from
here tenders went out to ships anchored in Dublin Bay. They were
being taken out of the country. In Kilmainham, Emmet had
received warning to leave and sent urgent messages to the Castle.
'I've been told to embark at 6am tomorrow for an unknown destination.' This was supposed to be by agreement, Emmet had a wife
and children. But departure remained set for the early hours of the
following day.[23]

In the grey spring dawn, sixteen prisoners were brought out of
three Dublin prisons and taken down to the quay. Light was growing in the east, illuminating the buildings of the old city and the elegant Georgian squares where servants were making up the fires, as
the leaders of the rebellion were escorted down to the waterfront, to
be taken out of Ireland. Horses' hooves clattered on the cobbles,
soldiers took charge of the prisoners, seamen messed with ropes.
The smell of salt blew at them. They stepped into the boat and were
rowed out onto the waters of Dublin Bay. The city fell away behind
them across the water as the sun rose. They came up alongside the
Aston Smith.[24]

Arthur was reunited with his brother Roger who despite his lively protests, was also being removed. So were Emmet, McNeven, McCormick, Sweetman and Chambers, Wilson, Sweeney, Hudson, Cummins and Cuthbert. There were sixteen of them, with their clothes, books and the provisions they had managed to buy in the rushed departure. There were clean berths prepared for them. The ship weighed anchor and sailed north.[25]

Arthur was only relieved to be with his brother again. Little human warmth had alleviated the last months. As they swayed to the motion of the ship, the prisoners exchanged news. They came into the mouth of Belfast Lough. Onto the ship came Tennent, Simms, Hunter and Dickson. It was something of a reunion. On the journey, Arthur gave his comrades copies of a poem he had written. It seemed a loyal production but was cleverly designed. If the lines of the second verse were read after the corresponding lines of the first, it gave a very different meaning:

> *The pomp of courts, and pride of Kings*
> *I prize above all earthly things;*
> *I love my country, but the King*
> *Above all men his praise I sing;*
> *The royal banners are display'd,*
> *And may success the standard aid.*
>
> *I fain would banish far from hence*
> *The 'Rights of Man' and common sense;*
> *Confusion to his odious reign,*
> *That foe to princes, Thomas Paine!*
> *Defeat and ruin seize the cause*
> *Of France, its liberties, and laws!*[26]

At 4am on 26 March, they set sail from Belfast in a hard gale and left the coast of Ireland behind them.[27] In nine hours they were in the Firth of Clyde in Scotland. Two days of difficult sailing brought them near Greenock. From the ship, they could see a train of carriages waiting for them on the beach, with a group of soldiers on horse and foot. They were Angus-shire Fencibles under Captain Ewing.

Neilson was in a fever but the other prisoners came ashore in good order and were handed into four carriages. With infantry to front and rear, with 44 horsemen alongside they proceeded to the Assembly Rooms in Greenock while crowds followed along the road and watched from the adjacent fields. In Greenock, their money was confiscated but there was a good fire and fine dinner with a pint of port per man. The prisoners cheered up. They soon concluded they were treated far better in Britain than they were in Ireland. In Scotland, the Irish rebellion had been reported as a 'Popish' one; when the Scots heard that only four of the twenty prisoners were Catholic there was surprise. Throughout their journey, people turned out to see the Irish rebels.[28]

It was a long journey. From Greenock through Glasgow, across the central lowlands and along the east coast, they made their way to Aberdeen. Their meals were good, at night they had feather beds, sheets, bolsters, blankets and pillows. The soldiers bought warm clothes for them with the confiscated money. The bleak hillsides, sparse grazing, biting wind and bleached sky were harsher than the mild climate and lush pastures of Ireland. In Aberdeen, magistrates, military men and gentry came in to meet them. It was a rare opportunity to meet Irishmen and a novelty; here were leading Irish rebels quartered in the town. Since Bonnie Prince Charlie's failed rebellion in 1746, no such troop of horse, nor any political prisoners had been seen in the Highlands.[29]

Arthur O'Connor cast his eagle eye over the landscape and the towns. They were travelling north, to a promontory near Inverness where Fort George had been built after the last Stuart rising. O'Connor had no time for the Stuarts but Scotland was dear to him as the home of Hume, Adam Smith and the Presbyterians, a country where first-class education was the standard. On arrival at Fort George it was Lt Col James Stewart who welcomed them.[30]

Fort George and Fort Augustus had been built at either end of the Great Glen to hold the Highlands after the first Jacobite rebellion. Following the second rising in 1745-6, a new fort was begun outside Inverness. The new Fort George was completed in 1769 and used as a barracks by a succession of Highland regiments. On a low promontory in the Moray Firth, it was surrounded by sea on three sides, the fourth side was defended by rampart and out-works.[31] The prisoners entered through a tunnel and came into the open space of the fort. The buildings, of red brick and slate were in wide rows. The clear air and spacious lay-out gave their new prison a healthy aspect;[32] but it was cold.

They were given one room each, allotted by ballot. The rooms were 16'x18' with plastered walls, ceilings and wooden floors. There were large windows with external bars and a fireplace. Each room had a four-poster bed with mattress, sheets, blankets, pillows and coverlet. There was a table and chair, bowl and basin, commode, fuel and candles. Four servants brought their food, served at table, supplied fuel and changed the sheets. The food was good, plenty of fresh herring and salmon. They were supplied with beer and wine. Mrs McGregor at the Inn in Ardesier supplemented their fare at the prisoners' expense.[33]

It was a great relief to walk on the open ramparts and enjoy the long view across water to the distant mountains. Books were sent from Inverness and the daily London newspapers. They could write letters, walk out ten at a time and as the summer came, they bathed in the sea, played ball games and rackets, hurling and football. Some days they were racing and leaping for six or seven hours a day.[34]

When the Irish State Prisoners arrived in April, the Fife Militia had just been stationed in the barracks. The following year the Ayrshire Militia moved in and in 1801 the Perth Militia took over.[35] Lt Col The Hon James Stewart remained Deputy Governor and the man in charge throughout their confinement. Several prisoners remarked on his kindness to them.[36] When stricter regulations arrived from Ireland, Stewart did not always enforce them. They were only to exercise two at a time, pen and ink were to be limited, they were not to meet at dinner but eat in their rooms. The exercise restrictions were never enforced.[37]

Even so, Arthur O'Connor wrote to Lady Lucy that he could not get enough exercise. She was a faithful friend and wrote to him frequently. She advised him to use a skipping-rope.[38] He wrote back that he didn't know what that was. 'I bathe every day be it frost or snow,' he told her. 'I do so to keep myself from being too tender which is one of the worst consequences of close confinement.'

Pamela was in Hamburg. She had left her son in England with the Duchess of Leinster and her youngest daughter with Edward's sister when she struggled to Hamburg and the refuge of Mrs Mathiessen. Lord Edward's property had been confiscated by a Bill of Attainder[39] and the FitzGeralds were lax in providing for her. In the spring of 1800, she married the American Consul in Hamburg, Mr Pitcairn,[40] and settled with her daughter Pamela. It was not a happy marriage. 'Let me hear how poor Pamela does,'[41] Arthur wrote to Lady Lucy. 'Pray remember me to her when you write to her.'[42] Later; 'it is so long since I heard from her, I fear she has forgotten me ...'[43]

On the cool Scottish coast, the noise and passion of rebellion over, the Irishmen found themselves face to face with each other on alien territory. What really bound them together? How did they see each other now, man to man, on the ramparts of the fort, playing ball games, swimming in the cold water? What did they have in common? Twenty men had come to Scotland, four were Catholic, six were Presbyterian, the rest were Protestants of the Established Church.[44] Some had known each other a long time and were close friends, others had only been brought together by pressure of politics. Their backgrounds varied; most were professional or businessmen from Dublin or Belfast. Only the O'Connors came from a family with large landed estates. Very few of the men had Gaelic names, most were descended from plantation families from Scotland and from seventeenth-century British settlers.

There were already splits and rivalries which had arisen before the rebellion. The difference of attitude, temperament and background between Arthur O'Connor and Thomas Addis Emmet grew into a poisoned rift. It was witnessed by their fellow prisoners. John Sweetman left a record of it.[45] According to him, Arthur O'Connor stated that Emmet, 'from nearly the first of their acquaintance acted towards him with the utmost duplicity, that he made a party against him in Kilmainham and that he gave information of the letter which O'Connor was writing through which means Government became acquainted with the circumstance'. Sweetman records O'Connor's contention that after he was moved to Newgate,

Emmet endeavoured to make a party against him; and that O'Connor could have proved Emmet base and treacherous except that Emmet was a United Irishman. O'Connor said that when the people were ready to rise, Emmet had warned it would be necessary to give information to the Castle to prevent it.[46]

What had been said in those hectic days when O'Connor was organising militant societies, pikes were being forged and messages arrived from France? Did Emmet panic and threaten O'Connor with the only weapon he had? Whatever Emmet said in those desperate meetings, O'Connor repeated in Fort George[47] and in his personal memoirs[48] that Emmet was a coward and threatened to inform. In Ireland, their common political allegiance kept them together. In prison in Scotland, there was nothing to bind them. Emmet retaliated strongly, apparently called O'Connor a liar. O'Connor challenged him to a duel. The matter could not be resolved in the fort and was left to hang.

There were other rifts. Emmet and Hudson had a row, Sweetman was cool with Arthur, O'Connor and McNeven threatened to duel. Because the prisoners exercised in two groups, Emmet and his friends could avoid the O'Connors who were in the other party. Each group now went out for three hours daily, from ten until one and from one until four.

The Irish State Prisoners occupied rooms on the second floor of the officers' quarters in the main block of the fort. On the south side, the rooms were opposite the Grand Magazine. Level with their apartments was an enclosed bastion approached by a gallery.[49] They exercised on the bastion but they were also allowed to swim in the surrounding Moray Firth.

Roger O'Connor's behaviour only exacerbated grievances. He had never signed the Kilmainham Treaty and had not, therefore, been included in the Banishment Act, nor had he been charged. He was an anomaly and on special terms. The others complained that Roger had the liberty of the garrison if accompanied by a sergeant and that he occasionally rode by carriage into Inverness.[50] Roger was in poor health in the summer of 1799. His wife was allowed to visit him at Fort George.[51] Despite pleadings he was not allowed to go to Ireland to visit her. But at the end of 1800 he was permitted to go to London for treatment, on condition that he did not return to Ireland without the express permission of government.[52]

O'Connor wrote to Lady Lucy:

... it has so happened that there are none of the persons imprisoned with whom I could form any friendship ... so that I am utterly devoid of society ... In prison every object is as it were brought under the microscope and you know how coarse even the finest objects appear when viewed through the microscope ... I therefore know the value of guarding against a too near approach.[53]

Thomas Addis Emmet's wife came to live with him at Fort George and two of their children were born there.[54] Samuel Neilson's son also joined him in Scotland.[55] Robert Hunter petitioned for his wife to live at Fort George as he had no funds to maintain her elsewhere. Recurrent requests for release were sent by individual prisoners. Three were released early with pardons and on condition of going abroad.[56]

In November 1799, by a coup d'état, Napoleon Bonaparte had become First Consul and effectively sole ruler of France. Gradually, Britain's war allies capitulated before the power of the French armies, the genius of Napoleon's command. The remaining State Prisoners were thought by government to pose a threat to the state and would be held until the war ended.

Arthur O'Connor sank into deep introspection. The long nights of winter, the pale clarity of the summer days that never faded, left little room for illusion. The frenzy of the years which had climaxed in rebellion were suddenly ended. In the silence of the Highlands, he considered his position, went over the sequence of events that had brought him there, thought about politics, pondered philosophy, read and re-read the Bible, meditated on the nature of God.[57] Everything his mother had taught him came back to him, he remembered her clearly and asked himself whether he had been true to her principles. The old, insoluble questions began to obsess him. The omnipotence of God, was that true, what did it mean? If God was all powerful, where did evil come from? He thought about David Hume and the great advances in human reason, perhaps here was a glimmer of a solution. In his heart, he felt bitterly all he had lost, wealth, land, privilege, the promise of high office, his country, his family, almost all human affection had been stolen from him. The cold air mirrored the cold sorrow inside.

To Lady Lucy he wrote:

> ... a being that has been so many years out of the world, has nothing but questions to put about those who are in it ... For God's sake send me a line, saying how you all are.' Emily, Duchess of Leinster had been very distressed at O'Connor's imprisonment. 'In your mother's society you have indeed the most amiable of companions, few so blessed with a well regulated mind ... You may well say your mother was always a great favourite of mine, it is a rare thing to meet a person from whose conversation it is possible to derive so much pleasure.[58]

He found the climate difficult to bear: 'all is covered in snow and coldness ... I take up my pen, dear Lucy, but what can I say, surrounded as I am with frost and snow ... what an element for a hot house plant like me.' Lucy sent him violets, 'they have perfumed my prison'. He was very solitary. 'I am a perfect hermit and I fear the habit will be so strong for me, that I shall continue one all my life. I have become such a philosopher that I shall forget I am a man.' He told her he seldom left his room and by submitting to everything, achieved a kind of detachment.[59]

Out on the ramparts, the Scottish soldiers went about their duties. Scots voices made a different rhythm to that of his Irish comrades who ran and raced, leapt for a ball, laughed and joked. The Irish voices were softer, more melodic. They were men in their prime, Arthur was 36 when the new century began. But he was slightly aloof, apart from the other men. In the curious combinations of race and culture which created the Irish nation, he was in a small minority, a Protestant landowner from an old Gaelic house.

The differences between the State prisoners were reported in Ireland. Arthur O'Connor was already a loaded name in England; that of a gentleman turned rebel, an inflammatory orator, complicit with French Jacobins, friend of Fox. In Ireland, his reputation was different. To the loyal gentry he was a traitor. To the people, he was Lord Edward's friend, the MP who took up the cause of Irish freedom. The administration worked hard to darken his name, the gentry already despised him. In England, *Portrait of a Traitor by his Friends and Himself* was published and went into a second edition. Evidence given by Fox and his friends at Maidstone was published alongside O'Connor's testimony to the House of Lords. 'I always thought Mr O'Connor to be perfectly well affected to his country,' Mr Fox had said, while O'Connor told the Lords that he joined the United Irishmen in November 1796 when the military organisation was already established and assistance from France arranged. Gillray's cartoons depicted O'Connor in court with the testimony of the Whigs floating from their mouths to save him. Secret service money was used to print *The Beauties of the Press*, a selection of material from O'Connor's paper, chosen to throw the worst possible light on its imprisoned proprietor.

Among the loyal and law-abiding subjects of King George in both islands, the name of Arthur O'Connor was linked with double-dealing, sedition, aiding the enemy, dishonour to friends and treason. Lord Moira had testified for him, albeit very tersely. Now Lady Moira reported with some glee to her friend Lady Granard,'they are all quarelling in Fort George'. Only four, she said, were in O'Connor's party. Beside the two brothers there was only Dowling and Hudson. She repeated cruel remarks supposedly made by O'Connor about Lord Edward, that he had called Emmet 'a sensualist and voluptory', and McNeven 'a pratting mixture of duplicity and meanness'. She said his own party had written an epigram on him that went:[60]

> O'Connor has merit I'm bound to confess
> He wrote well, he spoke well and printed the Press
> The faults of O'Connor I will also maintain
> He's envious, malignant, a liar and vain
> Of O'Connor in power then Erin beware
> For O'Connor in power would act Robespierre.[61]

In prison, little rumour reached him and O'Connor could not retaliate. He was indeed a very proud man, impatient, ambitious, often dominating. The rebellion had failed and some of its finest men had died. Splits opened up. The recriminations which followed found in him a natural target. The Establishment had been betrayed by him, one of their own. The United Irishmen were anything but united. O'Connor had come late among them and taken over. But the people who did not read pamphlets or even the public prints, knew only that a gentleman had risked his life for them and they remained warmly attached to his name.

If he could not defend his reputation, he also had little opportunity to organise his property. During 1799 his agent sold land he owned on Lapp's Island in Cork city.[62] The remainder of his property was in the hands of Burdett and the income was used to meet his needs in prison or accumulated with his agent. But he had given no time to his land, his house, his woodland or his tenants during the turbulent years, many matters were badly neglected and his fortune had been heavily drawn on.

More of his property was to be put up for sale. A young lawyer from Kerry thought of buying it. Daniel O'Connell wrote to his uncle in December 1800:

> Arthur O'Connor, the famous Arthur, is going to sell his estate in the County of Cork. It is about £600 per annum, as I am told. He could make out a clear unemcumbered title. Nor would there be any danger of forfeiture in the hands of a bona fide holder. But then it is at a distance from you and he is not a candid or fairdealing man. But I shall learn more of the matter shortly.[63]

In Ireland great changes had been proposed. Pitt was determined that an Act of Union would bring the Irish members into a single parliament in Westminster. There would be 28 Irish peers sitting in the House of Lords of the United Kingdom, elected for life from among the Irish peerage. The Union would also allow for a measure of reform. Rotten boroughs could be cancelled during the transfer of power and regulations imposed on placemen. In Dublin, discussion deepened on the likely effects while individuals jostled for representative peerages. Lord Longueville mentioned that Lord Westmoreland had recommended him for a peerage in 1794 and reminded the government of his strenuous loyalty during the insurrection.[64] Lord Barrymore wrote to Castlereagh 'how much I felt for fear so very old a peer and of so ancient a family as I am ... should now be passed over'.[65] Longueville was made a Viscount in 1800 and became a representative peer for Ireland.[66]

Pitt was convinced that Catholic emancipation should be a part of the Act of Union. Dubliners were concerned that their city would lose status as second city of the Empire and that its growing role as a second financial centre to London would be arrested. Merchants in Cork believed the Union would be good for trade. Castlereagh managed the Irish MPs very skilfully. The Act of Union passed both Irish Houses of Parliament in the summer and became law on 1 August 1800. Grattan's parliament was extinguished and members of the new parliament began looking for lodgings in London. The parliament house became empty. Castlereagh transferred to Westminster. But for Pitt, the Union was a failed policy. George III remained implacably opposed to Catholic emancipation. It was not included in the Act. Pitt believed it essential and resigned. George III had another attack of porphyria which brought on his recurrent madness. On his recovery in February 1801, Pitt stepped down as British Minister.

Lord Cloncurry was imprisoned for High Treason in 1801 and held in the Tower of London but later released.[67] William Corbet the printer had been briefly jailed in Kilmainham and in 1801 was out and informing again, this time on Putnam McCabe,[68] 'a handsome genteel figure' with 'a great fund of humour', son of a republican watchmaker from Belfast. McCabe was a master of disguise, a young businessman who had been active in the United Irishmen but fled the country in time to elude capture. John Stockdale, who had printed the *Press* for Arthur O'Connor, had been imprisoned for it, then released. He was re-arrested in August 1801.[69] Ireland was still restive. Republican and United men were active and still under surveillance.

The war with France, however, was brought to terms. In March

1802 Britain and France signed the Treaty of Amiens. O'Connor immediately enquired how he was to arrange his affairs, what plans had been made for them?[70] For some months, the government officials had been corresponding about the prisoners at Fort George.[71] Five were not in the Banishment Act. They were sent back to Ireland. Leaving on 30 December 1801, they travelled around the north coast of Scotland and sailed from Greenock to Belfast in January 1802.[72] The remaining eleven would be pardoned, taken to the continent and released.

It was July when they sailed for Hamburg. Arthur O'Connor, Emmet, McNeven, Russell, Dowling, Sweetman, Chambers, Wilson, Sweeney and Cuthbert were taken aboard the frigate *Ariadne* to leave 'His Majesty's dominions'. Just before the *Ariadne* anchored near Cuxhaven, Matthew Dowling took Arthur aside and said that Emmet would now be in Hamburg for some time. O'Connor replied that he would chose a time and place to call on Emmet.[73] Other prisoners felt it was time to look to the future and put old grievances behind them. They were taken ashore at Cuxhaven and released. Here they took a passage boat up the Elbe to the port of Hamburg further up river.[74]

On the boat John Chambers and John Sweetman discussed the differences which had arisen among the United Irishmen while at Fort George. They were slightly older than the others, perhaps they should attempt reconciliation. The rift between O'Connor and Emmet was at least two years old; if it could be resolved, other disagreements might be sorted out too. Chambers approached O'Connor. Sweetman talked to Emmet. Arthur said he certainly agreed the rift should be bridged. Emmet and O'Connor met on the foredeck. O'Connor spoke out, said he had never 'harboured any rancour in his breast' towards the other and withdrew his challenge. Emmet said he was right to do so. O'Connor 'expressed the purity of his motives' in all he had said. Emmet was annoyed, said the purpose of their speaking together was to give O'Connor the opportunity to explain what he had said to Patten about himself. O'Connor said he never meant to disparage Emmet who retorted that was impossible, he should explain himself properly. O'Connor repeated that he in no way meant to disparage the other's moral or political character.

This was all that could be achieved. The two men shook hands. O'Connor said he hoped the differences were behind them. They would not want their enemies to have the satisfaction of finding that the first thing they did on being liberated was to fight each other. Emmet made it clear that he was glad that any hostile relations had been put behind them but O'Connor should not expect 'any renewal of intimacy between them'. They bowed to each other and parted.[75]

Chambers and Sweetman each wrote an account of this incident and gave them to Thomas Addis Emmet in case O'Connor should ever publish anything injurious about him. Emmet later gave the reports to his son when it was known that O'Connor was writing his memoirs. Emmet's son[76] lodged them with Dr Madden who archived them.

With this partial reconciliation behind them, the men watched the boat negotiate the wide river. There was traffic of all kinds in and out of the port. The old trading city was ahead of them. The last time O'Connor had seen Hamburg he had been with Edward, returning from his meeting with Hoche. Both the other men were now dead. In the city, Edward's widow was living with little Pamela. The buildings became more distinct as they approached. Late in the afternoon on 5 July 1802 they drew up to the quays and O'Connor stepped ashore in Hamburg. He was 39 years old and an exile. He could not return to Ireland. He must make for himself whatever life he could.

After several disappointments, Lady Lucy Fitzgerald would soon marry. In 1802 she became the wife of Admiral Sir Thomas Foley and moved to his country house in Wales. She had no children.

—————— *Chapter 16* ——————

NAPOLEON'S IRISH GENERAL

Arthur had last seen Pamela FitzGerald when he left Dublin in those frenzied days of January 1798. Her daughter was five years old now. The girl later recalled: 'I once saw Arthur O'Connor at Hamburgh, when I was a child, and just remember a very handsome man patting my head and crying over me.'[1]

It was a hard meeting for Arthur. How often had Pamela begged him not to encourage Edward, not to urge him further into conspiracy? Now Edward was dead and Pamela, with almost no income and keeping only one of her three children with her, had accepted an offer of marriage which brought her no joy. Still lovely, she was a sad figure.[2] Arthur himself had spent the best years of his manhood in prison. Now he was an exile, vilified in his homeland. They could offer each other little comfort.

Money was a pressing problem for O'Connor too. Peace between Britain and France made it possible to get funds sent out from Ireland. But he had not set eyes on his own property for over four years. Attempts to sell the estate were confounded. It was not, as Daniel O'Connell thought, unencumbered. Arthur's brothers were of little assistance. He had given Roger power of attorney when the latter left Fort George.[3] Now Roger was back in Cork but he was very unreliable. Arthur would have to depend on his agent but no one had checked over the accounts for years and the agent was known to be bad at book-keeping.[4] Even more difficult was the question of his career. O'Connor had ceased to be a politician, was no longer an Irish landed gentleman. He had no business experience, nor a profession. What was he to do?

Hugh Bell sent out the income from his property. O'Connor

had some time to consider. Meanwhile the first pleasure of liberty was meeting his old friends. The peace, after so many years of war, enabled the English to cross the Channel. Sir Francis Burdett was in France.[5] More urgently, Charles James Fox was about to come over.

O'Connor needed to talk to Fox, whose friendship meant a very great deal to him. The leader of the Opposition had risked his own reputation to save his friend from a verdict of High Treason at Maidstone. Since then, O'Connor had testified to government and the Report of the Committee of Secrecy had been published. Since his letter to Fox from prison there had been silence. The years in Scotland had not allowed him to put the matter to rest.

O'Connor travelled south through Holland and was in Calais when Mr Fox and his wife Elizabeth stepped off the boat. They dined and supped together that day,[6] causing scandalous gossip. To the British political establishment, O'Connor was a rank traitor and even many of the liberal Whigs saw treachery in his conduct. Fox was a kind and broad-minded man. He was more concerned about his wife's health than public opinion, more interested in seeing some fine paintings than worrying what the political gossips said.

Two weeks later, Fox was in Paris and O'Connor dined with him several times.[7] The British liberals had arrived in Paris in force that summer. Arthur was reunited with Burdett. Also in Paris were Lord and Lady Holland, Lord Henry FitzGerald and Mr George Ponsonby. Not long afterwards Lady Bessborough arrived.

Old friends were meeting again. Fox and his FitzGerald cousins had known Talleyrand before his rise in the early Revolution, during his subsequent exile in London. They had similar backgrounds and political ideals. Talleyrand was back in Paris, an intimate of Napoleon and in a pivotal political position. Lafayette too, had returned to France and settled at his wife's chateau La Grange, south-east of the capital, where Fox went to stay.

O'Connor moved among this company. Some received him warmly, others treated him with contempt as a traitor, liar and conspirator. Fox was welcoming. Sir Francis Burdett was travelling with Lord and Lady Oxford. This lady took O'Connor with her on social occasions.[8]

Burdett and Lady Oxford had become lovers several years before; by 1798 their liaison was the talk of London.[9] Burdett was constantly with the Oxfords and the three of them had arrived in France that May to see how the country was progressing under Napoleon. Lady Oxford was a great beauty. Burdett was supposed to be her first lover and Lord Byron her last. When the poet knew her in 1813 she was almost twice his age but he was reported as saying of her, '... the autumn of a beauty like hers is preferable to the spring in others'.[10] Lord Oxford seems to have been unmoved by her infidelities although it was never certain that her children were actually his. Lady Oxford was not intimidated by the opinion of society and went where even the Whig ladies would not go.

She dined with Madame Cabarus and O'Connor accompanied her. Thérése Cabarrus gave great dinners to the English gentlemen. She dined with Fox but Lady Bessborough did not dare visit her – 'she is amiable, generous, delightful I am sure, but I am told it is impossible to go – and she is by this exposed to the worst set of English women here'.[11] Thérése Cabarrus had been divorced twice, firstly by the Marquis de Fontenay and secondly by Tallien, a Girondist. In 1802, she was the lover of Barras, a radical politician who had survived several stages of the Revolution. Fox thought her house and garden pretty and the dinner he received there very good.

Sir Robert Adair, Fox's friend, travelling companion and political associate was furious at the gossip about Fox and O'Connor. He wrote to Lady Melbourne in London:

I had before written to Lady Elizabeth Foster, and given her some account of a dinner we had at Madame Cabarrus's. In my letter to her I did not say a word about O'Connor, but between my writing to Lady E and my writing to the duchess, it was all about Paris that Mr Fox had brought him in his hand, and introduced him as his particular friend. Such an abominable lie made me determine to contradict it, so I wrote to the duchess, to state the fact exactly as it was. It seems that O'Connor is travelling about with lady Oxford, in company with a strange sort of a man whom she has with her to teach her Greek, having heard, I suppose, that it is nothing for a lady to have a turn for philosophy and metaphysics unless she can read the Greek alphabet. From her rank and her pretended enthusiasm with respect to Fox, Madame Cabarus thought she could not do better than to invite her, and lady O thought she could do nothing so well as to invite O'Connor. She brought him therefore, greatly to the annoyance of everybody there, especially Erskine who carried the matter too far on the other side. Since this, the gossips of Paris have talked of nothing else, and I have no doubt that, among ten thousand other misrepresentations, a fine story will be made out of it for the old women of London ... If Fox is commonly civil to a man who is proscribed by the rest of the world, then it is instantly said that he is making common cause with him, and is just as bad and dangerous a person himself.[12]

Fox said, 'It don't signify but by God I have not a heart to meet a man in distress whom I once knew when he was worthy of esteem and not take notice of him'.[13] In any case, Fox was researching the reign of James II and spent hours in the National Library. He showed little interest in the antagonisms of his associates but others believed O'Connor had betrayed the support they gave at Maidstone. There was almost a duel with Tierney. Fox was more concerned about France. He had an interview with Bonaparte which confirmed his suspicions. The nature of the First Consul was all too obvious to O'Connor. The liberals: British, Irish and French, meeting in Paris after war, exile and prison had dispersed them, realised all too quickly that Napoleon was not one of them. He was autocratic, relied on his massive army and distrusted freedom of speech.

On 12 October Lord and Lady Oxford dined with Mr and Mrs Fox at their lodgings at Hotel Richelieu. Arthur O'Connor was also a guest, as was Madame Cabarrus and several others. Fox left Paris on 13 November and arrived at 'dear, dear home' on 17 November.[14] O'Connor had no home and watched his English friends leave Paris one by one, as he continued in lodgings, gazing at a blank future.

Few men have felt what it is to make the sacrifice of parents, friends and country, to be disinherited, detested, calumniated by all those he loved and cherished and what no man can know but he who has made the perilous leap, the balm, the all healing cure is ever found in man's self-esteem.[15]

O'Connor's mental and physical strength buoyed up his confidence. His early habit of self-examination gave him self-discipline. Rage often clouded, almost obscured his reason but the energy with which he dominated others could also be used for self-command. The effort produced a sort of brooding charisma but O'Connor had retained friends. He had been tested to the limits but he still believed in himself.

The Oxfords were still on the Continent and he set out with them to Italy.[16] He travelled up into Switzerland too.[17] He liked mountain country, the clear air, the sense of being above the clamour of human society. Switzerland reassured his political beliefs, he approved its republican system. However, this had now been brought under French control. O'Connor had last been there with Edward in 1796, before the meeting with Hoche. In Switzerland the past was close, touched the raw places of his grief.

Back in Paris, O'Connor established a circle of friends. He became a regular visitor to Madame Helvetius. He was soon a close friend of Cabanis, through whom he met Cabanis' sister-in-law, Sophie de Condorcet. They were liberal gentry who had supported the original concepts of the Revolution. Many had been active in it. They recognised the administrative order of Napoleon, were glad of the peace. But no one was confident that the peace would last. When O'Connor returned to Paris, Britain and France were in contention over its terms. Instead of withdrawing troops from Holland, Napoleon stationed more. Britain refused to give up Malta. In May 1803 Britain declared war on France. In many ways this clarified O'Connor's position. It closed the commercial channels by which Hugh Bell was getting money to him. It made his chances of selling his property in Ireland very slight, he could not organise it. His English friends would not return to Paris. Once more Britain was France's enemy and this time it seemed that Napoleon seriously meant to invade. That, once more, raised the military stakes for Ireland.

In Ireland, the United Irishmen had struggled back into action. A small committee was active in Dublin. The Irishmen in France took stock. Thomas Addis Emmet had arrived in Paris and was actively engaged in getting military assistance from the First Consul on behalf of Ireland.[18] His younger brother Robert Emmet had already heard from Napoleon that he planned an expedition for Ireland in August 1803; Robert hastened back to Dublin to plan a rising. The position of the Irish in France was extremely difficult. If they could prove their affiliation to the French government they were secure and might be employed. If not, they were British subjects and liable to be held as prisoners of war.

O'Connor made use of the contacts he had. Before leaving Paris in November 1802, he had written to Talleyrand.[19] He already knew Lafayette and the great French liberal was once more in Paris after his imprisonment in Austria. General Emmanuel Grouchy had been Hoche's second in command on the 1796 expedition to Ireland. He was also the brother of Sophie de Condorcet. O'Connor's radical credentials were well known in Paris and he used them. On his return early in 1803 he wrote to the Minister of Justice, claiming his position as the United Irish ambassador to France. He gained the confidence of General Dalton, a French officer of Irish descent who had known Tone.[20] The Irish who fought for King James in the seventeenth century had formed the core of the Irish Brigade and fought for France in many wars. A new Irish Legion was envisaged by Napoleon and the Irishmen enlisted for it were the republicans of the 1798 rebellion. It was important to recruit men who had recently left Ireland, understood the current situation and could mobilise support there. Obviously the newly 'enlarged' United Irish leaders were vital to his plans. Dalton saw O'Connor frequently and wrote a long letter of recommendation on his behalf.[21]

O'Connor saw clearly that he had a second chance of liberating Ireland with the support of Napoleon. He also saw that a military command was his only likely chance of employment.

The presence of Thomas Addis Emmet in Paris complicated O'Connor's position. Miles Byrne was a United Irish leader from Wexford who arrived in Paris at this time and very much wanted to call on O'Connor. As a friend of Emmet, he felt he could not and regretted it very much.[22] Their fellow countrymen, both in France and at home in Ireland, looked on those two as their best agents with the French government. The enmity between them was bad for the United Irish cause. The French soon realised there were factions and became irritated at having to deal with two parties, even having to try to bring them together.

T.A. Emmet's own diary gives a clear account of how this relationship developed.[23] Dalton called on him in May 1803, said he came from the Ministry of War, the French government had determined on an expedition to Ireland. 25,000 men were to be embarked under General Massena. Emmet wanted to know if Dalton was talking to O'Connor and on hearing he was, Emmet insisted he and O'Connor must act separately. Dalton apparently told Wolfe Tone's widow that if they were unable to work together, sooner or later the French government would chose between them.

In June, Emmet heard that O'Connor was asking McCabe to go to Ireland, to prepare the North for a French expedition. O'Connor had seen Massena. Emmet wanted to see Napoleon but could not get an interview. He also needed official assistance to get his own messages to Ireland but this help was not given. The remnants of the Dublin United Irish organisation had appointed Emmet as their representative in France. The people who had appointed O'Connor in 1797 were now either dead or exiled. Emmet suspected that O'Connor did not even know there was a new Executive. To Emmet, the important thing was to 'ascertain my appointment and silence O'Connor's pretensions'.[24]

Among the Irish exiles in Paris, this proved difficult. O'Connor had influence and several key Irish leaders such as Chambers, Sampson and McMahon remained firmly attached to him. O'Connor had been asked by the French to make a list of the United Irishmen among the prisoners of war held in France. This put him in a powerful position. These men would then be freed and might be recruited for the expedition. According to Emmet, O'Connor was saying there was no Executive in Ireland and Emmet had been unable to collect enough signatures in Paris to support his position. His envoy to Ireland had a passport for only eight days, not nearly long enough to get to Dublin and back. On 19 July, T.A. Emmet saw the Minister of War, pressed his position, insisted that O'Connor had no United Irish accreditation and got a passport for his envoy.[25]

Robert Emmet's rising in Dublin came on 23 July. With little planning and small numbers, the insurgents were dispersed quickly. Robert fled. Caught when he returned to see his sweetheart, Sarah Curran, daughter of the famous lawyer, Robert Emmet secured his place in history by his famous speech in court. Sentenced to death, he spoke again from the scaffold before he was hanged. Emmet had criticised France. When the French landed in Ireland, they would depend on Irish support. Paris would be angered by the premature attempt, and also by Emmet's words.

O'Connor was apprised of Emmet's plans by Allen who had been tried with him at Maidstone and who was often with Robert Emmet.[26] Allen was not caught in the 1803 attempt. O'Connor had no part in it and looked on it as an act of madness.[27] He disapproved of both the Emmets, 'one for his cowardice, the other for his folly and rashness that ruined the Union'.[28] His comment to Madden was 'how call that a plan that vanished in smoke the moment it saw the light and that instantly ended in the ruin of all those in Ireland that were engaged in it'.[29]

News of the abortive attempt in Dublin reached Paris early in August. By then a committee was being set up regarding the prisoners of war, but news of the Dublin débâcle ruffled the French. Dalton told Emmet that he and O'Connor simply must work together. They could not have more splinter groups. Success required one concerted military effort. O'Connor was willing to work with Emmet but Thomas Addis refused to co-operate with this 'bad and dangerous man'. O'Connor had seen Humbert, was confided in by the Departments of the Marine and of War, by General Bernadotte, by Trugnet and Garat. It was Garat's idea that O'Connor should go with the expedition and Emmet remain in Paris as United Irish Minister. To this, Emmet would agree.[30]

On 18 September, Emmet was out making calls when 'Mr O'Connor and I met plump at the turn of a street. To my surprise,' Emmet recorded, 'he instantly saluted me and enquired very tenderly after my family. I answered him as coldly as I could with politeness, but he was not to be rebuffed.' O'Connor said it was obvious that the French government were communicating with both of them but not saying the same things. The French had pressed him to send messengers to Ireland too, but he had not done so as he was not convinced of French sincerity. He believed the French were deceiving both of them. His fortune, character and connections gave him access to information which showed up inconsistencies.[31]

Emmet listened with deep suspicion as O'Connor proposed they exchange information, within a vow of secrecy in order to protect lives. Emmet found this discourse 'in some parts very arrogant, but on the whole containing a very artful proposal'.[32] He declined to disclose anything but said if O'Connor wanted to confide in him, he would 'give him every obligation of secrecy'. O'Connor could not see why Emmet should feel bound not to discuss his relations with the French. No such tie had been put on him. The French, said O'Connor, treated him as the principal person and an *homme d'Etat*. The First Consul had empowered officials to sign agreements with O'Connor but had never asked for secrecy. He made clear to Emmet that he was acting as an individual, but could find a group to call themselves an Executive and endorse him, if he so wished.

Emmet heard this dig without riposte. They had been standing outside the Palais Royal for three-quarters of an hour and he was sure he was being delayed because O'Connor wanted them to be seen together. The depths of his suspicion and paranoia regarding O'Connor had no bottom; in every word he saw a plot or scheme. He told O'Connor he was acting for other people and could not disclose their communications. Emmet 'very politely concluded this extraordinary interview'.[33]

The news from Ireland was bad, persecution of rebels, troops everywhere. Robert Emmet's execution was confirmed. Thomas Addis continued to negotiate with Dalton, while the Irish in France were being drafted into a new corps, the Irish Legion. O'Connor was fully in Dalton's confidence and was able to procure commissions for his friends. The corps was ordered to Morlaix in Brittany during December. Those Irish who did not join were made prisoners of war and sent to Verdun.

Early in 1804 Napoleon was demanding a committee of the Irish leaders with both Emmet and O'Connor on it. He refused to deal with the Irish on any other terms. Emmet was obliged to give up his role as sole Ambassador from Dublin. There were arguments about who should be on the committee. Emmet thought too many of O'Connor's friends were included.[34] The French wanted O'Connor to take a leading military role, Emmet to be reserved for the civil administration.

On 24 February 1804, O'Connor was made Général de Division and posted to Morlaix,[35] under Général Augereau. He was an officer of the Irish Legion, part of L'armée de Côte at Brest. His orders came from 'Bonaparte, premier Consul de la République' and were dated 4 Ventose an 12. 'The First Consul made me the grade of General de Division Irlandais which I refused. I asked for and received the grade of General de Division Francais, also with the rights of a citizen of France'[36] he later reminded the Minister of War. McNeven was also at Brest. Emmet felt himself slighted and confided to his diary: 'I shall therefore avoid doing anything and keep myself in the background unless Government choses to show me some little civility and to convince me that they wish for the continuance of my communications.'[37] There was a silence. In October, Emmet left for the United States where he pursued a very successful legal career and became Attorney-General to the State of New York.

McSheehy had been appointed Adjutant-Géneral of the Irish Legion stationed at Brest. He was under Donzelot. They moved several times, to Quimper on the coast and to Carhais in Finistere.[38] The Irish Legion became part of La Grande Armée. Napoleon was building a large invasion fleet at Boulogne for a single strike, aimed immediately at London. As always, the Irish expedition would be a side-show of the attempt on Britain. O'Connor's recommendations had been followed in the appointment of officers. Many promotions were given to soldiers of the old Irish Brigade and to long-time French residents. Bonaparte wanted a fighting force but many of the United Irishmen felt over-looked. Factions developed. A ceremony for taking an oath of loyalty to the Emperor and constitution provoked a quarrel and an affray. O'Connor arrived at Carhais soon afterwards and blamed MacSheehy.[39] The Minister of War, Berthier sacked MacSheehy. O'Connor was now in full command of the Irish.

In September 1804, Major William Corbet who later distinguished himself fighting for France, wrote: 'Arthur O'Connor is General of Division in the French service, we are under his command and he is our very close friend.'[40]

In May 1804 Napoleon proclaimed himself Emperor of the French, an hereditary title. In December, he was crowned with pomp and magnificence. Although he took an oath to unhold equality of rights, civil and political liberty, many saw this as the collapse of the Revolution. The intelligentsia took stock. O'Connor watched this change with gloom; 'Bonaparte's despotism had made so many imagine liberty was a dream that mankind was not capable to realise.'[41]

But Bonaparte was set on conquest and Bonaparte was O'Connor's only hope of liberating Ireland. O'Connor impressed Bonaparte with his drive and confidence. The disagreements among the Irish exiles had forced Napoleon to choose an Irish leader. He chose O'Connor. In Brittany, progress was not as quick as General O'Connor would have liked. He set about laying in supplies and munitions.[42] Preparations for the expedition went on, but no orders for mobilisation arrived.

O'Connor published a new work in 1804. Printed in Paris, *The Present State of Great Britain*[43] was a more purely economic discussion than *The State of Ireland.* O'Connor's scornful critique of Britain's economic management lacked the raging polemic of the Irish pamphlet. He had had much time for quiet reflection at Fort George, where he was away from the twisting cross-currents of Irish politics. Much of the manuscript may have been written there. It was certainly written before Bonaparte was crowned. O'Connor describes the enlightened government of France: 'The republic stands broad as the soil and high as the heavens, and time must give it consolidation.'[44] He draws attention to the rapid increase in the number of poor in Britain and the way in which male primogeniture locks up land, making much of it unusable and agriculture less productive. This increases the urban population who depend on manufacturing, which in turn depends on buoyant trade. O'Connor lost no opportunity for advocating free trade.

'The first principle,' says O'Connor, 'in legislation and in political economy is to identify the interest of the individual with the interest of the nation.'[45] He loftily addresses himself to the British:

You are sacrificed as consumers to the preposterous project of producing for the rest of the world. The end of production is consumption, and you have reversed it, the object of all your means of production should be the most abundant supply for the people of Great Britain; and yet the whole of your system goes to furnish everything cheaper to the rest of the world than to yourselves.[46]

The rebellion, the appalling loss of life had clearly made a shift in his ideas. He points out that the days of heroic conquest are over, 'the nations of Europe seek to exchange the science of destruction for the science which teaches the increase of comfort, enjoyment and happiness.' He goes on: 'The most absolute freedom is the principle upon which the whole of this first of all sciences is founded;' ... 'establish a system of reciprocal benefits, and live in peace with the world.'[47]

Bonaparte was not concerned with philosophy. He had drawn up his Civil Code for the administration of France. It was highly efficient. The position of women was put firmly back in subordination to men. Rights of succession were defined. Now he turned back to beating Britain, conquering Europe, his plans for Egypt. Writing to his Marshal at Boulogne for a report on preparations for the British descent, he told him not to send a metaphysical reply, 'but go and look at the different stores and warehouses.'[48]

O'Connor's vision was of civil society, based on equality. This would create prosperity and peace. He was still willing to prosecute war to achieve it. He had few options. Only Napoleon could liberate Ireland. If O'Connor did not join the Irish Legion, in theory he could become a prisoner of war. He needed to build up his position in France if ever he was to become naturalised. He was glad of the salary. His income from Ireland was not sufficient and with war again blocking commerce, it became difficult to send funds from Cork via London to Paris. He was actually rather old to begin a military career. He declared himself a veteran of the Volunteers, saying he had joined in 1782 and he gave his date of birth as 1767.[49] Dalton gave him a splendid reference, recapitulating his position as an important member of the Irish parliament, Sheriff of County Cork, the man who had made the Treaty with Hoche. Dalton gave O'Connor's fortune as £20,000 sterling which he had risked, together with his life, in the service of his country in association with France.[50]

In Ireland Arthur O'Connor had become a spectre and a threat. There were constant sightings. Reports came into Dublin Castle – O'Connor had been seen in Chester and at Tralee,[51] was said to be in Dublin[52] and in County Cork.[53] Information reached Mr Marsden. Sampson had written to associates in Ireland, denigrating the Emperor and saying that Arthur O'Connor was very anxious and determined on an invasion.[54] In February 1805, he was said to be the only one of the Irish in France who kept up any hope.

To the militant peasantry he seemed the long-awaited saviour. In September 1804, a notice on the door of the Catholic church in Wicklow read: *The day is near approaching when O'Connor, the apostle of Liberty will be on our oppressed shore with an army, that will root out Tyranny from the impoverished land of Ireland.*[55] Others, terrified and demoralised, may have prayed he would not come.

In May 1805 Mr Marsden was informed that Emmet, McNeven, Loury and O'Connor had sent word that 'a Fatal Blow will be immediately struck',[56] although Emmet was by then in America. But by June, McNeven, Chambers and the others had left Bordeaux for the United States. Of the Fort George prisoners, only Sweetman, in ill health, and Arthur O'Connor were still in France.[57] In August 1805, William Corbet the printer told the Castle that O'Connor was in Spain.[58] This was untrue.

Corbet got most of his information from John Stockdale. Imprisoned in 1798 and released, Stockdale had been re-imprisoned in 1801. Informers were among the prisoners. By 1805 his liberty depended on William Corbet, who pumped him for information which he took to the Castle. In May, Corbet impressed on Stockdale that he was answering to the Castle for both of them; if either fell foul of the government, both would. Stockdale swore no insurrection was contemplated. But in June a letter arrived from Arthur O'Connor. Still no invasion was expected.[59] Meetings of United men were held to decide what to do, if the fleets at Toulon and Brest sailed. Corbet reported all of this. He also informed the Castle that 'Stockdale's female friend sailed yesterday for Bordeaux'.[60] She had visited relatives in Wexford. Stockdale had told Corbet that she was very intelligent. Corbet does not identify the woman. She may have been O'Connor's former mistress.

Stockdale was very important to the Castle. In July 1806 O'Connor's only child in Ireland was in his care.[61] This boy was about twelve and may have been left with Stockdale by his mother when she went abroad. The beleaguered printer had been imprisoned again that year. In May Hannah Stockdale was pleading for mercy from the Lord Lieutenant; her husband was very ill and she had seven children to support.[62] He was released and recovered, returned to Dublin by July where he was once more set upon by Corbet.[63]

Republican meetings went on in Dublin and the Castle was still obsessed with finding arms dumps and hidden pikes. But by 1806 Bonaparte was no longer a threat to the status quo in Ireland. Nor was Arthur O'Connor. The previous year the Emperor had re-engaged with the Austrians and the Russians, had beaten them at Austerlitz. Once more he had abandoned the expedition to Britain. In September 1805 the army at Brest was disbanded and O'Connor was free to return to Paris on full pay.[64] In October, Nelson crushed the French fleet at Trafalgar, off southern Spain. At the end of 1805 Napoleon abandoned the republican calendar. Thereafter O'Connor's military records, as all others, use the same calendar as the rest of Europe. Napoleon, impatient of metaphysics, had no time for an Empire run on incomprehensible dates.

General Arthur O'Connor returned to Paris and took lodgings. He was moving in intellectual circles and it was a pleasure for him to be back in the capital, able to meet and converse with his friends. But as his social circle in Paris opened up, the political world he had known in London utterly changed. In January 1806, his hated adversary William Pitt died. The death of his enemy left a curious vacuum. After 22 years in opposition, Charles Fox came into the government as Foreign Secretary. He was already ill but still believed he could achieve peace by negotiation with his old friend Talleyrand, now Foreign Minister in France. He was unsuccessful.

That autumn, Charles James Fox became terminally ill. The death of this genial and forgiving friend was a great loss to O'Connor. Without Pitt and Fox, the political dynamic of London was changed utterly. It had set the scene for Grattan's parliament, had been in play when O'Connor first visited parliament in London. With the death of Fox, the eighteenth century truly ended.

In Britain and in France, the new century was developing new concerns as technology advanced. From intellectual ideals, educated people turned their attention to manufacturing, commerce and Empire. Ireland remained in the shadow of failed rebellion. In 1807, James Trail wrote to Sir Arthur Wellesley that a very shrewd man who had been engaged in the rebellion

> ... says the whole population of Ireland is decidedly hostile to the government and to the English connection; that the people, even the labouring poor, talk and think of nothing but Bonaparte's success on the Continent, and rely with certainty on his invading this country and separating it from England ...
>
> O'Connor is looked to as a leader, and many expect that Bonaparte will make him King of Ireland ...
>
> This antipathy to England is ancient and has never varied.[65]

In France, expectations of a French expedition to Ireland faded. Arthur O'Connor, free from his military duties, pursued his intellectual interests among new friends. There was much to concern liberals within Bonaparte's France. Among the men and women of letters in Paris, O'Connor began to find his place. He saw he could not return to Ireland, would probably never return. Like many Wild Geese before him, he began to get a command of the lan-

guage, heard his name become Artur, pick up the French intonation. Though the Fort George prisoners had gone to America, there
were still many Irish emigrés both recent and from previous generations, with whom he met and exchanged news.

If only he had some capital in France, he could buy a property.
He cast about him for a means to settle down.

Chapter 17

COURTING THE PHILOSOPHER'S DAUGHTER

Sophie, Emmanuel and Charlotte de Grouchy came from a distinguished family. Their home in Normandy was the Chateau de Villete, near Meulan.[1] Charlotte married Pierre Cabanis in 1796. He was a doctor and *philosophe*, one of those intellectuals who developed the concepts of civil society from which the Revolution was born. O'Connor had become his close friend. 'Your friendship is too precious to me,' Cabanis wrote to O'Connor at Brest, 'that every manifestation of it that you can give, can only touch my heart in the most lively way'.[2]

Emmanuel was a professional soldier who by default had led the aborted mission to Bantry in 1796. He fought at Friedland under Bonaparte but his sisters were not supporters of the First Consul.

Through Cabanis, O'Connor became an intimate of the family. He frequently visited the widowed Marquise de Condorcet. Sophie had an apartment in the Grande rue Verte in Paris, where she kept a salon. She was a year younger than O'Connor and she, like him, had survived violent political storms.

Sophie de Grouchy had had a quiet childhood in the family chateau where her mother instilled devout Catholic virtue.[3] The girl could not reconcile the huge number of the damned and small number of the saved with a good God. Two years in a convent only turned her mind to Voltaire and Rousseau. She was 22 when she met the established mathematician and philosopher, Marie Jean Antoine Caritat, Marquis de Condorcet; she was 23 when they married. He was twenty years older, permanent Secretary of the Academy of Sciences and part of the rationalist movement which so disturbed the *ancien régime*. Sophie embraced his ideas and held

them all her life. The Condorcets were central figures of the intellectual phase of the Revolution but were cut down by the Jacobins
who quickly followed.[4]

Their house at Auteuil became a refuge for Sophie after
Condorcet's fall. President of the Legislative Assembly in 1792
among the Girondins, the next year he was a hunted man. While
Condorcet hid at the house of Madame Vernet in Paris, Sophie supported herself, her mother, sister and child by painting portraits.[5]
She started a small lingerie shop in Paris. A noblewoman could not
spend a night in the city. Sophie dressed as a peasant woman and
walked into Paris from Auteuil each day among the crowds which
flocked to the guillotine. Above the lingerie shop she painted her
portraits, slipping away to see her brilliant, fugitive husband.[6]

Sophie sued for divorce to keep her husband's property but
much was confiscated. The Revolutionary army came often; Sophie
too expected to be arrested. To please them, she painted their portraits. Sophie was a woman of character. She gave help and hospitality to her friends, Garat, Laplace, Lacroix, La Roche and
Cabanis.[7]

Condorcet was arrested in 1794 and found dead in his cell two
days later. By the end of the next year, the Terror was ending, the
Directory established. Sophie claimed the property of Condorcet
which had not been sold.[8] Unable to find more portrait clients, she
translated Adam Smith's *The Theory of Moral Sentiments.* Slowly,
her life became more secure. She acquired a country house, la
Maisonette at Meulan, and an apartment in the city. But too many
friends and associates had suffered. Her husband was dead, her
father had been in prison. What the young woman suffered in
1793-4 profoundly affected her health.[9] People never spoke of the
Girondins in front of her, it produced such extreme emotion. Many
of her husband's colleagues had been guillotined.

Condorcet was an idealist, a rationalist and a philosopher of
great scope. Sophie was artistic, intellectual and brave. Their only
child was said to have been conceived on the night the Bastille fell.[10]
Alexandrine-Sophie-Louise de Condorcet, born in May 1790, was
known as Eliza.

When Arthur O'Connor met Sophie, she was the lover of

Claude Fauriel, Professor at the Faculty of Letters.[11] In honour of Condorcet's memory, Sophie refused to marry again but her liaison with Fauriel was deep and enduring.

O'Connor had no difficulty introducing himself into this circle. He came from an equivalent Irish background. He shared their education, intellectual passions and social ideals. Like them, he had experienced political eruption, state violence and imprisonment. Like them, many of his colleagues were dead. He was a frequent visitor to the Marquise de Condorcet, they had many friends in common.

Volney the philosopher had been imprisoned. O'Connor had long admired Volney's work, read it to Lady Lucy, published it in the *Press* and defended it against Irish priests. The two men corresponded. By 1805, when O'Connor was released from duty in Brittany and returned to Paris, they were on close terms and Volney was storing wine for O'Connor in his cellar.[12]

Lafayette was a close friend of the Condorcets. He had signed the certificate for the marriage of Sophie with the philosopher.[13] He had known O'Connor since 1792 at the camp at Sedan. He too had been imprisoned, for five years in Austria, and was now established at La Grange.

The great survivor, Charles Maurice de Talleyrand-Perigord was ten years older than O'Connor and had escaped prison. He had been at court during the ancien régime, had been a Bishop but as President of the Assembly in 1790 he attacked the church and was excommunicated. In London and America during the Terror, he was Foreign Secretary under the Directory but followed the rising star of Napoleon, became his Minister and confidante. In 1803, informers told the Irish government that Talleyrand, O'Connor and McNeven were constantly together in France. The source was Cox, who told Corbet, who informed the Castle.[14]

O'Connor always defended Cox as staunch,[15] but Watty Cox was informing, and had petty grievances. He described O'Connor as a miserable miser, passionately fond of money although he lost £3,000 in the Irish Union. Cox reported that O'Connor importuned Stockdale with letters for an old cocked hat, and an old pair of spurs which he left at the printer's house, until finally Stockdale sent them to France. They 'would not have sold for a guinée'.[16]

Perhaps O'Connor was homesick, the personal possessions nostalgic.

Among the *ideologues* and liberal gentry, O'Connor had a place. The brilliant Madame de Stael was also his contemporary. The daughter of Necker and friend of Talleyrand, Germaine de Staël was in Paris from 1797-1803 when Napoleon ordered her 'forty leagues from hence'.[17] She came and went, living in Switzerland, Germany and England. Her writing had made her famous and she congratulated Sophie on the Adam Smith translation.[18] Her sometime lover and intellectual intimate was Benjamin Constant. He dined with Sophie de Condorcet in 1805 and met O'Connor; 'O'Connor is a subtle fellow,' the Swiss recorded. 'When joking, he has a lighter touch than foreigners usually have and so has something of the French defect of joking about his own opinions. More ambitious than a friend of liberty and yet a friend of liberty, because to be so is the refuge of ambitious men who have missed success.'[19]

O'Connor was certainly ambitious but his passion for philosophy was genuine and extended to those liberal philosophers whose ideas inspired his beliefs. Of these, Condorcet had been a shining light. A great mathematician and social scientist, sensitive and unworldy, Condorcet had tried to live out his ideals by taking a lead in the Revolution. He had died as a result, though no one knew the real cause of death. He had left a huge body of work, papers and manuscripts. Sophie had published his collected works in 1804. Around her, these ideas were discussed. At the Grande rue Verte she was a charming and stimulating hostess. She had a teenage daughter.

Arthur O'Connor paid court. He had foresworn marriage while he was planning revolution, had spent years in prison. Now, aged over 40, he felt entitled to a full domestic life. To him the daughter of Condorcet carried a glorious name. Although he was the same age as her mother, he saw no difficulty in courting the sixteen-year-old Eliza. He was marrying for the first time and was a novice as a husband. Sophie had married an older man and Arthur had perfect revolutionary credentials. He had risked all for Ireland's freedom and paid for it. He came from a landed and influential family. Tall, physically strong and still handsome, he had the infectious charm and wit of the Irish. He was clever and had a private fortune.

Sophie had no objections. Eliza accepted his proposal. She had never had a father, an older man might give protection and support. Eliza had two highly talented parents. She had been educated by her free-thinking mother. She was said to have much of the strong body and looks of her father.[20] She spoke English. Her childhood, during the Terror, had been full of tension and fear. Revolutionary soldiers terrified Sophie at Auteuil when Eliza was an infant of three and four. Hunted relatives and family friends came and went from the house. Sophie was strained to breaking point supporting her family. There were many deaths. Safety came slowly, financial security only later. Sophie and Eliza were very close and the daughter rather old for her years. She agreed to marry the Irish General. But first of all he had to provide her with a home.

Arthur's affairs in Ireland were entangled and chaotic. Roger had appropriated a large part of his wealth, had created further complications and legal difficulties before Arthur realised and cancelled the power of attorney. He wanted to sell the property but could not visit Ireland. The continuing war interrupted communications. The sale was not straightforward.

His youthful friend, John Waller, was in France during the peace but had been interned at Verdun. He knew O'Connor was well placed with the French government and managed to send a message. Henri Clarke had become Duc de Feltre and was in the Ministry of War. On O'Connor's recommendation, he gave Waller a passport back to Ireland. Waller wrote to thank him:

> ... most sincerely for a proof of what indeed I never doubted, your friendship for me and goodness of heart. I came to France determined not to leave it without our meeting, but almost immediately on my arrival the war commenced, and tho' I have since longed much for some intercourse with you, I did not know whether under the present circumstances of the two countries you might desire it.[21]

On his return he tried to 'remedy the confusion' in O'Connor's affairs and R. French, a mutual friend, assisted him. 'We intend,' Mr French assured Arthur, 'conjointly to exert ourselves, in procuring the sale of your property.' French was also buying books on cotton manufacturing to send to O'Connor in France.[22]

It was impossible for the two friends to resolve Arthur's affairs. The property at Ballinroe, near Kinsale, and his house, Fort Arthur, were not wholly discharged from mortgage in which his nephew William had an interest. William was pressing to receive part of Arthur's income in payment. The property could not be sold without settling the mortgage.[23]

On the death of Arthur's father in 1798 there had been further bequests. Old Roger had squandered a great deal of his inheritance but he still owned tracts of land which he had divided between his sons. Arthur's and Roger's shares were adjoining which later caused trouble.[24] Robert had appropriated the remainder of his mother's estate.[25] Despite his hatred of Arthur and Roger, two of Robert's children married two of Roger's.[26] By 1807 Arthur was in open contention with Roger over the management of his property and referred to him as 'that wretched being Roger'.[27]

Arthur's elder brother Daniel was living in Bristol.[28] Arthur's trustees were friends of the family, Daniel knew them well. The brothers shared a solicitor and had received bequests under the same wills. Daniel would understand the details, be able to effect the sale of the property in Cork. It was to Daniel that Arthur now turned.

William Putnam McCabe had been an associate of O'Connor's for some years. His father was one of the original United Irishmen from Belfast and McCabe was active in reviving the Society after the rebellion. Clever at disguise, he travelled frequently between Ireland, England and France, meeting English radicals. He was active in the United movement both in Dublin and Paris. He attempted to set up a cotton manufactory at Rouen in 1802 with other Irish exiles but it never came into being.[29] McCabe, however, had capital in France, as well as access to both England and Ireland.

McCabe had brought capital into France for the aborted cotton manufactory and had no immediate reason to invest it there. He and O'Connor were close at the time, both were friends of Hugh Bell in London.[30] McCabe offered to forward £4,750 to O'Connor to buy a property. He would be repaid in Ireland from the proceeds, once the estate near Kinsale was sold.

Arthur wrote to Daniel on 7 February 1807:

My Dearest Daniel

The decree that prohibited all communication with your side of the water has prevented me from either writing to you or hearing from you these some months. This will be delivered to you by a real true friend who seeing the cruel situation I was reduced to has lent me £4,750.

Daniel was to pay McCabe £750 immediately and they had agreed 5 per cent interest on the £4,000 until it could be paid. O'Connor hoped that O'Grady and Evans would press the amicable foreclosure of William's mortgage. He already foresaw litigation with Roger. 'Nothing,' he wrote, 'delays my marriage but finding a farm where we may reside. Madame Condorcet and Eliza join me in love and wishes for you and yours.'[31]

In March, Arthur hoped for arbitration to be agreed with Roger but in case of a law suit, he asked for Daniel's choice of Attorney. McCabe only wanted £750 immediately; if any of the property had already been sold the balance was to be sent via Hugh Bell to France. 'If I had it at this time there is a most advantageous purchase that I could make but without three or four thousand more I durst not venture to make it,' Arthur told Daniel. He asked McCabe to collect the agreed interest payments through Bell and begged his friend not to put a bond on him for the loan. This would only further complicate the sale of the property.

Since I saw you last, I have found the most advantageous and eligible estate that I could have wished and if it slips through my hands for the want of £4,000 it will be a most grievous disappointment, in six years it will more than double in value. It is the place of all others where I would be happy, there is a rapid stream that tumbles down through the whole property.[32]

'Press Daniel,' Arthur wrote to McCabe, 'to procure me this sum, as yet he has done nothing for me. If it had not been for the money you lent me I should have been in a sad taking.'[33]

Daniel did not really see why this large and tiresome burden should be his. To McCabe he expressed his opinion. 'It is a maxim universally allowed that a man who is unfaithful to his King and country cannot prosper. This has been realised in respect to my wretched brother Arthur possessed of above £1500 a year Estate and a fifth son; it is all going to decay.'[34] However, he did what he could. Arbitration was agreed between Roger and Arthur but William the nephew was very aggressive about the mortgage. As McCabe pressed Daniel for payment, William asserted that his claim preceded McCabe's. In July 1808 Daniel put Arthur's estate on the market and promised that as soon as the £5,000 owed to William was paid, the debt to McCabe should also be settled.[35]

Unfortunately, meanwhile, McCabe had crossed the Atlantic and visited Thomas Addis Emmet in New York.[36] Emmet's opinion of O'Connor had fixed into a furious hatred and distrust. McCabe now became far more anxious about repayment. In early 1809, back in London and about to emigrate to the USA, he lodged a letter of Attorney for the sum of £4,394 and empowered Thomas McCabe to prosecute O'Connor for its recovery.[37] Daniel struggled on. He needed Arthur's letters to validate the sale, McCabe wanted them as proof of debt. Their correspondence grew more acrimonious.[38]

Arthur, having received McCabe's money in 1807, was able to buy the estate on which he had set his heart. Le Château de Bignon had been the property of Mirabeau. Since the great man's death in 1791, it had had several owners. The French economy had been in a critical state for decades. Land prices were low. The confiscations of the revolutionary years and the turmoil of government had also cut property values while causing a wide change in land ownership. As in Ireland, one of the great fears accompanying each convulsion in government was that land settlements would be overturned. The returning exiles attempted to reclaim confiscated estates but many had been broken up and bought by farmers. Church lands too had been confiscated. Mirabeau's estate was for sale at the bottom of the market.

Bignon is a small village near Montargis in the Loiret. It is some 100 kilometres south of Paris. The river Betz flows through Bignon to join the Loing, which enters the Seine at nearby Fontainbleau. Like that of the Paris basin, the soil is rich and deep. Large stands

of forest include trees of great height. The chateau was a fine seventeenth-century building in which Mirabeau had been born. With
its tall windows, end turrets and pointed roof, standing in parkland
with mature trees, it was an imposing gentleman's residence. This
was no farmhouse.

Once he felt sure of securing the property, O'Connor was free
to marry. Arthur and Eliza were wed on his forty-fourth birthday,
4 July 1807, at the mayor's office of the first arrondisement in
Paris.[39] Eliza had turned seventeen that April and was a 'fine,
sprightly animated young girl'.[40] Emmanuel Grouchy was at the
wedding. Sophie's sister Charlotte and her husband Pierre Cabanis
had introduced O'Connor to the family. Sophie's biographer
described the bridegroom as 'un grand rouquin corpulent, aux
epaules larges, aux longs favoris, aux yeux malicieux' – 'a large, stout
redhead, with broad shoulders, long side-whiskers and mischievous
eyes'.[41] Jovial, he loved to laugh and to make others laugh. He was
generous and a 'bon vivant'. Miles Byrne saw the couple soon after
their marriage and thought them 'a very handsome pair'. He
thought O'Connor had 'very distinguished manners'.[42]

Six months later, they were installed in the château at Bignon.
Eliza's mother was in Paris, in an all but marital relationship with
Fauriel, a distinguished intellectual and friend of Benjamin
Constant. The O'Connors were in constant touch with Sophie and
frequently visited her in Paris.

Arthur took his bride to the estate at Bignon with enormous joy
and satisfaction. After everything he had lost, he now began a new
life as proprietor of a French estate with an intelligent girl as his
wife. She carried a name reverberant with everything O'Connor
admired and believed in. He added this name to his own, becoming General Arthur Condorcet O'Connor.[43] Among a new circle of
friends, liberal men and women of letters, he had at last arrived in
his chosen milieu. He had a General's salary and an estate near Paris
with historic connections.

His Irish friendships and rivalries continued. The life of his
family in Ireland moved on. In 1811 Lord Longueville died and as
expected, left Arthur nothing. The Longfield estates went to
Longueville's cousins and the title died out.[44] By 1811, Roger

O'Connor was petitioning the government for compensation for Connerville, which he claimed soldiers had seriously damaged.[45] The house was falling into serious disrepair if not ruin. Roger moved to Dangan Castle in County Meath. He said he needed a suitable house in which to receive Napoleon.[46] Dangan was partially burned in 1809. Roger then attempted to claim for it on a recent insurance policy.

In 1812 Roger indulged in his most famous exploit, robbing the Galway mail coach.[47] With several men from his estate, they stopped the coach on its way to Ballinasloe the night before the horse fair. Blunderbusses and pistols made the highwaymen formidable, they shot the guard and stole the mail. Roger shared out all the bank notes contained in the post, together with the passengers' money. They each got about £500. Sir Francis Burdett had remained a loyal friend to Roger since Arthur introduced them in 1796. He came over and testified for Roger who was acquitted. Later, Roger let it be known that he had robbed the coach to regain embarrassing love letters of Burdett's.

In the United States, the republican Irish were becoming a clearly defined community. Glad to be away from Bonaparte's France, they inter-married and began to prosper. Emmet never softened towards O'Connor. In 1805 he wrote to Robert Simms in Belfast, complaining of O'Connor's willingness to make terms with Bonaparte. Emmet suspected that O'Connor would, 'I am convinced, be selected under the auspices of the Protecting Country to be a greater man than Schimmelpennick is likely to be in Holland, and to revive the ancient title of O'Connor, King of Ireland'.[48]

Cuming wrote to Simms from New York to mention O'Connor's marriage but expressed no antagonism.[49] Extracts from the *Press* had been published in Philadelphia in 1802, showing O'Connor's role in the paper in a positive light. The poisoned relationship between O'Connor and Emmet was not the only one among the once United Irishmen. There were also divisions among the Irish in New York. Cuming agreed with Simms that these rifts were regrettable.[50] With time, the old comrades grew further apart, divisions widened. Many were bitter at the failed rebellion.

Sometimes, that bitterness crept into their friendships. As they settled to their new lives, they did their greatest service to history by writing accounts of the United Irish movement. Neilson's account was published in 1802. McNeven published *Pieces of Irish History* in 1806. Emmet's son later wrote two works on the subject.

O'Connor remained in France. The intellectuals who inspired him were European and he showed less interest in the development of the new democracy in America. At Bignon he became a family man.

---------- *Chapter 18* ----------

MARRIED LIFE AT BIGNON

'The delicacy that forms the charm of the marriage union'[1] seems to have come easily to Arthur O'Connor. As Benjamin Constant noted, he had a light touch in humour, a subtle wit. Despite his analytical mind, despite his temper, he had emotional sensitivity and subtlety. Arthur was a devoted husband to his young wife. The year after their marriage she gave birth to a son, Arthur. Two years later a second son, Daniel, was born. A third surviving son was born in 1817 and named George.

Eliza took her husband's religion and became a Protestant. Their beliefs and practice were personal, Arthur had no time for sects or dogma. On Christianity he consulted the teachings of Jesus. The children were given a liberal education and taught the values of honesty and self-appraisal which Arthur's mother had taught him. Eliza had been brought up by Sophie, who had abandoned her parents' devout Catholicism as a young adult. Sophie had taught Eliza contemporary ideas and her daughter brought up her children on the same principles. Eliza was a straightforward character, influenced by the strong personalities of her mother and husband, as well as by the legend of her father. But she had her own views and could be stubborn.

Eliza spoke to her children in French, their father talked to them in English. The language of the family was both, but the household naturally operated in French. The children's tutors, the maids, gardener and farm labourers spoke to Arthur in their local dialect. For many years, O'Connor did not trust himself to write in French. His letters to officials, dignitaries and even close associates would be written by a secretary or translator, then signed by

O'Connor. He had been in France a long time before documents in French appeared in his handwriting.

He was 45 when Eliza's first child was born. When later, Arthur wrote to his eldest son, 'the love I bear you is as strong as the heart of a father can feel for his child',[2] there was no exaggeration.

Bignon was a wonderful environment for the growing boys. Their father put his considerable energy into the management of his estate. Much of the land was arable when he bought it, cultivated on a two-year rotation of wheat, with oats or barley. No potatoes had been grown. He soon changed that, introducing break crops and keeping cattle. The livestock produced manure which was used on the arable fields. The cereals became more productive and his neighbours took notice. He instigated the planting of lucerne, clover, sainfoin, vetches, turnips, potatoes and beetroot. The crops did well, yields increased and the value of land rose steadily. When he bought it, his estate was 1,000 acres. In 1812 he bought another 100 acre farm, planted half with acorns and half with artificial grasses as a green manure, followed by cereals. Over the years he added more land. At the end of his life, the estate had doubled in size and the land was worth ten times what he originally paid for it. He was scornful of large proprietors who thought it unworthy of a gentleman to be economical. 'Nothing,' he wrote, 'is so expensive as family pride.'[3] His style was based on political economy. The land was in good heart and the income rising. His household was comfortable and well provided for.

Eliza was joint heir, with her mother, to her father's estate.[4] Sophie had been able to reclaim some of her husband's property soon after his death. Under Napoleon, compensation was offered for the remainder. The issue was not closed. In 1843, the O'Connors were still writing to officials regarding Condorcet's estate.[5] Confiscations were an ongoing issue for governments in France. The date of Condorcet's death was contested because he had been found dead in custody and because the dates in the Republican calendar still caused confusion in public records.[6]

The capital from McCabe and that realised from O'Connor's various small land-holdings in Ireland purchased the Bignon estate. Compensation from government was paid to Eliza with which the

O'Connors bought adjoining land.[7] The estate was productive. Some income reached him from Hugh Bell and General O'Connor had his army salary. They could keep up Bignon and live in some comfort.

The boys learnt the classical languages, mathematics, European literature and history. When their parents went to Paris, they showed off their skills by writing to them in Greek and 'Carissima mater' to demonstrate the Latin. In a style of English which showed all the florid formality of the age, young Arthur wrote, 'for me, my ever dearest Mother, your birthday is the brightest of the year. Nature seconding my wishes, is in all her charms'.[8]

Young Arthur was fourteen when he wrote, '... if the time appears to you and Papa extremely long, it does also appear equally long to every one of us and it is with the greatest pleasure we learned yesterday, by Papa's letter, that he thought he would be able to determine his departure in a day or two.' The boys had been read-ing Voltaire and the *Odyssey*. Young Arthur's written English has some stumblings. Even though he spoke the language with his par-ents, his education was mostly in French. Famous texts and much of his parents' library were in the language of the country. When his grand-mother was ill in Paris, young Arthur worried that maman passed her time 'most disagreeably and extremely tristly'.[9]

George was much younger than his brothers. When Papa went away to Paris on business, the older boys reported to their father for him. 'George sends you and Maman his love, he is as gay as a lark and is very well but sometimes he put himself in a wrath and tells everyone he will throw his soup in their face but then Mr Monthus sends him out of doors and it is soon over.' The boy reported on the farm as well, the Rousillon clover had been sown.[11]

The children grew into lively boys. When young Arthur was seventeen and Daniel fifteen, George only eight, their father repri-manded them.

My dear children,

I cannot express to you the affliction it has caused me to learn that I had scarce left you when your conduct towards one another and towards your mother has forced her to forbid you her room. What a poignant affliction for a father that loves his children to see that they cannot be one instant alone without dispute and discord ... after looking into my conduct towards you and into the inmost recess of my heart to see if I had ever been wanting in love towards you, I cannot conceive how I have merited that you should do so little to make me happy.

He particularly wants them to respect their mother and states that 'the children that in quitting the state of infancy and entering on the state of men cannot render themselves amiable to parents that love them as yours do you, will never be either loved or respected by the world'.[11]

He had been remonstrating with them on and off for years. Young Arthur had written 'a mon cher papa', five years earlier, to say 'I am very sorry to have given you so much pain. I will make all my efforts in future never to be headstrong any more; for I see that obstinacy is very bad and unreasonable, and so I have resolved to break myself of it'.[12]

Generally, the O'Connors were warm in their affections. 'My dearest boys,' wrote their father in 1826, 'the presence of your dear mother has entirely cured me, the fever left me from the moment she came. I now require but a few days to prepare for my departure to you. Adieu my beloved children, ever and ever your loving and affectionate father and friend, A.C. O'Connor.'[13]

Eliza's letters to her sons were more practical, concerned with their health, education and transport. Her large, elegant handwriting showed on the folded letters brought to Bignon and later followed them when they went to tutors in Paris. She was direct both in opinions and regarding her emotions. Less volatile than her husband, she had her own firmness of character. She also learnt to manage his changeable temperament.

Their life at Bignon was comfortable and safe. Eliza's relatives were also Arthur's friends. In 1808 Arthur had lost a close friend when Pierre Cabanis died. In Paris, they frequently visited Sophie de Condorcet at the Grande rue Verte. The three boys, her only grand-children, were fond of their 'cher maman Condorcet'.[14] They sent little notes to Eliza, to ask her help in getting a birthday present for their grandmother. When Sophie became ill in 1822, they were very upset and worried. Was maman Condorcet getting better, would their mother soon be coming home?

Arthur kept up a long correspondence with Volney. The O'Connors often invited the Volneys to stay. Warm messages were sent back and forth between the wives.[15] O'Connor records a conversation regarding the French acceptance of priests. The anti-clericalism of the revolutionary years had soon worn off. Both Volney and O'Connor deeply distrusted the French clergy, considered them very corrupt. 'I have it from the lips of Volney, his conversation on this subject with Bonaparte. On seeing Bonaparte bring back the priests, he observed to him he did not know the men he was bringing to power, to which [Bonaparte] answered "how will you that I can govern men if I have not the priests to stultify them?".'[16]

O'Connor received a new overture from the Emperor in 1811 when Bonaparte decided on another invasion of Britain. He asked Henri Clarke, Duc de Feltre to get the opinion of O'Connor and the other Irish on the prospects for an invasion. General Arthur wrote Napoleon a careful report of eight pages, 'a sa Majeste L'Empereur et Roi'.[17] He rehearsed the grievances of Ireland, the severe deficiencies of government in that island and the Catholic issue. He said that if the expedition which 'Your Majesty prepared in 1804 had arrived in Ireland there is no doubt that it would have been received with joy and supported with ardour'.[18] But time had elapsed and the Irish had lost confidence in the French. It would be presumptuous to point out to His Majesty the strategic importance of Ireland in relation to England. Bonaparte was advised to establish new contacts with Ireland and to get an inside report.[19]

Napoleon told the Duc de Feltre, 'I have read with interest General O'Connor's letter.[20] This correspondence with Ireland must be established, it seems to me'. He was not averse to sending 30,000 men and 6,000 horses but his Ministers must determine the spirit of the country. An agent was to be dispatched. The agent reported more or less what the Emperor wanted to hear. If Ireland was to rise, county leaders must be appointed. Napoleon did not read this as discouragement and preparations continued. But in

1812, Napoleon marched on Moscow which was the beginning of his downfall. The long winter retreat, the desertion of his allies ended in 1814 with the fall of Paris to his enemies. Napoleon was deposed and Talleyrand became head of a provisional government. The British were determined to re-establish the French monarchy and Louis XVIII was brought back to Paris.

Arthur O'Connor was enraged. A British government imposing a King on Republican France, a King who believed in the old theory of divine right, was a goad to his temper beyond endurance. Also, O'Connor was put on half-pay.[21] He pressed for restoration of his salary, asked for a posting, suggested the National Guard in the Loiret. The Duc de Feltre gave him an excellent reference; O'Connor had been a leading MP and patriot in Ireland, had risked his life and left behind his Irish fortune. He had been awarded full pay even when not on active service as recompense. Berthier, now Prince of Wagram, was more cautious. Perhaps there were more notes on the file. Dalton confirmed that he had made the promise of a full salary to O'Connor on behalf of the government.[22]

Then, early in 1815, Bonaparte returned from Elba to France and marched north. On 19 March, Louis XVIII fled and Napoleon reached Paris. O'Connor, still in a temper, wrote to Bonaparte on 30 March, expressing his outrage that the English would use their wealth and power to reinstate a family that all France had rejected. 'At a moment like this, it is not enough merely to offer to serve your Majesty, I dare to demand the right to do so.' His language was as inflated as his temper. 'Having lost my country fighting the English for independence, I found a new country in France. Your immortal genius has need of support worthy of you ... will find it in the thousands of us who love liberty.' O'Connor will defend the independence of France and 'our sacred right to obey the leader of our choice'.[23] It sounded like a letter of deep loyalty. It was actually a cleverly worded assertion of the sovereignty of the people. Moreover, Napoleon would probably restore his full salary.

In June, Napoleon marched north to Waterloo. In July, Louis XVIII returned to Paris. O'Connor had several interviews with the Minister of War pressing now for naturalisation and the maximum pension. The King seemed inclined to agree, until his officers checked the files and discovered the letter to Napoleon during the 'usurpation'. For a few weeks, General Arthur was in a dangerous situation. The Minister advised the King to dismiss O'Connor entirely from the French service. After his written remarks, he could not hold a commission from His Majesty. An order was drawn up ordering him to leave France. The King did not sign it. O'Connor still had friends in positions of influence. The references he had received from the Duc de Feltre, from Berthier and Dalton gave a picture of O'Connor as an Irish patriot and a friend of France during the war with Britain. A report from the Ministry of War on 31 May 1816 secured his position. The King had received a report on Lt-Gen O'Connor and had decided that O'Connor should receive either half-pay or the maximum pension, whichever was more appropriate.[24]

His Majesty's reason for this decision was known only by the Minister but Lt-Gen O'Connor was therefore to be awarded the maximum pension, calculated on the basis of his retiring pay. He should also receive naturalisation. The pension was fixed at 6,000 francs a year.[25]

The other Irish officers had initially supported the Restoration but became suspicious of British influence and rallied to Napoleon during the Hundred Days. The Irish regiment was disbanded in September 1815. Several officers left for America.[26] O'Connor had been wise to press for a full French commission and for naturalisation. Other Irishmen were left with a very uncertain status.

After the fall of Napoleon, visitors from Britain and Ireland arrived once more in France. Sir Jonah Barrington, a colourful character, liberal MP and friend of the late Henry Sheares, arrived and contacted O'Connor.[27] He described the General as 'a remarkably strong-minded, clever man, with a fine face and a manly air. He had a great deal of the Irish national character, to some of the failings whereof he united some of its best qualities. I met him frequently and relished his company highly'.[28]

In 1815, Allen, who had stood trial with O'Connor at Maidstone and been acquitted, was arrested in France and ordered to leave the country.[29] O'Connor protested to the Duc de Feltre that Allen was worse treated in France than he had been in Kent.

Allen was released and allowed to retire to Tours on half pay.

Major William Corbet remained a close friend. Despite his military service, he received only a small pension. He and his brother spent several months 'on a visit to a common friend who lives in the country,' as he described his stay with the O'Connors at Bignon in 1818.

O'Connor's relationship with McCabe deteriorated. Still unable to resolve his affairs in Ireland, he could not pay off the outstanding debt. McCabe seems to have put a bond on him under Irish law, which further impeded the sale of Fort Arthur at Kinsale. When peace was made with Britain in 1814, O'Connor applied to travel to Ireland. Castlereagh was now British Foreign Secretary. He curtly refused.[30] After Waterloo and the peace settlement, an application was made for Madame O'Connor to visit Ireland. It was granted although the government wanted her carefully watched.[31] Eliza could not resolve the problem. Apart from the mortgage and McCabe's bond, Roger had swindled Arthur of both income and capital. He had made complications and evasions. Eventually they took the matter to court.[32]

The journey did have the benefit of introducing Eliza to other members of Arthur's family, his old friends and trustees. Later, their son Daniel went to Ireland annually and got to know his cousins well.[33] But the financial problems remained unsolved and Francis Burdett took Roger's part.[34] This caused Arthur great anguish, what could have so changed the affections of his once dear friend? Burdett saw Roger as a victim. Although he scolded him for his self-destructive behaviour, he also felt sorry for Roger and his family.[35] This was despite the fact that Roger was living, not with his wife and children, but with a Mrs Smyth at Dangan.[36] But Roger had charm, guile and many dependants. Perhaps Burdett had idealised Arthur too long and become correspondingly disillusioned.

Burdett visited Roger in 1817, when he testified for him regarding the Galway mail. Travelling in west Cork, he noted that the Irish were passionately fond of music. In the wild mountains, he passed some of the most pleasant days of his life with 'my companion young O'Connor ... his name was a passport to the inmost recesses of their cabins or caverns, and to intercourse void of all suspicions – many's the hour and night we passed in dance and merriment'.[37]

McCabe was a State Prisoner in Kilmainham in 1818.[38] The following year he got a court judgement against O'Connor in France. There was a sum of 5,000 francs outstanding which O'Connor was ordered to pay.[39] This he did in four annual instalments with interest. In 1820, McCabe was in custody in Scotland and in very poor health.[40] He died the following year and O'Connor settled the last of the debt with his daughter soon afterwards.

Later, O'Connor wrote to Madden the historian, that the French government had proved that McCabe was a double spy. He also claimed to have saved McCabe's life through the Duc de Feltre.[41] In 1803, Mrs McCabe had received Secret Service money for McCabe's subsistence but there is no record of any other payment.[42] In 1796, an informer had got information from McCabe but every leading United Irishman had unknowingly talked to informers. Perhaps the French were misinformed. Or perhaps O'Connor was embarrassed by his obligation to McCabe, felt that, by not discharging it dishonour or unmanliness reflected on him and repeated spiteful gossip to ease his sense of shame.

Arthur O'Connor was proud, emotional and easily wounded. His response was often anger. He considered himself of an equable temperament and, at home with his family, he was big-hearted, a loving husband and father. He had always got on well with his mother-in-law. Sophie was intellectual and agnostic, artistic and beautiful. Arthur had a great regard for her. In 1821 she became ill. She died in September the next year. Eliza had been with her mother often throughout her illness, although Fauriel shared her apartment. Sophie had inherited property from her father and husband although she was not wealthy. Her will left her estate to her daughter but there were other bequests. Fauriel was to take over the lease of Grande rue Verte, to receive 600 francs p.a. in perpetuity and 12,000 p.a. for his lifetime.[43] There were also bequests to employees and friends.

Fauriel visited the O'Connors. In Eliza's room they discussed the legacy. Fauriel demanded that a sum should be invested in government stocks sufficient to pay the 12,000 francs. Arthur remarked there was no certainty of finding enough in the estate to satisfy his demand. Fauriel must realise that a daughter's rights had priority over all others. O'Connor believed Sophie's estate had been pilfered during her illness. Fauriel said that the lawyer had given him a package containing the items alluded to. The interview ended without resolution.[44]

O'Connor wrote to Sophie's solicitors, who corresponded with Fauriel.[45] There was an unpleasant exchange of letters with O'Connor, who referred to the day when the legacy of 12,000 francs was ruled out, Sophie's note on the matter and her conversation with her friend Madame Lasteyrie. For two weeks, Eliza was prevented from seeing her mother and during that time, Sophie's will had been changed.[46]

The will was resolved at last. Sophie had left pieces of furniture to her son-in-law and grandchildren. Much later, Fauriel deposited the correspondence among literary letters he gave to L'Institut de France.

After two decades of war, peace had been established. Contact with Ireland became easier. Roger had left County Meath after his trial in 1817. He built himself a cottage on his land at Connerville. The mansion was almost derelict. In 1822 Roger published *The Chronicles of Eri* which claimed to be the history of the 'Gael Sciot Eri or Irish people', translated by the author from manuscripts in the Phoenician dialect of the Scythian language. Roger became increasingly eccentric. His children had grown up. General Arthur hardly knew his nieces and nephews in Ireland. Now they were marrying and starting families of their own.

But the important news from Ireland was the pressure for Catholic emancipation. The lawyer and Kerryman Daniel O'Connell was starting to make a name for himself.

Chapter 19

A MAN OF AFFAIRS IN FRANCE

The Christian religion consisted in loving our neighbour but both Protestants and Papists have reversed it by making it consist of mutual rancourous hatred. This papal dogma has brought the Catholics to maintain that the land of Ireland is their exclusive property and all others are intruders. By this a Barnacle or Kenmare of English birth are Irishmen and I, O'Connor am a Saxon.[1]

As the Restoration showed its character in France, General Arthur saw the ideas of the Enlightenment compromised, the principles of the Revolution struggle to survive. In 1815, a royalist Chamber of Deputies was elected; the long struggle for the constitution of France began again. Four French monarchs would reign before a brief Republic at the end of Arthur O'Connor's life. The efforts of the Catholic church to reassert its position were not welcome to him. Secondary education had been radically modernised in the early days of the Revolution. Under Napoleon, the system was consolidated with the title of the Imperial University. Primary education had not been revised, was generally done by Catholic teaching orders. Old liberals like Lafayette were active in encouraging a system of primary education, lay taught and open to more children. Louis XVIII died in 1824 and under Charles X the church began to gain ground. The Abbé de Lamennais was prominent among those clerics calling for suppression of the Imperial University. Lamennais was much influenced by Daniel O'Connell. The Kerryman had been given a Catholic education in France and a legal one in London before becoming a barrister in Ireland. His growing reputation as the first Irish Catholic MP, then as leader of the Repeal Association, aroused mixed feelings in O'Connor. He had risked everything for Catholic emancipation and reform. While he was reviled, another man pushed those through. O'Connor's contemporaries, fellow MPs in 1790, Arthur Wellesley and Robert Stewart were in power. The former was Duke of Wellington, the latter, Viscount Castlereagh, was Foreign Secretary. And O'Connell, the 'Liberator', undisputed leader of nationalist Ireland, was supported by a 'Catholic rent' collected by parish priests. These were not the terms on which O'Connor would have wished for political progress. The laurels had passed to others, the victory went to the old order. For O'Connor, this was bitter.

O'Connor suspected the Irish Protestant clergy just as violently. Still supported by tithes paid by the Catholic masses, to him they were the 'Protestant corporate priesthood'.[2] As for Rome, he thought the Jesuits had usurped papal power and that the Roman Catholic church undermined proper national governments. The Catholic priesthood was opposed to progress of knowledge and liberty, to equality and industry, to all the sciences. The Protestant priesthood upheld an aristocratic elite in Britain. In O'Connor's opinion 'the truest friends to Catholic emancipation were those who sought it, in the conviction that it was the only means of freeing the papists from bigotry, superstition and the tyranny of their priests, and enabling them to assert liberty and maintain it'.[3] In France, O'Connor was editor of *Journal de la Liberté Religieuse*.

'To God only, man gives his account.'[4] For O'Connor, if people abandoned their reason, the Republic could not exist.[5] How tirelessly his father-in-law, whom he revered but never knew, had worked for human reason, both as an academic and as a legislator. Now, here was the Catholic church in France trying to get control of education and O'Connell in Ireland condemning undenominational universities as 'godless', opposing mixed education. Arthur O'Connor was to live through more bitter disappointments.

In the early days of the Restoration, he was vulnerable. Reprisals were common against supporters of Napoleon during the Hundred Days. He was lucky to stay in France, much more so to keep his pension. Gradually the liberals were elected to the Chamber, Lafayette took a seat in 1818. O'Connor, having secured an income and naturalisation, lived a quiet life with his family at Bignon. At times, they kept an apartment in Paris, in the rue de Bac and later in rue de Tournan. Arthur visited Paris to arrange business with his banker, M Pillet-Wills at the Boulevard Poisonière. In Paris, he met his friends, bought books and kept in touch with politics.[6]

His attention was focussed on his wife and sons. 'We will chat round the snug fire of your dear mother and in the society [of] the dearest and nearest to my heart, I will enjoy better health and spirits'.[7] He took an active part in his children's education, bought them fine guns when they were older so that they could learn to shoot game in the forests of the estate. He sent the two older boys to tutors in Paris. They were keen students, eager to please and did commissions for their parents, visiting family friends, buying and delivering books.

With the peace and since Eliza's visit to Ireland, the O'Connors were in contact with their relations in Ireland. Arthur and his brother Daniel were on reasonable terms. Daniel's home was in Bayswater, Middlesex, but he was frequently in Bristol where he may have retained commercial interests from his ancestors' shipping business. Possibly Arthur received some benefit from these too. Daniel's son, Daniel, moved back to Ireland and in 1824 he began the construction of Manch House on the western-most portion of the old Conner estate near Ballineen.[8] This young Daniel Conner and Roger's son Feargus, came to visit their uncle in France in 1826 but did not impress him. First of all, they brought quantities of Irish butter, but a posset of onions cooked in it gave the General acute gastritis. Also, as he confided to his eldest son, still with tutors in Paris, 'your cousins pass all their time at Chariots Billiard table which is a miserable way of passing their lives, but I am not their tutor. Feargus,' he went on, 'is going with us in his way to London to make himself a lawyer. I do not think he will ever have application, entre nous, they are both terribly ignorant.' The young men did, however, endear themselves to their uncle by shooting the rats.[9]

Feargus did become a lawyer and, in 1832 MP for County Cork. He joined Daniel O'Connell's movement for Repeal of the Union, pressing him to propose it in the Commons in 1834 where it was defeated. Feargus had many of his father's skills and weaknesses. He went on to become leader of the Chartists, campaigning for one man one vote, peasant proprietorship and other egalitarian causes. An extreme radical on the left of the Chartists, Feargus became angrily opposed to O'Connell. To Sturge, a Quaker and more right-wing Chartist, O'Connor strongly criticised his nephew. Feargus became unstable, had a fit in the Commons and was pronounced insane in 1852. He died and was buried in London; a crowd of 40,000 crowded round the graveyard to honour the fiery champion of the people.

His brother, Roger's third son, Francis Burdett O'Connor had gone off to South America in 1819 to fight for Bolívar. After the liberation of Bolivia, he became Minister of War and Chief of the General Staff.[10] One of his descendants was a diplomat in the Bolivian Embassy in London.

Arthur's son, Daniel, entered the Faculty de Sciences at the Académie de Paris in 1827.[11] The elder boys were growing up. Arthur O'Connor felt the time had come to write about his struggle for Irish independence. He started the long and difficult task of writing his memoirs in 1828.[12] It was a bequest to his sons, a justification and a record for history.[13] The manuscript was addressed to his eldest son.

> My beloved Arthur, the hope that these memoirs of my life, which has been so checkered and much of it passed in important transactions, may be useful to you and your dear brothers is the principal object to induce me to write them; but there is another inducement: some of those important transactions were known only to General Hoche and to me. He is no more, they now rest solely with me and yet without them, the history of these events must remain incomplete or, as I see by the histories which have been written, be given incorrectly.[14]

O'Connor chronicled his family tradition, his childhood, education and youth. He started a new draft. As for many writers, it was difficult to give a single narrative without explaining Irish history, Britain's role and the religious divisions. It was difficult to be concise. He had talked to his sons about Irish history many times and reminded them of those stories as he wrote.

He had not reached the point at which he had left parliament and joined the United Irishmen when his work on the memoirs was interrupted by a terrible loss. In 1829, at the age of 21, his son Arthur died. Tuberculosis was rife and seems to have been the cause of death. O'Connor had married late and revelled in his family. The loss of his eldest son hit him like a rock in the chest. His own constitution had withstood shock, illness and imprisonment. Yet his son was dead almost before manhood. Eventually he recovered his spirits but it was twenty years before he returned to the memoirs.

The last bequest that O'Connor had received from his father was of land in east Cork adjoining Roger's and divided from it by a small tributary of the Bandon river named the Blackwater. Arthur's land was on the western bank. The Blackwater flows south-east before entering the Bandon river. Roger had the brilliant idea of making the river flow directly south, thereby appropriating a large area of Arthur's land. He built a bridge for the diverted river.[15] Arthur heard of this scheme and determined to stop it.

His son Daniel was a sensible young man. His father began to discuss matters of business with him, the estate at Bignon and the ongoing problems of his property in Ireland. Eliza made another journey to Ireland in 1830 and Daniel went with her.[16] Arthur's estate at Ballinroe near Kinsale was still encumbered. He had inherited parcels of land and property in west Cork and Cork city which he had gradually sold, the first during his incarceration at Fort George.[17] Like the majority of Irish land holdings, there were inherited claims on Arthur's property from mortgages, dowries and bequests to widows and daughters. In his case, Robert's daughters and Feargus had an interest.[18] Eliza and Daniel were able to pay these claims and cleared one part of the encumbrance.

George, still a schoolboy, visited London with his mother and stayed for a few months to learn English while she went on to Dublin. In 1830 George was with tutors in Paris.[19] His father was often in the capital. The political situation in France was not stable. Charles X was inclined to be autocratic, the constitution had not been settled and the Revolution remained unfinished, its form unresolved. O'Connor, determined to secure his position and with an eye to a new chance, applied to his friend General Dalton in 1828 for another reference.[20] Dalton rehearsed his own and O'Connor's distinguished careers and 'certified' that Arthur O'Connor had been promised that the salary of his rank 'would be constantly reserved and that, as a poor recompense' for all he had lost.[21]

In July 1830 Charles X was dethroned by a coup d'état. Amid rioting in Paris, Lafayette once more became Commander-in-Chief of the National Guard. Like parallel mirrors, the events of the past 40 years kept repeating. Charles X's cousin, the Duc d'Orléans, became King as Louis-Philippe I. General Arthur O'Connor, now aged 67, although on the French files he was 63, thought it worthwhile to try for his military rights. Lafayette was older but in a key position. He gave O'Connor an excellent character. 'Independent of my personal friendship with him and my high regard for him, I would like to give witness to his public life.' Influential in the Irish parliament, one of the chief patriots of Ireland, 'under the uniform of the Volunteers of Ireland he appeared with his friend Hutchinson at my army headquarters in 1792'. Hutchinson abandoned republican sympathies and became a British General in Egypt. 'O'Connor continued his patriot career and became one of the principal leaders of the party which wanted republican liberation, the alliance with France.' He had been the victim of British censure and imprisoned; Charles Fox stood witness for him. In France he was the official consultant for all Irish affairs during the war.[22]

It was a glowing reference and O'Connor added to it copies of those given by de Feltre, Wagram and Dalton, together with new ones from Lt-Gen Lamarque and Admiral Truguet. 'O'Connor showed courage and devotion to France.' O'Connor was a popular officer, regarded as the man who should be Irish commander-in-chief or lead the independence movement. With these, he applied for full naturalisation, to regain the rank of Major-General and full pay for that rank from June 1816. It was a bold demand but it was refused.[23]

In 1831, he published a pamphlet entitled *A Letter to General Lafayette, on the causes which have deprived France of the advantages of the Revolution of 1830*. He discussed the way in which France might settle her constitution. The choices were the old feudality, the English system or the French constitution of 1791. The revolution of 1688 gave the English the right to choose their representatives and created, in theory, a just balance of power. However, O'Connor believed the Executive in Britain had usurped powers of appointment and that primogeniture created great fortunes which could buy votes. The middle classes were tenants of these wealthy eldest sons and indebted to them. He did believe that 'England has had 143 years possession of constitutional liberty ...'

'Montesquieu said that the English monarchy was a Republic; and Aristotle proclaimed, 2200 years before him, that a Monarchy in the general interest was a Republic ... The nation is aware that Government in the general interest can be presided over by an hereditary King, as well as by an annual Consul, as at Rome, or a president for four years, as in America ... A truly great genius would have seen that he lived in an age when no Government could have stability, if it were not founded on the principle of *industry* and *public utility*. This principle has introduced amongst us a science unknown to our fathers, which is to the body politic what matrimony is to the human body.' 1830 had given France another chance to establish a sound democratic constitution but, once more, those with vested interest gained control. Liberty must stand on equality.

In the same year, Pamela FitzGerald died. She had grown very plump but kept her pretty femininity.[24] She died a devout Catholic. Her daughter Pamela had deep suspicions of Arthur O'Connor who she believed was 'not true' to her father. She received this impression both from her mother and her aunt Sophia, Lord Edward's sister.[25] The FitzGeralds blamed Lord Edward's fate on his co-conspirators.[26]

Lady Lucy Foley never for one moment entertained doubts of Arthur. She had the generous nature and quick affections of Lord Edward and kept her warm friendship with Arthur. In the year of Pamela's death she wrote to Lady Bute of Lord Edward, how he was thirty-one before he met the 'twin of his soul', Arthur O'Connor.[27] The first biography of Lord Edward, by Thomas Moore, was published in 1831. Lady Lucy did not approve of it; she thought it an inaccurate portrait of her brother.[28] The book treated O'Connor with respect but gave only a brief description of his role in Lord Edward's life.

In London, a Whig government was in power and with the help of Sir John Bowring, O'Connor at last got permission to go to Ireland. It was 35 years since he had sailed from Dublin as a prisoner. In 1834, he was a respectable gentleman of 71. His brother Robert was dead. Roger died that summer. He was living in a cottage at Ovens, near Ballincollig with a local girl who he called his 'Princess of Kerry'.[29] Roger was buried, at his request, in the friary of Kilcrea, in the ancient tomb of the McCarthys of Muskerry. The ancient Lords of Munster, the McCarthys were claimed as ancestors by Roger through their marriage to O'Connor Kerry. He died a Catholic.[30]

'Roger was greatly honoured about Kilcrea. His appearances and the constitutional generosity ... and impulsive honour of his character together with this question of a kingly descent formed the ... ideal of a gentleman in the mind of the peasantry', a contemporary observed to Dr Madden. By some deranged, perhaps drunken path, Roger had found his way back to the world of his forefathers.[31]

Ten years before, Arthur had filed a bill against Roger for misappropriated funds. Nothing had been paid.[32] As Roger's sense of reality unravelled, his land holdings were sold to pay the bills. Connerville was now a semi-derelict mansion but still in his name. Roger's affairs were in chaos. Arthur had stopped the diversion of the Blackwater. He sold his interest in the Manch land to his nephew. The little arch built by Roger for the diverted water had no purpose. Thereafter it was known as Idle Bridge.[33] There seem to have been plans to build a house for General Arthur at Manch. A well there is known as the General's well.[34]

His son Daniel was spending long periods of time in Ireland. They had found a buyer for the estate at Ballinroe. Part of it, Old Court was on a lease for three lives, indefinitely renewable. It had last been renewed in 1813 by Francis Burdett and Roger, on Arthur's behalf. This lease and all the lands of Ballynedown orte and orse, Ballynedon, Ballyroe, Ballyrea, Fort Arthur and

Kilcoleman were sold to James Sandys for £16,400 sterling. General Arthur paid off the remainder of the mortgage to his nephews.[35]

The government allowed the O'Connors to spend six months in Ireland in 1834. They visited old friends. John Waller was delighted to receive them.[36] They also visited Standish O'Grady, now Lord Guillamore, who had married Katherine Waller. After the three friends had travelled in Europe together as young men, O'Grady had gone on to become Attorney-General and had been one of the prosecuting counsel in the trial of Robert Emmet. He was known for his wit and learning. How curiously their lives had diverged and begun to run back together. Arthur and Eliza were staying at Lota Park near Cork when Katherine Guillamore wrote to say how sorry she was that they would not see each other again before the O'Connors returned to France, a letter had been delayed. Was there a hint of guile in Lady Guillamore's 'we regret that we have not had full enjoyment of your and dear Mrs O'Connor's company and are sorry to think we have been separated by a short distance when we might have passed the time in friendly intercourse'? But she expected 'a visit from your son before he leaves Cork, all here will be happy to see him on his own account, doubly so on yours'.[37]

O'Connor visited Daniel O'Connell at Derrynane.[38] They must have spoken freely to each other and got each other's true measure for O'Connor became violently hostile to O'Connell.[39] However passionately both men attempted to serve Ireland, their views and methods could not be more dissimilar. O'Connell reminded General Arthur of the gentlemen of the Catholic Association whom he had found so difficult in 1797. A lover of symbolism, monarchy and uniforms, the Liberator was the antithesis of O'Connor's rationalist ideals. Besides, O'Connell openly criticised the United Irishmen. Although he spoke well of the brotherhood of creeds, united in one Ireland, O'Connell condemned violent insurrection. He embodied the Gaelic Catholic gentry. Like O'Connor, his ancestors were Kerry clansmen who had made their money in shipping; O'Connell's uncle by the smuggling trade to France. But O'Connor was a Protestant republican, O'Connell a Catholic monarchist. And Arthur O'Connor was bitter at the criticism of his youthful comrades, their sacrifice. He fumed over 'the vile calumnies of O'Connell, his jealousy of everyone who serves Ireland disinterestedly'.[40] What would O'Connell be without the United Irishmen, he could not be a priest or even a hedge-school teacher? 'Ireland had lain for a century and more under the imputation of base, cowardly slaves that had not the spirit to vindicate her rights. It was imperatively essential we should show our oppressors we had the spirit to reclaim our rights[41] ... This we did, and by so doing we have convinced England it is impossible to longer withhold Catholic emancipation and reform. The United Irish will live in history as the fathers of Irish liberty when O'Connell will appear as their calumniator.'[42]

Dr Richard Madden was a physician who worked all over the British Empire from Cuba to Australia in the 1830s and 1840s. In 1837, he started compiling material for his account of the United Irishmen, a chaotic and sometimes unreliable series of volumes produced in the 1840s. His archives became invaluable, since he corresponded with all the United Irishmen he could track down. O'Connor wrote to him at some length in 1841 and answered a questionnaire for Madden in 1843. '*The Dictionary Biographique des Contemporains* is a work so full of error that it has no species of credit.' He considered Gordon's account of the Rebellion the most reliable.[43] 'I am occupied with my memoirs but what you may write will not interfere with them. My memoirs will take in all I know of the Union from the beginning to the end; there is a wide field and room enough for all that wish to write on the subject.'[44]

A second tragedy struck Arthur and Eliza. Their youngest son George died in his late teens. They buried him, alongside his brother Arthur, in the park at Bignon.[45] O'Connor would follow his beliefs to the last, he wanted no church ceremonies. Bignon was the scene of their happiness as a family. To his remaining son Daniel, he made over some part of his invested wealth.

In 1839 the O'Connors visited Ireland again.[46] Despite a court judgement in his favour, Roger's debt to Arthur was still unpaid. He filed a new claim.[47] Connerville was finally sold to Mr Lysaght in 1841 for £3,200. Part of the property was owned by Mr Bernard who was bankrupt. The proceeds of sale cleared Roger's remaining debt to Arthur, whose son Daniel had been in Ireland most of that year and was a signatory to the deed.[48]

There was a more liberal administration at Dublin Castle and some progress had been made on tithes and poor relief. But the population was growing alarmingly, was over eight million, of whom two million subsisted on potatoes, grown on tiny plots of land rented year by year. Government reports warned constantly that these people lived on the edge of starvation. The system of land holding required thorough reform. Middle men drove up rents, bankrupt estates were so encumbered they could not be sold, entails locked up properties. Everything that O'Connor knew of enterprise and economy raged in frustration. Changes in the Poor Law and Corporations would not produce wealth. The efforts of Whig governments and O'Connell's pressure for Repeal had not produced any economic change in Ireland. It had never been worse.

Nonetheless, there was a different style in Dublin. Lord Morpeth was Secretary and invited the O'Connors to dinner at the Lodge. Lord Edward's daughter was at Drumcondra but was not invited. She had doubts about O'Connor. Afterwards both she and Lord Morpeth received anonymous letters accusing them of dining with the betrayer of Lord Edward.[49]

O'Connor's wealth and lifestyle in France aroused suspicion in Ireland. Men whispered that he had been bought by the British government. The men of 1798 were disappointed men. To O'Connor, the use he made of his inherited resources was proper economy and enterprise. To many of his former comrades, with no inheritance and the bitterness of defeat, it was additional cause for mistrust. Throughout the nineteenth century, speculation continued over who had been the spies and informers, causing a hostile paranoia to fester.

Arthur O'Connor was too proud to be bought and was detested by British governments from Pitt to Peel. His reputation had suffered from the constant efforts of governments to denigrate him. The feuding between the once United Irishmen cast a shadow over his name in some circles. His irascibility, impatience and dominance alienated many.

When the Repeal Association published an address referring to the United Irishmen: 'as to 1798, we leave the weak and wicked men who considered force and sanguinary violence ... to the contempt and indignation of mankind',[50] the bitterness deepened. In April 1841 the New York Irish Repeal Association held a meeting at Tammany Hall and Robert Emmet, son of Thomas Addis, resigned as President amid angry scenes.[51]

O'Connor had no doubts about his ideals. He was a rationalist and republican. From childhood, he had studied modern sciences, of which economics and politics were so vital. Eliza was heir to her father's literary estate.[52] Between 1847-49 the *Oeuvres de Condorcet* were published by A. Condorcet O'Connor, Lt-Gen and M.F. Arago, permanent secretary of the Academy of Science in Paris. More complete than Sophie's edition of 1804, it contained the mathematical essays of Condorcet. O'Connor and Arago had researched the biographical essay and Eliza contributed personal detail.

O'Connor was working on a long treatise which was published in three volumes in 1848. *Monopoly: The Cause of all Evil* encompasses economics, social science and religion. 'The only difference I have been able to discover between the poor of England and of Ireland is, that the poor of the former can still descend lower, while the latter have long since arrived at the lowest stage of social life, where a farther descent is impossible.' The Industrial Revolution was well under way in England and O'Connor had been reading reports on the urban working class. He quotes M. Buret and the Commission of Physicians who reported on malignant fevers in the slums. Although the great famine had devastated Ireland from 1845-48, O'Connor does not specifically mention it. He may not have received reports of it in France before he delivered his manuscript, or he may not have known that it was any greater than the famine which had ravaged Ireland on and off throughout the century. In his view, urban poverty in England and rural poverty in Ireland were both the result of *Monopoly: The Cause of all Evil.*[53]

'The formation of poor laws on their true principles is perhaps the most difficult thing in the whole of economical science.' The poor relief had certainly failed in Ireland. Why, asked O'Connor, were there such numbers of poor when Britain had become so rich? Because land and resources were locked up by monopoly. It was inefficient. If land and capital were in more hands, far more wealth would be created. O'Connor was arguing for Smith's free trade. His concerns for the industrial working classes would echo throughout the nineteenth century.

In France, the laws of succession outlawed primogeniture. With much leeway, parents must divide their property. More people owned land, women owned property in their own right, new enterprises had started, prosperity was increasing. O'Connor attacked monopoly of power; and monopoly of thought. His target was aristocratical society on the one hand and the Jesuits on the other. He railed against confession. He believed it an intolerable intrusion, why should a priest hear from a woman the intimate secrets of her marriage? Confession creates an inappropriate intimacy between a celibate priesthood and women, even young girls. O'Connor approved of the Quakers but belonged to no sect. His religion was taken directly from the teachings of Jesus, considered in depth during his prison years. He had read and re-read the Gospels, suggested that certain passages were forgeries. He was scathing about church services: what had they to do with the teachings of Christ?

O'Connor admits the omnipotence of God but believes it too distant for man to appeal to or understand. That there is much suffering in the world, war and injustice; he cannot deny. This is not the presence of evil. Rather, as man progresses in knowledge, as society increases in equality, suffering will be reduced.

As an author, O'Connor tends to rant, then suddenly to jolt the reader with a lucid and original insight. His views connect two ages because he had lived so long. 'All men are created equal,' the Americans asserted in 1776. A century later, Victorian socialists struggled with urban slums. O'Connor's philosophy was rooted in the first, resonated with the second. He had missed the position of power for which he was well fitted. He never stopped reading and questioning. True to his principles, he would always challenge himself and others.

Of Arthur and Eliza's three sons, only Daniel was still living. He was a mild-tempered young man with pleasant manners. The intellectual interests of his parents and grandparents had made no especial impact on him. In 1843 he married Ernestine Duval de Fraville, from a conservative Catholic family. They bought a house at Bazoches, not far from Bignon. Arthur's health was not always good, he was 80 years old. But he was delighted to hear that Ernestine was pregnant.

---- Chapter 20 ----

MEMORIES

It is not from pride of family I mention my descent. I might say I have been a republican from my birth, I have no recollection from the dawn of my reason of ever having entertained other principles.[1]

Thomas Addis Emmet suspected O'Connor of ambitions to become King of Ireland. Napoleon had put General Bernadotte on the throne of Sweden, his relations on the thrones of Spain and Italy. Why not instate an O'Connor on the Irish throne? Arthur always said a French invasion of Ireland must be immediately followed by elections. He preferred an elected head of state, but he would have accepted constitutional monarchy. Government must be at the will of the people, that was the point of democracy. He would have stood for elections with his customary vehemence. He was certainly no regicide: 'what interest had I in the King's death?'[2] Emmet's fears were unfounded, O'Connor had no designs on a throne. If Bonaparte had foisted him onto the Irish as a monarch, he would have been insulted and furious.

He was conscious only of his ancestry and bloodline. O'Connor does concede that 'nothing is more natural, than that a man should feel pride from being the son of a man who had illustrated his name, from the virtues by which he rendered signal services to his country'. He was proud of O'Connor Kerry, he hoped his descendants would be proud of him.[3]

Daniel's wife Ernestine had conceived soon after their marriage. Although the young O'Connors lived a short distance from the château at Bignon, the General and his wife felt excluded from

269

Daniel's married life. Ernestine did not have an easy pregnancy. Eliza wrote to her son to reassure him that cholic would stop after the birth. 'The extreme directness of my character,' Eliza wrote, 'obliges me to tell you, that it was in my heart not to write to your wife, but to go and embrace your wife and the child,' after the birth. Eliza was worried that 'an invitation to come and see the old parents and introduce them to the child' might not be welcomed. To Ernestine, 'daughter and wife', Eliza wrote that 'all the calls that I had made on your heart since your marriage were useless'. Daniel was their only remaining son, yet his whole life seemed now to belong only to the family of his wife, 'while his respectable father and his mother (who solely alas compose all his family) would no longer be but the object of some official visits, as you would make to the most banal acquaintances'.[4]

Ernestine came from an aristocratic family. Eliza was concerned that O'Connor's life as a rebel who had suffered imprisonment was not acceptable to Ernestine and her relations. The letter must have touched Daniel and Ernestine. There was a change of mood. The young couple did not mean to be inattentive. The birth of their son Arthur caused joy and soon Eliza wrote, 'ma chere fille, I'm so happy you've had the baby and that you're well', and before long, 'we're pleased to hear from Daniel that you plan to visit us at Bignon. The good air of the country will be good for the baby'.[5]

Arthur's family were in Ireland. Eliza was an only child. Daniel was the only one of their sons to survive. On him and his children were focused all Arthur's hopes. He was 80 when his son married, had outlived most of his friends and all of his brothers, except Daniel the eldest, who survived to the great age of 94, only dying in 1848.[6] Starting a new life in France in his forties, General Arthur did not have the web of connections he would have had in his native country.

His family solicitor became an intimate friend. M. Isambert was counsellor at the court of appeal in Paris.[7] He dined with the O'Connors, knew the details of their financial plans, arranged the inheritance for Daniel and looked into the details of Condorcet's estate for Eliza. 'Madame,' he wrote to Eliza when he reported what he could discover in 1829, but by 1844 she was 'Madame et amie'.[8]

The railways were under construction and the O'Connors might invest in railway stock. Isambert was a gentleman and a Catholic, he discussed religion and philosophy with the ageing General, until he believed he understood his views.[9]

Arthur Condorcet O'Connor made his will. He had already given to Daniel half of his fortune. 'Everything that I own at the time of my death, whether in goods and chattels or in real estate, I bequeath to my dear wife.'[10] The property bought in his name with her indemnity money was to be entirely hers. All these properties were to be merged with the Bignon estate. They had made an agreement about furniture and effects in their marriage contract which she would now inherit. Eliza was also his residual legatee.

The reign of Louis-Philippe was punctuated by unrest and assassination. Instability and dissatisfaction put pressure on the King and his Ministers. In 1847 O'Connor presided over meetings for electoral reform in Montargis, the nearby town.[11] He had started a school in Bignon.[12] It was a common theme among the men of 1789 in France and of 1798 in Ireland that education was essential, as an end in itself and to fit people for voting. O'Connor's friend Lafayette had worked for this and Arthur was faithful to the principle, put it into practice at Bignon.

The pressure for electoral reform led to the deposition of Louis-Philippe in 1848. The Second Republic was proclaimed and for a brief period there was civil war in Paris, the workers manning the barricades. The bourgeoisie, however, had had enough of revolutions and the country people were alarmed. In December a right-wing Chamber was elected and Prince Louis-Napoleon, nephew and heir of Bonaparte, was elected President.

O'Connor was better loved by Bonapartists than by Bourbons. He wanted to assure Eliza's position and his descendants' inheritance. Daniel and Ernestine now had a second son, Ferdnand. O'Connor applied for full naturalisation and was granted it.[13]

The unfinished pile of papers in the library disturbed him. The past was full of pain and rage which he felt compelled to face. Eliza dreaded the memoirs.[14] When Arthur talked of them or worked on them, he became furious, distressed and impossible to calm. But he was determined. He owed it to Daniel to leave a complete record. He owed it to himself.

In 1849, he took up the story again. 'I come to present the case before a third generation who will judge us with the impartiality of men who live at a time when all the furious passions, all the violent prejudices are dead.'[15]

> In looking back upon the 86 years I have lived, I am led to agree with Solomon that all or nearly all is vanity. In 1784, was ever King or Queen more universally loved, revered, obeyed than were Louis XVI and Marie Antoinette. Yet in a few years after, was ever fall more ignominious. Then came their successors and each in turn passed under the axe of the Guillotine. Sudden fall attended the Directory. Then came Bonaparte, did ever the despotic will of one man rule so widely, was ever despot hurled from such a height to such a depth. With what exaltations did Louis XVIII mount his throne, was ever fall more humiliating than his on 20 March 1815? Then his brother's fall, the fall of Louis Philippe.[16]
>
> Who must not despise human greatness? Scenes looked back on from the eminence of an independent philosophical mind present a world more of headless creatures than of rational beings.[17]

Now he wrote with urgency and without digression. From time to time, he lifted his splendid head and gazed down the park. As his focus lengthened, the park became less distinct, his memories more real. From outside the library door, the sounds of his wife's voice reached him. Daniel's sons played outside in the sunshine, aged five and two, until Ernestine came calling them. She spoke to them in French. His grandsons heard very little English. Ernestine was conservative and Catholic. Her attitudes were difficult for her father-in-law to accept.

Arthur wrote of the campaign for reform, Fitzwilliam's recall, the defeat of Catholic emancipation. The United Irishmen re-invigorated in Belfast, Lord Edward and the journey to Switzerland, the meeting with Hoche: it all became vivid to him once more. He went into detail over Quigley's greatcoat at Maidstone, his training as a lawyer made him precise about evidence.[18]

Then the unbearable and the unthinkable happened. Daniel, aged 41, in the prime of his life, sickened. In 1851 he died. Arthur and Eliza stood together in the park at Bignon, with Ernestine and the two small boys. The casket was put into the vault where young Arthur and George were already buried.[19]

At the end of the year there was a coup d'état. Early in 1852 Louis-Napoleon was re-elected President with sweeping powers under a new constitution. At the end of the year, by a vote of the people, he became Emperor Napoleon III.

Arthur O'Connor never saw the Second Empire. He survived Daniel by one year. On 25 April 1852 at six o'clock in the morning, the old rebel died in his bed. Dr Beauregard was at the château, as was Isambert.[20]

He was buried with his sons. The household servants and farm labourers carried the coffin.[21] Arthur O'Connor had been mayor of Bignon. The Deputy mayor, the son of O'Connor's estate manager, spoke beside the tomb. He and his brother Etienne both knew the General well. M Isambert gave an address. There was only a small gathering of people: Eliza, Ernestine and the little boys, the servants and employees, a few local friends. Isambert pointed out that 'an entire people of 7-8 million souls would render their last homage', if O'Connor had not lost his native land fighting for civil liberties.

They should not worry that no minister of religion was present. O'Connor fought for Catholic emancipation and it was due to him that it was finally wrested from the English. He was not irreligious, he believed in a benevolent Providence.[22]

'Pray for this noble daughter of Condorcet who, at the age of seventeen years, consecrated her life to the happiness of this illustrious older man.'[23]

O'Connor had loved to employ the local people, said Isambert, he devoted the better part of his income to helping families by encouraging work.[24]

'Farewell, good citizen. Never have you belied your beliefs, never have you flattered the powerful. You were faithful, to the times, to the cause of your native land and to France, your adopted country.'[25]

The death of General Arthur Condorcet O'Connor was reported in the Dublin and London papers. He had outlived Daniel O'Connell. Ireland was in the shadow of famine and mass emigration. O'Connor seemed like a figure from a distant age. The *Illustrated London News* gave a warm verdict on 'this celebrated leading partisan of the Irish Rebellion of 1798, a man of daring yet chivalrously consistent spirit'. 'The Old Republican was true to his faith to the last.'[26]

> Had he lived in times more genial to his better feelings, he might, instead of being a rebel to England, have had the honours not of France, but of his own country, thick upon him, and might have added another hero to that glorious roll of warriors who have achieved the united greatness of the British Empire.[27]

Eliza applied for and received his military pension, due to her as his widow.[28] Unknown to her, a petition reached Isambert from Ireland via Dr Madden. A man there claimed to be Arthur O'Connor's son. Isambert replied that the documents he produced were not sufficient to prove his claim under French law.[29] Besides, the lawyer continued, O'Connor had been to Ireland, as had his wife and son, but this man never contacted them. A certificate from the General's brother, Roger, was the worst recommendation. In fact, he appeared to be the son of Daniel, the General's eldest brother and had taken that man's name. He produced no birth nor baptism certificate nor seemed sure where he was born. His early life was not compatible with the dates of O'Connor's captivity at Fort George. Isambert was acting on behalf of O'Connor's grandchildren and refused to put the claim forward.[30]

Eliza lived on for another seven years. She died on 7 April 1859 in Paris.[31] She was brought home to the château and buried, as her will requested, 'beside my husband in the park at Bignon'.[32]

Ernestine moved to Bignon and brought up her sons. A devout Catholic, she was horrified by the tomb in the grounds. A family vault was constructed in the Roman Catholic cemetery at the edge of the village. Ernestine had the five coffins taken for proper Christian burial in consecrated ground.

Arthur O'Connor's grandchildren grew up as French Catholics. Ferdnand became a Général de Division but did not marry. Arthur married Marguerite de Ganay and had two daughters. Marguerite was well-off and well connected. The old château, which had seen the birth of Mirabeau and the death of O'Connor, was dilapidated. In 1880, Marguerite had it demolished and a new château constructed in the style of the late nineteenth century. Her daughter married Count Francis de la Tour du Pin, whose son Patrice was a respected poet. Arthur O'Connor's descendants continue to live at Bignon.

Every man may look in the mirror and Arthur O'Connor frequently turned his penetrating gaze upon himself.

Was it I or was it Pitt, he asked himself? 'Either I have been the author of the greatest ... evil or ... it is Pitt.'[1] Even the question was a reflection of his sense of importance. There were other culprits, perhaps they were beneath his notice. There was Lake, a barbarous General. There was Beresford, the epitome of corruption. Camden was head of government when martial law was proclaimed. King George III refused Catholic emancipation because he was unaware of its necessity.

O'Connor understood political power, he had experienced it. For a brief period, he led the United Irishmen and set the pace in Ireland. He recognised the power that Pitt exercised as head of the British government and the skill with which he used it. The slim, high-stepping British Minister had resolute determination. O'Connor had energy, the energy which rage breeds in intellect. In the contest, thousands died.

O'Connor relates how in the compact with Hoche, the terms were based on Washington's with Rochembeau. 'Many will sneer,' he told his son, 'to hear your father speaking of taking the place of Washington. He succeeded and I failed ... Washington is a great man, a great patriot and hero, and deservedly, and I, in the eyes of the world, a traitor.'[2]

Nonetheless, he had an eye on the judgement of history. His actions alone would not sway the verdict. His character too, left a strong impression. He was a man of powerful intellect and determination. He could be ruthless, override others, hardly hearing their protests. His intellect was coherent; but there were blind spots in O'Connor. The beauty of the light in Ireland is matched by dense shade. Within O'Connor was just such a place of shadow. An extreme disjunction of cultures plagued Ireland. The reckless heroism of old Gaelic culture, the administrative order demanded by England, the symbolism and emotional power of the Catholic church, the Protestant emphasis on truth and probity; these cultures were in conflict. No accommodation had been found. Individuals carried combinations of these urges, and felt the disjunction. The instability in his brothers may come from this source. O'Connor's anger against the system of government and the part played by England received some added energy from the internal split.

In 1998, a memorial was erected in the Four Courts in Dublin, 'in honour of the members of the legal profession who in 1798 sacrificed their lives or their careers in pursuit of their vision of a free Ireland, uniting Protestant, Catholic and Dissenter'. Arthur O'Connor's name was inscribed with Theobald Wolfe Tone, T.A. Emmett and others. The judgement of history is constantly revised.

O'Connor's religious views were deeply held. They were the result of long periods of study, meditation and introspection. He had his reasons for his antipathy to any priesthood, and in particular the Roman Catholic one.

It was an irony that his daughter-in-law had his body re-buried in a Catholic cemetery. How angry he would have been. Somehow the old religion of his ancestors, which he considered a conspiracy to enslavement, had reached out and taken back his earthly remains.

Nothing could contain his spirit. For 88 years, Arthur O'Connor set his course towards liberty and for him, liberty of the mind brought freedom of the spirit. Nothing that Ernestine could do would change that. She completed her rituals. The spirit of Arthur O'Connor had gone free.

———— APPENDIX ————

Arthur O'Connor's address to the free electors of the county of Antrim [published as a pamphlet through the presses of the *Northern Star* on 27 January 1797]

To The Free Electors of the County of Antrim

Fellow Citizens,

The Post Office is so immediately dependent on the Government, that any anonymous production issuing from thence, must be looked on as coming from the Administration itself; in this light I have viewed the anonymous paper which has been so industriously distributed through the Post Offices of the North, avowedly to deprive me of whatever share of your confidence I might have gained, and in this light I have given it an answer. Had I treated it with silent contempt, I should have hoped that its coming from an Administration which had so deservedly forfeited the confidence of every Irishman, who valued the liberties of his Country, would have insured me from suffering, in your estimation, from the falsehood and calumny with which it abounds; but my respect for those invaluable Censors, the Press and the Public Opinion, the conscious integrity of my own heart, and the most perfect reliance on the virtue of the cause I espouse, prompt me to seize any occasion which affords an opportunity of vindicating it or myself, from the aspersions of an Administration, whose heaviest charge, in their wretched production, is, that at any time of my life I had been the advocate of them or their measures. As the whole of the work is one continued tissue of misrepresentation and falsehood, a plain recital of facts, will be the best means of giving it a full refutation. After the question of Regency, that memorable display of the infamy and principles of the factions of Ireland, some of the most considerable of them were forced into *Irish Parliamentary patriotism*, by being stript of the wages of prostitution; I accepted a seat from my Uncle, Lord Longueville, in the chimerical hope, that this crash between the factions and the Government, might be improved to the advantage of Ireland; but experience soon convinced me, that nothing short of the establishment of a NATIONAL GOVERNMENT, A TOTAL ANNIHILATION OF THE FACTIONS, AND THEIR USURPATIONS, *and an entire abolition of Religious Distinctions,* could restore to my country those Rights, and that Liberty, which had been so long a subject of traffic, under a regularly organised system of treason; and acting up to this conviction, from the day I accepted the seat from Lord Longueville, to the day I resigned it, I earnestly intreated him to declare for a Reform of Parliament, and for the freedom of my Catholic countrymen. The thanks which were given me by the Delegates of the Catholics of Ireland, for my defence of them and their cause, so early as 1791, and the vote which I gave for their total emancipation, against Lord Longueville and the Government, in the beginning of 1793, give the lie to the assertion of Administration, that I was not the advocate of Catholic Freedom until my having spoke on that subject in 1795; and so wholly is it unfounded in truth, that I have exerted myself in defence of the liberties of my country, because the Government refused me a Commissioner's place, altho' Lord Longueville repeatedly pressed me to let him procure me a Commissioner's place, I as often refused it; assuring him that it was contrary to my principles, to accept the money of my impoverished countrymen, for the detestable treason of betraying their Rights, their Industry, their Manufactures and Commerce: that for the bribe of a British Pander, I should barely contribute to aggrandize *his* country, at the expense of every thing dear to *my own*; whilst so far from bartering my principles, to better my fortune, that tho' Lord Longueville pressed me to accept large sums of his own money, I declined them; – and it is notorious he has since disinherited me for the open avowal of my political sentiments on the Catholic Question. Being forced, in my own vindication, to speak of myself, I will leave you, my fellow-citizens, to judge of an Administration, that by falsehood and calumny, have attempted to widen a breach between me and connections that were but too widely extended before; yet whilst they have given me an opportunity of proving to you, that no consideration could induce me to abandon my principles, they shall never succeed in making me utter one unkind expression of a man, whose wishes to promote me in life, have left a grateful remembrance their malice shall never efface. Abandoned Administration! who have trampled on the liberties of my country, do you presume to accuse me of dissuading my countrymen from arming to oppose an invasion, which *your's and your accomplice's crimes have provoked?* Is it that the inalienable rights of free-born men to make their laws by delegates of their choice, should be bartered and sold by usurpers and traitors, that I should persuade them to arm? Is it that our markets, our manufactures and commerce, should be sold to that nation which appoints our Government, and distributes our patronage, that I should persuade them to arm? Is it to support the Gunpowder Bill, which deprives them of arms, or the *Convention Bill,* which aims at perpetuating the usurpation of rights, by proscribing the only obvious and orderly means to regain them, that I should persuade them to arm? Is it to support the suspension of the Habeas Corpus Bill, which has destroyed the bulwark of liberty by withholding the Trial by Jury, that I should persuade them to arm? Is it to rivet the bolts, or to guard the dungeons of their fellow-citizens, who, torn from their homes and their families by Administration, vainly demand that trial by Jury, which by proving *their* innocence must establish *its* guilt, that I should persuade them to arm? Is it that a vile Pander of national honour and legislative duty should be invested with uncontrouled power over the opinions and persons of an injured, a gallant and generous people, that I should persuade them to arm? or to crown all, is it under the auspices of the indemnified Carhampton, I should persuade them to arm? go, Impotents, to the Catholics, whose elevated hopes of all glorious freedom, you have been appointed to tauntingly blast, and if they should charge you with crimes of your mission, although you cannot plead the having raised them to equal rights with their fellow-citizens, you can at least boast that you have levelled those rights to the standard of Catholic thraldom! – Hence, then, contemptible Administration, from those you have insulted and levelled, to those you have raised! go to the monopolists of the representation of Ireland, and ask them to arm; go to those whom the continuance of the system of corruption enables to live in affluence at the expence of that poverty and misery their treason has caused, and ask them to arm; go to those hussars of fees and exactions in the revenue, whose regular pay bears no proportion to their pillage and plunder, and command them to arm; go to attorneys and lawyers, who live by villainy, chicane and fraud, under a system of complexity, finesse and fiction, at the expence and ruin of those who are forced to employ them, and tell them they ought to arm; go to those swarms of petty tyrants, perjured grand-jury jobbers, army contractors, tythe proctors and land sharks, and tell them how necessary it is for them to be armed; go to the *established* clergy, who pocket those monstrous funds for *Instructing* nine-tenths of the nation, which should provide decent establishments for three such countries as Ireland, and tell them to preach to the nine-tenths who are excluded from this *glorious* half of the constitution, to arm in its defence; or ask them to blow the expiring embers of religious dissention, and I will leave it to the inhabitants of Armagh, at length recovering from delusion, to judge of their zeal in this christian-like duty. These factions, Administration! are your natural allies; these are your strength; on these you may reckon; and although as devoted to systems which should be abolished, as apostates to national rights and national honour, they count but too high, thank Heaven they are as insignificant in numbers as in strength to those that are sound. Although the old Volunteers have been discouraged, because they boldly threw off the open avowed dominion of Britain, and that these Yeomen corps have been raised to support the concealed deadly influence she has gained by corruption and treason; although the old Volunteers have been rejected, because they extended the rights and liberties of their country, and that these corps have been set up to support laws subversive of both; yet when the systematic scheme of the British minister, and of those vermin that have nestled about the throne, to frame some new modelled despotism on the ruins of freedom, by the erecting of barracks, those bills that have been passed year after year, the late contempt of that only privilege of the Commons which was left them, the granting of money, and the correspondent conduct of their creatures in this country, shall have been developed to that degree which would make resistance an indispensable duty, from my soul I believe that they would find themselves widely mistaken in the support they will meet from many of these corps they have raised. Are the people of Ireland so weak as to convert a threatened invasion from France into an expiation of the injustice, the crimes and oppression by which the temptation to make it was caused? or shall an invasion from France act like magic in changing the present ardent affection of the people of Ireland for liberty, into an unbounded display of loyalty to a system of corruption and treason, by which the most happily gifted nation on earth has been made to contain more misery than any country in the creation? Away with delusion! Are the people of Ireland sure that the factions and Administration, who so earnestly press them to arise to repel the invasion of France, are not *invaders themselves?* Are we sure that their masters and maker, the Minister of Britain, has not invested them with enormous funds of corruption to which our wretchedness has been made to contribute! Are we sure that these funds have not been distributed amongst traitors, in the heart of our island, for betraying the industry, manufactures and commerce of the people of Ireland, to aggrandize those of Great Britain? Nay, are we not certain that every market in Great Britain is shut against every species of Irish industry, with the solitary exception of linen, whilst every manufacture of England has free access to every market in Ireland, without any exception whatever? With these facts in our view, what Irishman can doubt that to support the worst of invasions - the invasion of *rights and of commerce,* 15,000 English and Scotch have not been sent to invade us already? or can we be certain that the shambles of Germany have not been resorted to, to invade us with more? Compare the few troops they left us in the war against American freedom, when they had all Europe their foe, with the numbers they have sent us this war against the freedom of France, when they had all Europe their ally; – compare the weakness of Ireland, divided by religious dissension, *when troops were so few*, with that strength which UNION has given, *when troops are so many*, we cannot but see with whom they seek to contend. Could French invaders do worse than establish a system of pillage and treason *within*, that they may pillage and plunder *without?* – Could they do worse than reject laws an unanimous people had fought, or than pass those they detested? – Could they do worse than commit the personal liberty of the people of Ireland to two men, without connection or interest in the country, without responsibility or controul? – Could they do worse than with-hold trials from Irish citizens cast into dungeons, to the destruction of their health and the ruin of the property? Could they do worse than establish military Magistrates throughout the nation, and indemnify those, whose unfeeling souls had torn hundreds of Irish citizens from every endearing connection in life, after depriving their habitations of every privilege due to the residence of free-born men, consigned them to the flames, turning their wives and their children to beggary and famine, exiled their husbands to fight against that freedom of which they had robbed them on an element they disliked, and in a cause they abhored? or could any thing be more alarming to a people who valued their liberties, than the appointment of a man, that could require such an indemnification, to be commander in chief of the army? or to crown all, could any invaders do worse, that with powers to legislate for a limited time, under the form of constitutional order, destroy the constitution itself?

In vain shall the accomplices of the author of carnage inveigh against French fraternity, as long as Ireland exhibits so melancholy a picture of the fraternity they have adopted themselves. I will not compare the systems of fraternity in East or West Indies, adopted by England and France; but I will compare the alliance which England had formed with France, she calls her natural enemy, with that she dictates to Ireland, she calls her brother and friend. In her alliance with France, she gave what she got, and reciprocity was the equitable basis on which it was made; whilst in her alliance with Ireland, she has taken all she could have asked or demanded and she has given us EXCLUSIONS in grateful return. On this scale of British fraternity, let her hirelings boast of British connections - On this scale of British fraternity, may my country no more be cursed with the friendship of Britain! Too long a tyrant, she forgets her dominion has ceased – Too long her slaves, we must shew her we are resolved to be FREE! Had she ceased to maintain power by the accursed means of fomenting religious dissension; – had she ceased to support factions, usurpers and traitors; – had she abandoned the false illiberal notion, that she gained more by our depression than by our exaltation; – had she treated us like brothers and friends, I may, with confidence affirm, a more affectionate generous ally, never existed, than she would have found Ireland to her. But if the existing fraternity, my fellow-citizens, be the bonds by which you wish a connection with Britain, I am not a Delegate fit for your choice; for though I stood alone in the Commons of Ireland, I would move the repeal of every law which binds us to England, on those, or on any such terms. I will neither be conquered by England or France; nor are we any more bound to a disadvantageous alliance to one than we are to the other; and before England, the factions of Ireland, and the Administration, I speak it, if it is more the true interest of Ireland to form an alliance with France than with England, she is free to adopt it. The jargon of standing or falling with Britain is false: in the days that are past, we have always been *down* – it is time we should seek to be *up*! Rich in a population of 4,000,000 of a healthy intelligent people – rich in her fertile soil — rich in her harbours and navigable rivers – rich in her favourable position between the old and new worlds – rich in her insular situation, without usurping dominion over any people upon earth – what interest, what cause, what pretext can the Administration of Ireland assign for the blood and the wealth they have lavished, in a war commenced in despotism, conducted in ignorance, and ending only by ruin? With 800,000 gallant Citizens, able to arm, is it that the English and Scotch have more to fight for in Ireland than the Irish themselves, that we cannot be trusted with self-defence? when, in the unanointed Republics of Swiss, they can defy the invasion of Germany, of France and Sardinia, those warlike and powerful nations by which they are bounded, by that law which *obliges* every Citizen from 18 to 60 years old, to be provided with arms, why cannot Ireland defy the whole world by a like *obligation*? Why has the Gun-powder Act, which disarms our people, been passed? The answer is too plain for infatuation to mistake it. Happy for Ireland if the prime mover of mischief had borrowed the councils of that great and intuitive mind, England is ruined by having neglected – Happy could he and his minions be taught, in the language and wisdom of Fox, that there is more strength to be gained by gaining the confidence of the people of Ireland, than in 40,000 of the best forces of Europe. Let them give up corruption, and they may safely disband the troops it has furnished; – let them cease to narrow the limits of freedom, as the expansion of intellect demands that they should be extended; – let them rest assured, that a system which cannot be supported without spies and informers, must soon be abandoned; instead of buying, of bribing, or of persecuting the PRESS, let them strip falsehood of the advantages she gains by concealment and misrepresentation, and give to truth that light and publicity with which she must ever prevail; let them recall those base orders throughout the Post Offices, for violating the secrets of friendship, and betraying the credit of commerce; let them open the dungeons, by repealing those laws by which they are crowded; let them abolish what the Chief Magistrate's Deputy calls the mildness of Government, and give us an adequate representation for the basis of liberty, and I will stake my life on it, *no nation shall ever invade us!* But, alas! my fellow-citizens, I lament that the same infatuation, usurpation and folly, which have been so much the order of the day, will still prevent those equitable terms from being conceded: But mark me, the whole Irish fabric is supported by that of Great Britain, whose progress in ruin can only be equalled by her infatuation. If the principles of the French Revolution are as wicked, as destructive, and as diabolical as the Minister has represented them, why was it necessary to involve the people of England in the horrors and ruin of war, that they may not be *persuaded* to adopt them? Is it that the extreme of vice is so seducing, that the most violent of remedy only could prevent a wise people from rushing to meet it? And although the Minister has assigned, day after day, different objects for having involved them; and that every assertion on which he has founded his arguments of the day, have been belied by the facts of the morrow. Still they have been deaf to the councils of his glorious opponent, which, as long as tradition continues, must ever remain a wonderful instance of the efforts of genius and patriotism, to rescue a besotted and misguided people from ruin: but the privileged and the rich, yielding to fear and corruption, have deserted this champion of liberty, to prostrate themselves at the feet of that Minister it was once their province to control; placing terror in the seat of reason, and sacrificing every species of industry to the manufacture of soldiers, they have looked to the bayonet of the mercenary for their only salvation. Presumptuous delusion! Do they imagine they can force back the current of public opinion? Is it by that corruption, whose necessities must increase by geometrical measure, whilst its means must decrease in the same rapid proportion? Is it by a carnage which would exhaust the creation? Is it by oaths wrung from oppression? know they not that the first oath of allegiance is from the King to the Laws, the Constitution and the People; and that if swearing *without consideration,* was binding, Charles could never have suffered, James have been excluded, nor a Brunswick have sat on the throne! We know that King, Lords and Commons exist but by the people's permission; if useful, their titles can never be questioned – if not, they can never be bolstered by swearing. Vain efforts, to change the current of the human mind, like the noisy winds, which to the shallow sight, give a seeming current to the troubled face, whilst with ponderous weight great ocean moves the tide, with slow majestic pace to its predestined limits.

Altho' it were in nature to rescue Britain from impending destruction, it is not in nature that Ireland can be longer held by the disgraceful and ruinous vassalage by which she is bound. Much has been said of the loyalty of the South, contrasted with that of the North; if they mean loyalty to that system of Government which this Administration have adopted – to the connection with England on the present conditions – to the actual state of representation – to the prostituted sale of the right to legislate in one house, by the still more prostituted sale of the right to legislate in the other – to the jobbing and perjury of Grand Juries – to tythes, tythe-proctors and land-pirates – to the annual exportation of two millions worth of the produce of Ireland, to pay Absentees, without any return - to the immoderate high rents and the low rate of wages – or to the enormous expence by which these corruptions are mov'd and maintained; I will answer for it, that the people of Leinster, of Munster and Connaught, are as sensible of the misery and poverty these grievances have caused, and that they will go as far as the people of Ulster to get them redressed. I know the means which have been used to persuade the Catholics in the South, that the persecutions of the Catholics in the North, which have been so diabolicaly fomented and protected in Armagh, were the acts of the Presbyterians of the North; but I stake whatever credit I possess with my Catholic and Presbyterian countrymen, on the assurance I give to the Presbyterians, that the Catholics of the South have buried in eternal oblivion all religious distinction; and in the assurance I give to the Catholics that the crimes with which their Presbyterian countrymen stand charged, and for which so many are dungeoned at this instant, is *their zeal for the Union of Irishmen amongst one another without distinction of sect or religion*; it is the essence of Christianity, it is the essence of all morality, and cannot by human laws be abolished. Trust me, my fellow-citizens, that as the Minister of England perceives the dying convulsions of a country, on the destruction of whose liberty he has so long supported his power, he will be obliged to change his system in Ireland of tyranny and force, into concession and conciliation; you will then see his minions exchanging the saucy flippancy with which they now insult and traduce you, into humiliation and meanness, with which they will endeavour to soothe you: the insolence of the coward, the sport of the drol, and the petulance of the puppy, will soon evaporate into the insignificance from whence they have risen; but let no wretched palliative induce you to ally your cause with corruption; let nothing short of a perfect Representation satisfy you. With this admonition I leave you; but that I may be suspected of seeking your confidence by any other means than the fullest disclosure of my political sentiments, I promise you, as soon as time will permit, that I will lay before you the best account of the state of our country my poor abilities will allow me to furnish. The best assurance I can give of my fidelity to you and your cause is, that I believe in a better order of things; that those who violate the property and rights of others, will forfeit their own; whilst those who respect the rights and property of others, will be certain to have their's respected in turn. With these sentiments, knowing that you had widely determined never to interfere any more in elections, *under* the system of corruption and undue influence, I have offered my services to use every means in my power to effect its destruction, and finding that from the monopoly of one aristocratic faction or other, yours was the only place of popular election I could hope to succeed in.

Think it not presumptuous, my countrymen, that one who lives liberty, should seek her in the only assylum she has left; – think it not presumptuous, my fellow-citizens, that one who will never out-live the threatened liberties of his country, should seek an advanced post where he may triumph in her cause, or fall in her defence. In contempt of calumny, UNITED with you in brotherly love and affection, and in the glorious cause of REFORM, I will ever remain your faithful friend and fellow-citizen,

ARTHUR O'CONNOR
Belfast, Jan. 20, 1797

BIBLIOGRAPHY OF ARTHUR O'CONNOR
(ARTHUR CONDORCET O'CONNOR)

The Measures of Ministry to prevent a revolution, are the certain means of bringing it on, (D. Eaton. London, 1794)

Speech of Arthur O'Connor, Esquire, delivered in the House of Commons of Ireland, on Monday, May 4 1795, upon the important question of Catholic emancipation, (London, 1795)

A letter to the Earl of Carlisle, (London, 1795)

Address to the Free Electors of the County of Antrim, (Belfast, Jan 1797)

The State of Ireland, (Dublin and London 1798)

Defence of the United People of Ireland

Arthur O'Connor's letter to Lord Castlereagh, (Dublin, 1799)

The Rise and Progress of the Irish Union, as stated to Government, in August 1798 by Arthur O'Connor etc. etc. together with such parts of the examination of Arthur O'Connor, T.A. Emmet, and Doctor McNeven, before the House of Lords, as they themselves took note of, (Dublin, 1800?)

Memoire, or detailed statement of the origin and progress of the Irish Union, delivered to the Irish government by Messrs Emmet, O'Connor and McNeven, together with the examinations of these gentlemen before the secret committees of the houses of lords and commons in the summer of 1798, (Dublin, 1802)

The Present State of Great Britain, (Paris, 1804)

Etat actuel de la Grande Bretagne, (Paris, 1804)

A Letter to General Lafayette, on the causes which have deprived France of the advantages of the Revolution of 1830, (London 1831, Paris 1831 2nd ed)

Marie Jean Antoine Nicolas, Marquis de Condorcet. Works. *Oeuvres. Publiees par A. Condorcet O'Connor et M.F. Arago*, (Paris, 1847-49)

Monopoly, the cause of all evil, (Paris and London, Firmin Didot, 1848)

Description of Irish Priests – extracted and translated from his work Monopoly the cause of all evil, (London, 1852)

BOOKS PUBLISHED ABOUT ARTHUR O'CONNOR BY THE GOVERNMENT

The Trial at large of Arthur O'Connor Esq., John Binns, John Allen, Jeremiah Leary and James Coigley for high treason, before Judge Buller, etc. under a special commission, at Maidstone, in the County of Kent. Taken in shorthand, (London, printed for James Ridgway, 1798)
Evidence to character, being a portrait of a traitor by his friends and himself, (London1798)
The charge of Sir Francis Buller, Bart. one of the commissioners appointed in Kent for trying Arthur O'Connor, Esq., James O'Coigly, John Binns, Allen and Leary on a charge of High Treason at Maidstone, on Wednesday 11 April 1798, to the grand jury who were sworn on that commission, (Dublin, printed by John Exshaw, 1798)
The Beauties of the Press, (London, 1800)

Notes

PROLOGUE
1. O'Connor, Arthur, Memoirs, Bignon papers

CHAPTER 1
1. O'Connor, Arthur, Memoirs, Bignon papers
2. Ibid
3. O'Conor, Rt Hon Charles Owen, Don, *The O'Conors of Connaught* (Dublin, 1891)
4. Leland, *History of Ireland* (Dublin, 1773)
5. Williams, Ronald, *The Lords of the Isles* (1984)
6. MacLysaght, Edward, *Irish Families, their Names and Origins* (Dublin, 1957)
7. O'Connor, Charles of Belenagare, *O'Conor's Memoirs* (Dublin, 1990)
8. The Four Masters, *Annals of the Kingdom of Ireland* (Dublin, 1990)
9. *Calendar of the Irish patent Rolls of James I*
10. *Book of Survey and Distribution*
11. Conner family papers
12. Registry of Deeds, Dublin, Book 27, Page 39, No: 15069
13. PRONI, D2707/A1/1 and A1/2
14. Registry of Deeds, Dublin, Book 37, Page 359, No 62093
15. Burke, Sir Bernard, *Second Series of Vicissitudes of Families* (London, 1860)

CHAPTER 2
1. Bignon papers
2. Ibid
3. Ibid
4. Ibid
5. Ibid
6. Ibid
7. Ibid

8. Burke, Sir Bernard, *Second Series of Vicissitudes of Families* (Dublin, 1860)

9. Quoted by Madden, R.R., *The United Irishmen*, from O'Donovan, *Book of Rights*

10. Devonshire Wills and Administrations

11. International Genealogical Index

12. *Kingdom of Ciorraige Luachra*, video by Bertie O'Connor

13. Ibid

14. O'Donovan, *Book of Rights*

15. O'Connor, Kerry genealogy in both Conner family papers and in Bignon papers

16. Ibid

17. Ibid

18. Gillespie, Raymond, *The Transformation of the Irish Economy 1550-1700* (Dublin, 1991)

19. Davies, K.G., *The Royal African Company* (London, 1957)

20. Ibid

21. PRO Kew T70/309

22. Conner family papers

23. Burke's Irish Family Records

24. Ibid

25. Madden, R.R., *The United Irishmen*, (Dublin, 1842-46)

26. Ibid

27. Registry of Deeds, Dublin, Book 27, Page 39, No 15069. Also, *Book of Survey and Distribution*

28. Longfield family papers

29. Ibid

30. Bignon papers

31. Burke, Sir Bernard, *Second Series of Vicissitudes of Families* (Dublin, 1860)

32. *Country Life*, among Rosse papers in PRONI

33. Burke, Sir Bernard, *Second Series of Vicissitudes of Families* (Dublin, 1860)

34. *Calendar of State Papers of Ireland*

35. Registry of Deeds, Book 15, Page 230, No. 7333

36. Registry of Deeds, Book 16, Page 246, No. 7395

37. Longfield family papers

38. Bignon papers

CHAPTER 3
1. Bignon papers
2. Ibid
3. Ibid
4. Ibid
5. Ibid
6. Ibid
7. Ibid
8. Ffolliott, Rosemary, *The Pooles of Mayfield*, Hodges Figgis (Dublin, 1958)
9. Bignon papers
10. Ibid
11. MacLysaght, Edward, *Irish Families, their Names, Arms and Origins* (Dublin, 1957)
12. O'Conor Don, Rt Hon Charles Owen, *The O'Conors of Connaught* (Dublin, 1891)
13. Bignon papers
14. Ibid
15. Ibid
16. PRONI, Drennan letters, T765/1 13.12.1777
17. Bignon papers
18. Ibid
19. Ibid
20. Ibid
21. Ibid
22. Ibid
23. Ibid
24. Ibid

CHAPTER 4
1. Leland, *History of Ireland Vol II* (Dublin, 1773)
2. Lecky, W.E.H., *The History of Ireland in the 18th Century* (London, 1896)
3. Bignon papers
4. Ibid
5. Ibid
6. Burtchael, G.D. and Sadlier, T.U., *Alumnii Dublinensus 1593-1846* (London, 1924)
7. Bignon papers
8. Ibid

9. Becket, J.C., *A Short History of Ireland* (London, 1987)
10. Bignon papers
11. Ibid
12. Quoted in Becket, J.C., *A Short History of Ireland* (London, 1987)
13. Bignon papers
14. Ibid
15. Ibid
16. Ibid
17. Ibid
18. Ibid
19. Ffolliott Rosemary, *The Pooles of Mayfield* (Dublin, 1958)
20. Bignon papers
21. Ibid
22. Ibid
23. Quoted in Bignon papers
24. Bignon papers
25. Ibid
26. Ibid

CHAPTER 5
1. Biography of Roger O'Connor, Conner family papers
2. Burke's Irish Family Records
3. Will of Richard Longfield, Lord Longueville, Cork City Archives
4. Burke's Irish Family Records. Parliamentary Debates, Ireland
5. Truxes, Thomas M., *Irish-American Trade 1660-1783* (Cambridge, 1988)
6. King's Inn Admission Book. King's Inn Library, Dublin
7. Bignon papers
8. Ibid
9. Ibid
10. Bignon papers. Also: Curtin, Nancy, *The United Irishmen* (Oxford, 1994)
11. Bignon papers
12. PRONI Drennan letters T765/1
13. Bignon papers
14. *The Trial of James O'Coigley, otherwise called James Quigley, otherwise called James John Fivey, Arthur O'Connor Esq., John Binns, John Allen and Jeremiah Leary for High Treason at Maidstone in Kent May 1798* (London, 1798)
15. Bignon papers

16. Harrington James, *Oceana and other Works* (London, 1737)
17. Bignon papers
18. Burke's Irish Family Records
19. Burke, Sir Bernard, *A Second Series of Vicissitudes of Families* (1860)
20. King's Inn Admission Papers, King's Inn Library, Dublin
21. Bignon papers
22. Ibid
23. Ordnance Survey of Ireland, 1" series No 25 1987. Registry of Deeds Book 352, 353
24. Bignon papers
25. Ibid
26. PRONI T/3393/25 Grey/Ponsonby papers
27. Bignon papers
28. See PRONI D562/14705 on Mic 500/63
29. Bignon papers
30. Ibid
31. PRONI D2707/A3/3/1-191
32. Cusack MF, *The History of Cork* (1875)
33. PRONI D/3030/31515 Castlereagh papers No 38
34. PRONI T765/1, 3 May 1790

Chapter 6
1. Bignon papers
2. Quoted in Lecky, W.E.H., *The History of Ireland in the 18th Century* (London, 1896)
3. PRONI D2707/A3/3/1-191
4. Parliamentary Registers Ireland
5. Bignon papers
6. Quoted in Furet Francois: *Revolutionary France 1770-1880* (Oxford, 1988)
7. PRONI T765/2/2
8. Tone Theobald Wolfe: *Life of,* ed Bartlett Thomas (Dublin, 1998)
9. Burke, Edmund: *Reflections on the Revolution in France* (1790)
10. Paine, Thomas, *Rights of Man* (1791)
11. Quoted in Bignon papers
12. See Curtin, Nancy: *The United Irishmen* (Oxford, 1994)
13. Bignon papers
14. Parliamentary Registers Ireland
15. Ibid
16. PRONI D2707/A3/3/1-191

17. Parliamentary Registers Ireland
18. Bignon papers
19. Parliamentary Registers Ireland
20. Bignon papers
21. Ibid
22. Ibid
23. Ibid
24. Ibid
25. Ibid
26. Ibid
27. Furet, Francois, *Revolutionary France 1770-1880* (Oxford, 1995)
28. Bibliotheque de L'Institut de France, Ms 848
29. Bignon papers
30. Ministere de la Guerre, Vincennes, Paris, Dossier 393 GD 2/j
31. Bignon papers
32. Ibid
33. Ibid
34. Ibid
35. Ibid
36. Ibid
37. Ibid
38. Quoted in Lecky WEH, *The History of Ireland in the 18th Century* (London, 1896)
39. Ibid

CHAPTER 7

1. Bignon papers
2. PRONI T765/2/3/387
3. Patterson, M.W., *Sir Francis Burdett and his Times* (London,1931)
4. Bignon papers
5. MacDermot Frank, 'Arthur O'Connor', *Irish Historical Studies* XV (1966)
6. Will of Richard Longfield, Lord Longueville, Cork City Archives. Longfield papers
7. Bignon papers
8. Ibid
9. Ibid
10. Ibid
11. Ibid
12. Ibid

13. Campbell, Gerald: *Edward and Pamela Fitzgerald* (London, 1904)
14. Ibid
15. Stuart, Dorothy Margaret, *Dearest Bess* (London, 1955)
16. Ibid
17. PRONI T765/2/4
18. Bignon papers
19. Ibid
20. PRO Kew, PRO30/8/104
21. NA Dublin, Rebellion papers, 620/41/112
22. PRONI, D2707/A3/3
23. Bignon papers
24. Lecky, W.E.H., *The History of Ireland in the 18th Century* (London, 1896)
25. Parliamentary Registers Ireland
26. Tone, Theobald Wolfe, *Life of,* ed Bartlett Thomas (Dublin, 1998)
27. Quoted in O'Brien Conor Cruise, *Edmund Burke,* abridged by McCure, Jim (Dublin, 1997): from O'Brien, Conor Cruise, *The Great Melody* (1992)
28. Ibid
29. NA Dublin, Rebellion Papers, 620/15/3/1-20
30. Bignon papers
31. Ibid
32. Ibid
33. *Report from the Secret Committee of the House of Commons* (Dublin, 1798)

CHAPTER 8

1. Bignon papers
2. Ibid
3. Ibid
4. NA Dublin, 620/15/3/5
5. Bignon papers
6. Ibid
7. Ibid
8. Ibid
9. Ibid
10. Ibid
11. PRONI T765/1 Dec 1783
12. Bignon papers
13. Ibid

14. See O'Connor's speech in Parliamentary Registers Ireland (1791)

15. Bignon papers

16. *The Shorter Oxford English Dictionary*

17. PRONI T1210/1-23

18. Bignon papers

19. Ibid

20. Ibid

21. Ibid

22. Quoted in Foster, R.F. *Modern Ireland 1600-1972* (London, 1989)

23. Bignon papers

24. Ibid

25. Ibid

26. Ibid

27. PRO Kew, HO/100/77. *Journal of the Cork Historical and Archaeological Society* (1948, 1949)

28. Bignon papers

29. Trinity, Dublin, Ms. Dept. Ms 873/576-578

30. Bignon papers

31. Ibid

32. NA Dublin, 620/15/3/7

33. Bignon papers

34. Bodleian Library Oxford, Duke Humphries Ms Dept. Diary of William Godwin

35. Bodleian Library Oxford, Ms. Eng. lett. c144

36. Bodleian Library Oxford, Diary of William Godwin

37. O'Connor Arthur Condorcet, *Monopoly: The Cause of all Evil* (London and Paris, 1848)

38. NA Dublin, 620/15/3/5

39. Bignon papers

40. Ibid

41. Ibid

42. Campbell Gerald, *Edward and Pamela Fitzgerald* (London, 1904)

43. Archives Nacionale, Paris, Corr. Pol. Ang. 590 fos. 217-23

44. Campbell, Gerald, *Edward and Pamela Fitzgerald* (London, 1904)

45. Bignon papers

46. Bignon papers

47. Tone, Theobald Wolfe, *Life of,* ed Bartlett Thomas (Dublin, 1998). Also Bignon papers

48. Tone, Theobald Wolfe, *Life of,* ed Bartlett Thomas (Dublin, 1998)

49. Ibid.

50. Ibid
51. Taylor IA *Life of Lord Edward Fitzgerald* (London, 1903)
52. Tone, Theobald Wolfe, *Life of,* ed Bartlett, Thomas (Dublin, 1998)
53. Bignon papers

CHAPTER 9
1. Tone, Theobald Wolfe, *Life of,* ed Bartlett, Thomas (Dublin, 1998)
2. Ibid
3. Bignon papers
4. Ibid
5. Ibid
6. Ibid
7. Ibid
8. Ibid
9. Ibid
10. Ibid
11. Ibid
12. Ibid
13. Ibid
14. Ibid
15. Ibid
16. Ibid
17. Ibid
18. Ibid
19. Ibid
20. Ibid
21. Ibid
22. Ibid
23. Ibid
24. Ibid
25. *Journal of the Cork Historical and Archaeological Society* (1948, 1949)
26. Bignon papers
27. Ibid
28. Taylor, I.A., *Life of Lord Edward Fitzgerald* (London, 1904)
29. PRONI D2707/A3/3
30. Tone, Theobald Wolfe, *Life of,* ed Bartlett, Thomas (Dublin, 1998)
31. Bignon papers
32. Taylor, I.A., *Life of Lord Edward Fitzgerald* (London, 1903); Also Bignon papers
33. Bignon papers

34. Campbell, Gerald: *Edward and Pamela Fitzgerald* (London, 1904)
35. Taylor, I.A., *Life of Lord Edward Fitzgerald* (London, 1903)
36. Campbell, Gerald, *Edward and Pamela Fitzgerald* (London, 1904)
37. Bignon papers
38. Ibid
39. Ibid
40. Ibid
41. Ibid
42. NA Dublin, 620/18A/17
43. Bignon papers
44. Campbell, Gerald, *Edward and Pamela Fitzgerald* (London, 1904)
45. Ibid
46. PRONI T765/1

CHAPTER 10
1. PRO Kew, HO/100/62/64
2. Ibid
3. Bignon papers
4. Ibid
5. Quoted in B. Library Ms Dept. Fox letters Ms 47569
6. NA Dublin, 620/15/3/7
7. Bignon papers
8. Trinity, Dublin, Ms. Dept. Ms 873, 744
9. Bignon papers
10. NA Dublin, 620/15/3/22
11. Ibid
12. NA Dublin, 620/15/3/23
13. Ibid
14. NA Dublin, 620/15/3/4
15. NA Dublin, 620/15/3/16
16. NA Dublin, 620/15/3/26
17. NA Dublin, 620/15/3/8
18. PRO Kew, HO/100/62
19. Archives Nacionale Paris AF 111 186B
20. Tone, Theobald Wolfe, *Life of,* ed Bartlett, Thomas (Dublin, 1998)
21. Bignon papers
22. Bignon papers
23. *Journal of the Cork Historical and Archaeological Society* (1915)
24. Bignon papers
25. *Journal of the Cork Historical and Archaeological Society* (1915)

26. PRO Kew, HO/100/62
27. Lecky, W.E.H., *The History of Ireland in the 18th Century* (London, 1896)
28. Bignon papers
29. Campbell, Gerald, *Edward and Pamela Fitzgerald* (London, 1904)
30. Lecky, W.E.H., *The History of Ireland in the 18th Century* (London, 1896)
31. Bignon papers
32. Ibid
33. Ibid
34. Biography of Roger O'Connor, Conner family papers
35. Bignon papers
36. Bignon papers
37. Ibid
38. Ibid
39. PRONI T765/1/
40. NA Dublin, 620/15/3/11
41. Campbell, Gerald, *Edward and Pamela Fitzgerald* (London, 1904)
42. N. Library, Dublin, Ms. Dept. Ms 18994
43. PRONI T765/1
44. NA Dublin, 620/28/200
45. NA Dublin, 620/15/3/13
46. NA Dublin, 620/15/3/26
47. Bignon papers
48. PRONI T3765/11/3/6
49. PRONI T/3393/25, Grey-Ponsonby papers

CHAPTER 11
1. Trinity, Dublin, Ms Dept. Ms 873 No 156
2. NA Dublin, 620/3/31/5
3. Campbell, Gerald, *Edward and Pamela Fitzgerald* (London, 1904)
4. Ibid
5. NA Dublin, 620/1/2/10
6. Ibid and 620/1/2/7
7. Ibid
8. Bignon papers
9. Campbell, Gerald, *Edward and Pamela Fitzgerald* (London, 1904)
10. Ibid
11. Ibid
12. MacDermot, Frank, 'Arthur O'Connor', *Irish Historical Studies* XV

(1996)

13. Campbell, Gerald, *Edward and Pamela Fitzgerald* (London, 1904)

14. Ibid

15. N. Library, Dublin, Ms. Dept. Acc 5348 Nos 81, 93 & 113

16. Campbell, Gerald, *Edward and Pamela Fitzgerald* (London, 1904)

17. Quoted in Patterson: *Sir Francis Burdett and his Times* (London, 1931)

18. Bignon papers

19. *Report of the Secret Committee of the House of Commons* (Dublin, 1798)

20. Emmet, Thomas Addis, O'Connor, Arthur and McNeven, William James, *Memoire* (Dublin, 1802)

21. See Elliott Marianne, *Partners in Revolution* (Yale, 1982)

22. Campbell, Gerald, *Edward and Pamela Fitzgerald* (London, 1904); Lecky, W.E.H., *The History of Ireland in the 18th Century* (London, 1896); PRO Kew, HO 100/70; PRONI D3030/185-212

23. Ibid

24. PRONI D3030/185-212

25. NA Dublin, 620/31/15

26. PRO Kew, HO/100/70

27. NA Dublin, 620/2/6

28. NA Dublin, 620/1/2

29. PRO Kew, HO/100/70

30. PRONI Drennan letters T765/

31. Emmet, Thomas Addis; O'Connor, Arthur; McNeven, William James, *Memoire* (Dublin, 1802)

32. Ibid

33. Bignon papers

34. Ibid

35. Ibid; Trinity Dublin Ms Dept. Ms. 873 No 744

36. Lecky WEH *The History of Ireland in the 18th century* (London, 1896)

37. *Extracts from the Press* (Philadelphia, 1802)

38. *Extracts from the Press* (Philadelphia, 1802)

39. Curtin, Nancy, *The United Irishmen* (Oxford, 1994)

40. NA Dublin, 620/61/140

41. NA Dublin, 620/10/125/5; 620/23/98

42. NA Dublin, 620/34/35; 620/37/24; 620/23/98

43. *Extracts from the Press* (Philadelphia, 1802)

44. Ibid

45. Trinity Dublin, Ms Dept. Ms 873 No 744

46. PRONI D3217/14/1

47. *Extracts from the Press* (Philadelphia, 1802)

48. Ibid

49. Ibid

50. Bignon papers

51. Ibid

52. Quoted in Lecky, W.E.H., *The History of Ireland in the 18th Century* (London, 1896)

53. Bignon papers

54. Ibid

55. Ibid

56. Trinity, Dublin, Ms. Dept. Ms 873 No 744 and NA Dublin, 620/37/24; 620/11/138/35; 620/32/183

57. Bignon papers

58. Ibid

59. Ibid

60. Ibid

61. Ibid

CHAPTER 12

1. N. Library, Dublin, Ms. Dept. Ms 886-7

2. PRO Kew, HO 100/75

3. Ibid

4. Fitzpatrick, W.J. *The Secret Service under Pitt* (London, 1892)

5. Patterson, M.W., *Sir Francis Burdett and his Times* (London, 1931)

6. Bignon papers

7. *Trial of O'Coigley* (London, 1798)

8. Bignon papers

9. Ibid

10. NA Dublin, 620/35/139

11. Ibid

12. Biography of Roger O'Connor, Conner family papers

13. PRO Kew, HO 100/69

14. NA Dublin, 620/35/126

15. Biography of Roger O'Connor, Conner family papers

16. Fitzpatrick, W.J., *The Secret Service under Pitt* (London, 1892)

17. Bignon papers

18. Ibid

19. Ibid

20. *Beauties of the Press,* p478-480 (London, 1800)

21. Quoted in Lecky, W.E.H., *The History of Ireland in the 18th Century*

(London, 1896)

22. *Trial of O'Coigley* (London, 1798)

23. PRO Kew, HO 100/75

24. *Trial of O'Coigley* (London, 1798)

25. Bignon papers

26. Elliott, Marianne, *Partners in Revolution* (Yale, 1982)

27. Bignon papers, *Trial of O'Coigley* (London, 1798)

28. Ibid

29. Elliott, Marianne, *Partners in Revolution* (Yale, 1982)

30. NA Dublin, 620/35/139

31. Bignon papers; Elliott, Marianne, *Partners in Revolution* (Yale, 1982)

32. PRO Kew, HO 100/70

33. Bignon papers

34. PRO Kew, HO 100/75

35. *Trial of O'Coigley* (London, 1798)

36. Ibid

37. Bignon papers

38. Ibid

39. Ibid

40. Ibid

41. Ibid

42. Bodleian, Oxford, Ms. Eng. lett. C 66 Burdett

43. Bignon papers

44. Ibid

45. PRO Kew WO/94/4

46. 24 February 1798, *Beauties of the Press* (London, 1800)

47. PRONI D2707/A3/3/1-191

48. *Trial of O'Coigley* (London, 1798); NA Dublin, 620/18A/17; Trinity, Dublin, Ms. Dept. Ms 869/9

49. *Trial of O'Coigley* (London, 1798)

50. Bodleian, Oxford, Ms. Eng. lett. C66

51. Bignon papers

52. *Trial of O'Coigley* (London, 1798)

CHAPTER 13

1. Bignon papers

2. PRO Kew HO 100/75; NA Dublin, 620/4/29/7

3. *Trial of O'Coigley* (London, 1798)

4. Bignon papers

5. Ibid

6. Ibid

7. Campbell, Gerald, *Edward and Pamela Fitzgerald* (London, 1904)

8. PRO Kew, HO 100/75

9. Bignon papers

10. Ibid

11. NA Dublin, 620/4/38

12. PRONI D2707/A3/3/1-191

13. For a full account of the rebellion see Pakenham, Thomas, *The Year of Liberty* (London, 1969)

14. NA Dublin, 620/4/38

15. PRO Kew, HO 100/69

16. 'The United Irishmen in Cork', see *Journal of the Cork Historical and Archaeological Society* (1948, 1949)

17. Bignon papers

18. Ibid

19. Ibid

CHAPTER 14

1. N. Library, Dublin, Ms. Dept. Ms. 886-7

2. Ibid

3. Ibid

4. Bignon papers

5. Trinity, Dublin, Ms. Dept. Ms. 873 No 476

6. Bibliotheque de L'Institut de France, Ms. 2475 No 5

7. Trinity, Dublin, Ms. Dept. Ms. 873 No 744

8. PRONI D/3030/263

9. PRO Kew, HO 100/77

10. B. Library, Ms. Dept. Add. Ms. 47569

11. Ibid

12. Ibid

13. Ibid

14. NA Dublin, 620/41/112

15. NA Dublin, 4/29/15

16. B. Library, Ms. Dept. Add. Ms. No 47569

17. PRONI D/3030/263

18. Ibid

19. Pelham Ms. quoted in Lecky, W.E.H., *The History of Ireland in the 18th Century* (London, 1896)

20. PRO Kew, HO/100/77

21. PRONI D/3030/263

22. Holt, 'Memoirs', in *Journal of the Cork Historical and Archaeological Society* (1950)

23. PRONI D3030/184A

24. NA Dublin, 620/7/79/21/5

25. NA Dublin, 620/41/112

26. NA Dublin, 620/14/211/1-5

27. PRONI, D/3030/263

28. PRONI D/3030/263; PRO Kew, HO 100/78

29. Emmet, Thomas Addis; O'Connor, Arthur and McNeven, William James, *Memoire* (Dublin, 1802)

30. PRO Kew, HO/100/78

31. NA Dublin, 620/4/29/15

32. PRONI D/3030/263

33. NA Dublin, 620/41/112

34. *Report of the Secret Committee of the House of Lords and of the House of Commons* (Dublin, 1798)

35. PRO Kew, HO/100/77

36. Emmet, Thomas Addis; O'Connor, Arthur and McNeven, William James, *Memoire* (Dublin, 1802)

37. Ibid

38. PRO Kew, HO/100/78

39. Ibid

40. PRONI D3030/263

41. Ibid

42. Quoted in Lecky, W.E.H., *The History of Ireland in the 18th century* (London,1896)

43. N. Library, Dublin, Abercrombie Ms 886-7

44. PRO Kew, HO/100/78. McNeven, William James, *Pieces of Irish History* (London, 1802)

45. *Report of the Secret Committee of the House of Lords and the House of Commons* (London, 1798)

46. N. Library, Dublin, Ms. Dept. Abercrombie Ms. 886-7

47. N. Library, Dublin, Ms. Dept. Ms. 35,005/9

48. PRONI D2707/A3/3/1-191

49. *The Journal of Elizabeth Lady Holland* (London, 1908)

50. Ibid

51. N. Library Dublin, Ms. 35,005/14

52. Ibid

53. Statutes 38 Geo. III Chapter 78

54. McNeven, *Pieces of Irish History* (London, 1802)

55. PRO Kew, HO 100/78
56. Longfield papers
57. NA Dublin, 620/15/3/29
58. NA Dublin, 620/15/3/31
59. Ibid
60. See Gillray's Cartoons
61. B. Library, Ms. Dept. Add. Ms. 47569
62. Ibid
63. Ibid
64. Ibid
65. Ibid

CHAPTER 15
1. NA Dublin, 620/7/74
2. PRONI D/3030/296
3. O'Connor, Arthur *Letter to Lord Castlereagh* (Dublin, 1799)
4. PRONI D/3030/ 263
5. Ibid
6. McNeven, William James, *Pieces of Irish History* (London, 1802) O'Connor, Arthur, *Letter to Lord Castlereagh* (Dublin, 1799)
7. PRONI D/3030/296
8. Quoted in Lecky, W.E.H., *The History of Ireland in the 18th Century* (London, 1896)
9. Trinity, Dublin, Ms. Dept. Ms. 873 No 655; PRO Kew, PRO 30/9/156
10. PRO HO 100/78
11. PRO Kew, PRO 30/9/156; 'Prisoners from Cork', *Journal of the Cork Historical and Archaeological Society* (1948)
12. Preamble to published version of O'Connor, Arthur, *Letter to Lord Castlereagh* (Dublin, 1799)
13. PRONI D1748/B/3/9
14. PRO Kew, PRO /30/9/156; PRO Kew, HO/122/6
15. PRONI D/1748/C
16. PRONI D/1748/B/3/9/1-10
17. NA Dublin, 620/4/29/7
18. NA Dublin, 620/4/29/32
19. NA Dublin, 620/15/2/12
20. NO Dublin, 620/7/74
21. NA Dublin, 620/18/13
22. Trinity, Dublin, Ms. Dept. Sirr Ms. 868/1

23. NA Dublin, 620/15/2/12

24. Dickson, William Steel, *Narrative of a Confinement* (Dublin, 1812)

25. Ibid

26. Fitzpatrick W.J., *The Secret Service under Pitt* (London, 1892)

27. Dickson, William Steel, *Narrative of a Confinement* (Dublin, 1812)

28. Ibid

29. Ibid

30. PRO Kew, Army Lists

31. Fort George Publ: text by MacIvor, Iain for Historic Scotland (1996)

32. See Trinity, Dublin, Ms. Dept. Russell Ms 873 No 655

33. Dickson, William Steel, *Narrative of a Confinement* (London, 1812)

34. Ibid

35. From *The Fort George Garrison* supplied by Lt-Col A.A. Fairrie of Regimental Headquarters, The Highlanders, Inverness, Scotland

36. Emmet, T.A., *Ireland under English Rule* (New York, 1903) McNeven, William James, *Pieces of Irish History* (London, 1802)

37. Dickson William Steel, *Narrative of a Confinement* (London, 1812)

38. McDermot, Frank, 'Arthur O'Connor', *Irish Historical Studies* XV (1966)

39. N. Library, Dublin, Ms Dept. Acc 5348

40. Trinity, Dublin, Ms. Dept. Ms 873 No 353

41. N. Library, Dublin, Ms. Dept. Ms 35,005/11

42. Ibid

43. Ibid

44. Dickson, William Steel, *Narrative of a Confinement* (London, 1812)

45. Trinity, Dublin, Ms. Dept. Ms 873 No 557

46. Ibid

47. Ibid

48. Bignon papers

49. Trinity, Dublin, Ms. Dept. Ms. 873 No 578

50. Ibid

51. PRO Kew, HO 122/5

52. PRO Kew, HO 122/6

53. N. Library, Dublin, Ms. Dept. Ms 35,005/11

54. Emmet, T.A., *The Emmet Family* (New York, 1898)

55. Dickson, William Steel, *Narrative of a Confinement* (London, 1812)

56. PRO Kew, PRO 30/9/156; PRO Kew, HO122/6

57. O'Connor, Arthur Condorcet, *Monopoly: The Cause of all Evil* (Paris and London, 1848)

58. N. Library, Dublin, Ms. Dept. Ms 35,005/11

59. Ibid
60. PRONI T3765/J/9/2/8
61. Ibid
62. Registry of Deeds, Dublin, Book 15, P115, No 347787
63. O'Connell, Maurice ed, *Correspondence of Daniel O'Connell Vol I*, for the Irish Manuscripts Commission (Dublin, 1972)
64. PRONI, D3030/410
65. PRONI, D/3030/551
66. *The Complete Peerage,* Doubleday and de Walden
67. PRO Kew, WO 94/4
68. NA Dublin, 620/49/125
69. Trinity, Dublin, Ms. Dept. Sirr Ms. 868/1
70. NA Dublin, OP129/10
71. PRO Kew, HO122/6; PRO30/9/156; PRO30/9/123; NA Dublin, 620/10/120/10
72. Dickson, William Steel, *Narrative of a Confinement* (London, 1812)
73. Trinity, Dublin, Ms. Dept. Ms. 873 No 557
74. Ibid
75. Ibid
76. Ibid

CHAPTER 16

1. Campbell, Gerald, *Edward and Pamela Fitzgerald* (London, 1904)
2. Trinity, Dublin, Ms. Dept. Ms. 873 No 353
3. MacDermot, Frank, 'Arthur O'Connor', *Irish Historical Studies,* XV (1966)
4. NA Dublin, 620/35/139
5. Patterson, M.W., *Sir Francis Burdett and his Times* (London, 1931)
6. B. Library, Ms. Dept., Add. Ms. 51475a Journal of Charles James Fox
7. Ibid
8. Airlie, Mabel, Countess of, *In Whig Society* (London, 1921)
9. Patterson, M.W., *Sir Francis Burdett and his Times* (London, 1931)
10. Ibid
11. Airlie, Mabel, Countess of, *In Whig Society* (London, 1921)
12. Ibid
13. Aspinall, A., *The Correspondence of George, Prince of Wales,* Vol IV. p354, McMahon to Duke of Northumberland, 1 Jan 1803, quoted in Mitchell, LG, *Charles James Fox* (London, 1992)
14. B. Library Ms. Dept., Add. Ms. 51475A Fox diaries
15. Bignon papers

16. MacDermot, Frank, 'Arthur O'Connor', *Irish Historical Studies* XV (1966)

17. Bignon papers

18. Emmet, T.A. *Ireland under English Rule* (New York, 1903)

19. MacDermot, Frank, 'Arthur O'Connor', *Irish Historical Studies*, XV (1966)

20. Ministere de la Guerre, Archives Vincennes, Paris Dossier 393 GD 2/j

21. Ibid

22. Byrne, Miles, *Memoirs* (Dublin, 1906)

23. Emmet, T.A., *Ireland under English Rule* (New York, 1903)

24. Ibid

25. Ibid

26. Trinity, Dublin, Ms. Dept. Ms. 873 No 744

27. Ibid

28. Ibid

29. Ibid

30. Emmet, T.A., *Ireland under English Rule* (New York, 1903)

31. Ibid

32. Ibid

33. Ibid

34. Ibid

35. Ministere de la Guerre, Archives Vincennes, Paris, Dossier 393 GD 2/j

36. Ibid

37. Emmet, TA, *Ireland under English Rule* (New York, 1903)

38. Byrne, Miles, *Memoirs* (Dublin, 1906)

39. Ibid

40. N. Library, Dublin, Ms. Dept. Ms 5966

41. Bignon papers

42. Ministere de la Guerre, Archives Vincennes, Paris, Dossier 393 GD 2/j

43. O'Connor, Arthur, *The Present State of Great Britain* (Paris, 1804, An XII)

44. Ibid

45. Ibid

46. Ibid

47. Ibid

48. Quoted in Furet, Francois, *Revolutionary France 1770-1880* (Oxford, 1995)

49. Ministerre de la Guerre, Archives Vincennes, Paris, Dossier 393 GD 2/j

50. Ibid
51. NA Dublin, 620/67/173
52. NA Dublin, 620/11/130/15
53. NA Dublin, 620/11/130/11
54. NA Dublin, 620/14/188
55. NA Dublin, SOC 1030/100
56. NA Dublin, 620/14/188
57. NA Dublin, 620/14/188/31
58. NA Dublin, 620/14/188/41
59. NA Dublin, 620/14/198/13
60. NA Dublin, 620/23/98
61. NA Dublin, 620/14/198/1-10
62. NA Dublin, 620/13/172/14
63. NA Dublin, 620/14/188
64. Ministere de la Guerre, Archives Vincennes, Paris, Dossier 393 GD 2/j
65. Wellesley, Arthur, Duke of Wellington, ed. by his son, *Supplementary Despatches* Vol 5 (London, 1858-72)

CHAPTER 17

1. Bibliotheque de L'Institut de France Ms 2475 no 42
2. Ibid No 2
3. Ibid No 42
4. See Baker, K.M., *Condorcet* (Chicago, 1975)
5. Bibliotheque de L'Institut de France, Ms 2475 No 42
6. Ibid
7. See Boissel, Thierry, *Sophie de Condorcet, Femmes de Lettres (1764-1822)* (Paris, 1988)
8. Bibliotheque de L'Institut de France Ms 848 Nos 7-8; Boissel, Thierry, *Sophie de Condorcet* (Paris, 1988)
9. Guillois, Antoine, *La Marquise de Condorcet* (Paris, 1897)
10. Baker, K.M., *Condorcet* (Chicago, 1975)
11. Boissel, Thierry, *Sophie de Condorcet* (Paris, 1988)
12. Bibliotheque de L'Institut de France, Ms 2475 Nos 6-21
13. Bibliotheque de L'Institut de France Ms 848
14. NA Dublin, 620/64/147
15. Trinity Dublin Ms. Dept. Ms 873 No 744
16. NA Dublin 620/64/147
17. Furet, Francois, *Revolutionary France 1770-1880* (Oxford, 1995)
18. Bibliotheque de L'Institut de France, Ms 2475 No 44-45

19. Constant, Benjamin, *Journaux Intimes* ed Paris 1952, quoted in MacDermot, Frank, 'Arthur O'Connor', *Irish Historical Studies* XV (1966)

20. Guillois, Antoine, *La Marquise de Condorcet* (Paris, 1897)

21. O'Connor, Arthur, Correspondence from Bignon papers

22. Ibid

23. Trinity, Dublin, Ms. Dept. Ms. 873 No. 768

24. Conner family papers

25. Longfield papers

26. Burke's Irish Family Records

27. Trinity, Dublin, Ms. Dept. Ms. 873 No 767

28. Ibid No 768

29. Ibid No 768

30. Ibid

31. Ibid

32. Ibid

33. Ibid

34. Ibid

35. Ibid

36. Ibid

37. Trinity, Dublin, Ms. Dept. Ms. 873 No 761

38. Trinity, Dublin, Ms. Dept. Ms 873 No 768

39. Bibliotheque de L'Institut de France, Ms 848-849 Papiers Condorcet

40. Byrne, Miles, *Memoirs* (Dublin, 1906)

41. Boissel, Thierry, *Sophie de Condorcet* (Paris, 1988)

42. Byrne, Miles, *Memoirs* (Dublin, 1906)

43. Archives de Loiret, Certificate of Death No ADL 4072 No 7

44. Will of Richard Longfield, Lord Longueville, Cork City Archives

45. NA Dublin, 620/14/211

46. Conner family papers

47. NA Dublin, OP 314/2; OP 481/11; newspaper reports

48. PRONI D1759/3B6

49. Ibid

50. Ibid

CHAPTER 18

1. O'Connor, Arthur Condorcet, *Monopoly: The Cause of all Evil* (Paris and London, 1848)

2. Bignon papers

3. O'Connor, Arthur Condorcet, *Monopoly: The Cause of all Evil* (Paris

and London, 1848)

4. Guillois, Antoine, *La Marquise de Condorcet* (Paris, 1897)

5. Bibliotheque de L'Institut de France, Ms. 848

6. Ibid

7. Bibliotheque de L'Institut de France, Ms. 2475 No 22

8. O'Connor, Arthur, Correspondence of, from Bignon papers

9. Ibid

10. Ibid

11. Ibid

12. Ibid

13. Ibid

14. Ibid

15. Bibliotheque de L'Institut de France, Ms. 2475 Nos. 6-21

16. Bignon papers

17. N. Library, Dublin, Ms. 10961

18. Ibid

19. Ibid

20. Ibid

21. Ministere de la Guerre, Archives Vincennes, Paris, Dossier 393 GD 2/j

22. Ibid

23. Ibid

24. Ibid

25. Ibid

26. Elliott, Marianne, *Partners in Revolution* (Yale, 1989)

27. MacDermot, Frank, 'Arthur O'Connor', *Irish Historical Studies* XV (1966)

28. Barrington, Sir Jonah, *Personal Sketches* (London, 1827)

29. Byrne, Miles, *Memoirs* (Dublin, 1906)

30. Trinity, Dublin, Ms. Dept. Ms 5966 No 44

31. MacDermot, Frank, 'Arthur O'Connor', *Irish Historical Studies* XV (1966)

32. O'Connor, Arthur, Correspondence of, from Bignon papers

33. Registry of Deeds, Dublin, 1842, Vol 2, No 24

34. Trinity, Dublin, Ms. Dept. Ms. 873 No 750

35. Bodleian, Oxford, Ms. Eng. lett. C66

36. Ibid

37. NA Dublin, OP 481/11

38. Bodleian, Oxford, Ms. Eng. lett. C64-66

39. NA Dublin, 620/14/213/1-2

40. MacDermot, Frank, 'Arthur O'Connor', *Irish Historical Studies* XV (1966)

41. NA Dublin, 620/4/29/44

42. Trinity, Dublin, Ms. Dept. Ms 873 No 744

43. Gilbert, Sir John Thomas (ed), *Documents Relating to Ireland 1795-1804* (Shannon, 1970)

44. Bibliotheque de L'Institut de France, Ms 2328 No 511B

45. Bibliotheque de L'Institut de France, Ms 2328 No 511F

46. Bibliotheque de L'Institut de France, Ms 2328

47. Ibid

CHAPTER 19

1. Bignon papers

2. O'Connor, Arthur Condorcet, *Monopoly: The Cause of all Evil* (Paris and London, 1848)

3. Bignon papers

4. Bignon papers

5. Bignon papers

6. Ibid

7. Ibid

8. Conner family papers

9. Bignon papers

10. Burke's Irish Family Records

11. O'Connor, Arthur, Correspondence of, from Bignon papers

12. Bignon papers

13. Ibid

14. Ibid

15. Conner family papers

16. Bignon papers

17. Registry of Deeds, Dublin, Book 531, P115, No 347787

18. Registry of Deeds, Dublin, Volume 857, P12, No 572012

19. Bignon papers

20. Ministere de la Guerre, Archives Vincennes, Paris, Dossier 393 GD 2/j

21. Ibid

22. Ibid

23. Ibid

24. Trinity, Dublin, Ms. Dept. Ms. 873 No 353

25. Campbell, Gerald, *Edward and Pamela Fitzgerald* (London, 1904)

26. N. Library, Dublin, Ms. Dept. Acc. 5348

27. Campbell, Gerald, *Edward and Pamela Fitzgerald* (London, 1904)
28. Ibid
29. Biography of Roger O'Connor, Conner family papers
30. Trinity Dublin, Ms. Dept. Ms. 873 No 770
31. Ibid
32. Registry of Deeds, Dublin, 1842 Vol 2 No 24
33. Conner family papers
34. Conner family papers
35. Registry of Deeds, 1834 Book 21 No 113
36. MacDermot, Frank, 'Arthur O'Connor', *Irish Historical Studies* XV (1966)
37. Bignon papers
38. MacDermot, Frank, 'Arthur O'Connor', *Irish Historical Studies* XV (1966)
39. Ibid
40. Trinity Dublin, Ms. Dept. Ms 873 No 742
41. Ibid
42. Ibid
43. Trinity Dublin, Ms. Dept. Ms 873 Nos 742 & 744; Bignon papers
44. Trinity Dublin, Ms. Dept. Ms 873 No 742
45. *Paroles sur la Tombe de M. le General Arthur Condorcet O'Connor* (Paris, 1852)
46. MacDermot, Frank, 'Arthur O'Connor', *Irish Historical Studies* XV (1966)
47. Registry of Deeds, Dublin, 1842, Vol 2, No 24
48. Ibid
49. Campbell, Gerald, *Edward and Pamela Fitzgerald* (London, 1904)
50. Quoted in Trinity, Dublin, Ms. Dept. Ms. 873 No 584
51. Ibid
52. Bibliotheque de L'Institut de France, Ms. 2328 No 511B, also Guillois, Antoine, *La Marquise de Condorcet* (Paris, 1897)
53. O'Connor, Arthur Condorcet, *Monopoly: The Cause of all Evil* (Paris and London, 1848)

CHAPTER 20

1. Bignon papers
2. O'Connor, Arthur, *The State of Ireland,* ed Livesey, James (Dublin, 1798) Bignon papers
3. Bignon papers
4. Bibliotheque de L'Institut de France, Ms 2475 No 39

5. Ibid No 40-41

6. Burke's Irish Family Records

7. *Paroles sur la Tombe de M. le General Arthur Condorcet O'Connor* (Paris, 1852)

8. Bibliotheque de L'Institut de France, Ms. 2475 No 27-29

9. *Paroles sur la Tombe de M. le General Arthur Condorcet O'Connor* (Paris, 1852)

10. Bibliotheque de L'Institut de France, Ms. 2475 No 22

11. MacDermot, Frank, 'Arthur O'Connor', *Irish Historical Studies* XV (1966)

12. *Paroles sur la Tombe de M. le General Arthur Condorcet O'Connor* (Paris, 1852)

13. Ministere de la Guerre, Archives Vincennes, Paris, Dossier 393 GD 2/j

14. Notes and Queries June 10th 1852

15. Bignon papers

16. Ibid

17. Ibid

18. Ibid

19. *Paroles sur la Tombe de M. le General Arthur Condorcet O'Connor* (Paris, 1852)

20. Archives de Loiret, Certificate of Death No ADL 4072 No 7

21. *Paroles sur la Tombe de M. le General Arthur Condorcet O'Connor* (Paris, 1852)

22. Ibid

23. Ibid

24. Ibid

25. Ibid

26. *Illustrated London News* 1852

27. Ibid

28. Ministere de la Guerre, Archives Vincennes, Paris, Dossier 393 GD 2/j

29. Trinity, Dublin, Ms. Dept. Ms 873 No 750

30. Ibid

31. Trinity, Dublin, Ms. Dept. Ms. 873 no 741

32. Will of Mme O'Connor, Alexandrine-Louisa-Sophie

EPILOGUE

1. Bignon papers

2. Ibid

SELECT BIBLIOGRAPHY

Airlie, Mabel, Countess of, *In Whig Society* (London, 1921)

Baker, K.M., *Condorcet* (Chicago, 1975)

Beauties of the Press, (London, 1800)

Beckett, J.C., *A Short History of Ireland* (1987)

Boissel, Thierry, S*ophie de Condorcet, Femme des Lumieres (1764-1822),* Presses de la Renaissance (Paris, 1988)

Book of Survey and Distribution, Cork

Bottigheimer, *English Money and Irish Land* (Oxford, 1971)

Brady, W. Maziere, *Clerical and Parochial Records Cork, Cloyne and Ross* Vol 2, (Dublin, 1863)

Brogan, Hugh, *The Penguin History of the United States of America* (London, 1990)

Burke, Edmund, *Speeches and Letters* (London, 1886)

Burke, Sir Bernard, *A Second Series of Vicissitudes of Families* (1860)

Burke's Irish Family Records (1976)

Burke's *Peerage, Baronetage and Knightage*

Burtchael, G.D. & Sadleir, T.U., *Alumnii Dublinenses 1593-1846* (London, 1924)

Byrne, Miles, *Memoirs* (Dublin, 1906)

Campbell, Gerald, *Edward and Pamela FitzGerald* (London, 1904)

Census of Ireland for the Year 1851

Christie, Ian R, *Wars and Revolutions, Britain 1760-1815* (London, 1982)

Coupland, R. (ed), *The War Speeches of Wm Pitt* (1916)

Curtin, Nancy J., *The United Irishmen* (Oxford, 1994)

Cusack, M.F., *The History of Cork* (1875)

Dickson, William Steel, *A Narrative of the Confinement and Exile* (Dublin, 1812)

Dickson, David; Keogh, Daire and Whelan, Kevin *The United Irishmen* (Dublin, 1993)

Dictionary of National Biography

Drennan, William, *Selected Writings,* Belfast Historical and Educational

Society (1998)

Dunlop, Robert, *Grattan* (London, 1889)

Elliott, Marianne, *Partners in Revolution* (Yale, 1982)

Elliott, Marianne, *Wolfe Tone, Prophet of Irish Independence* (Yale, 1989)

Emmet, T.A., *Ireland under English Rule* (New York, 1903)

Emmet, T.A., *The Emmet Family, With some Incidents relating to Irish History* (New York, 1898)

Emmet, Thomas Addis, O'Connor, Arthur and McNeven, William James: *Memoire or detailed statement or the origin and progress of the Irish union,* Delivered to the Irish Government by Messrs. Emmet, O'Connor and McNeven August 4th 1798 (Dublin, 1802)

Extracts from the Press (Philadelphia, 1802)

Ffolliott, Rosemary, *The Pooles of Mayfield* (Dublin, 1958)

Fitzpatrick, W.J., *Secret Service under Pitt* (London, 1892)

Foley, Terence (ed), *Eyewitness to 1798* (1996)

Foster, RF, *Modern Ireland 1600-1972* (London, 1989)

Furet, Francois, *Revolutionary France 1770-1880* (Oxford, 1995)

Gilbert, Sir John Thomas (ed), *Documents Relating to Ireland 1795-1804* (Shannon, 1970)

Gilbert, Sir John Thomas, *Life of Lord Edward Fitzgerald with a selection of historical and biographical sketches and anecdotes of celebrated United Irishmen* (1836)

Gillespie, Raymond, 'The Transformation of the Irish Economy 1550-1700', Studies in Irish Economic and Social History (1991)

Glendinning, Victoria, *Jonathan Swift* (London, 1998)

Guillois, Antoine, *La Marquise de Condorcet* (Paris, 1897)

Haddick-Flynn, Kevin, *Orangeism, The Making of a Tradition* (Dublin, 1999)

Harrington, James, *Oceana and other works* (London, 1737)

Hull, Eleanor, *A Text Book of Irish Literature* (Dublin, 1910)

Hume, David, *An Enquiry concerning Human Understanding* (1993)

Irish Parliamentary Register

Jacob, Rosamund, *The Rise of the United Irishmen* (1937)

Kee, Robert, *The Green Flag Vol 1* (London, 1972)

King's Inns Admission Papers

Lecky, W.E.H., *The History of Ireland in the 18th Century* (London, 1896)

Leland, *History of Ireland* (Dublin, 1773)

Lewis, S, *A Topographical Dictionary of Ireland* (1837)

Grattan, Henry the younger, *Memoirs of the Life and Times of the Rt. Hon. Henry Grattan* (London, 1839-46)

MacDermot, Frank, 'Arthur O'Connor', *Irish Historical Studies* XV (1966)

MacLysaght, Edward, *Irish Families, their Names, Arms and Origins* (Dublin, 1957)

Madden, R.R. Dr, *The United Irishmen, their lives and times* (Dublin, 1842-26)

Maguire, W.A. (ed), *Up in Arms,* Ulster Museum (Belfast, 1998)

McNeven, William James, *Pieces of Irish History* (London, 1802)

Mitchell, L.G., *Charles James Fox* (London, 1997)

Moore, Thomas, *The Memoirs of Lord Edward Fitzgerald* (London, 1897)

Neely, Sylvia, *Lafayette and the Liberal Ideal 1814-1824* (Illinois, 1991)

O'Brien, Conor Cruise, *The Great Melody* (Dublin, 1992)

O'Brien, Conor Cruise, ab. McCue, Jim, *Edmund Burke* (Dublin, 1997)

O'Brien, Gerard, *Anglo-Irish Politics in the Age of Grattan and Pitt* (Dublin, 1987)

O'Connell, Maurice, (ed) *The Correspondence of Daniel O'Connell Vol 1,* Irish University Press for the Irish Manuscripts Commission (Dublin, 1972)

O'Connor, A. Condorcet Lt-General et Arago, F.M., *Oeuvres de Condorcet* (Paris 1847-49)

O'Connor, Arthur, ed. Livesey, James, *The State of Ireland* (Dublin, 1998)

O'Connor, Arthur Condorcet, *Monopoly: The Cause of all Evil* (London & Paris, 1848)

O'Connor, Roger, *The Chronicles of Eri* (London, 1822)

O'Conor Don, Rt. Hon. Charles Owen, *The O'Conors of Connaught* (Dublin, 1891)

O'Toole, Fintan, *A Traitor's Kiss, The Life of Richard Brinsley Sheridan* (1998)

Packenham, Thomas, *The Year of Liberty* (London, 1969)

Paine, Thomas, *Rights of Man* (London, 1985)

Patterson, M.W., *Sir Francis Burdett and his Times* (London, 1931)

Prendergast, John P., *The Cromwellian Settlement of Ireland* (1865)

Proceedings of the Society of United Irishmen (Philadelphia, 1795)

Read, Donald, *Feargus O'Connor* (1961)

Report from the Secret Committee of the House of Lords (Dublin, 1798)

Report from the Secret Committee of the House of Commons (Dublin, 1798)

Russell, Bertrand, *History of Western Philosophy* (London, 1995)

Smith, Charles, *The Ancient and Present State of the County and City of Cork* (1750)

Smith, Adam, *Wealth of Nations* (London, 1997)

Somerset Fry, Peter and Fiona, *The History of Scotland* (London, 1982)

St Clair, William, *The Godwins and the Shelleys* (London, 1989)

Stuart, Dorothy Margaret, *Dearest Bess* (London, 1955)

Swift's Irish Pamphlets, An Introductory Selection ed Joseph McMinn (1991)

Taylor, IA, *Life of Lord Edward Fitzgerald* (London, 1903)

Teeling's *Rebellion of 1798*

The Trial of James O'Coigley, otherwise called James Quigley, otherwise called James John Fivey, Arthur O'Connor Esq. John Binns, John Allen and Jeremiah Leary for High Treason at Maidstone in Kent May 1798 (London, 1798)

The Four Masters, *Annals of the Kingdom of Ireland* (Dublin, 1990)

Tillyard, Stella, *Citizen Lord* (1997)

Tone, William T.W. (Compiled and arranged by), Bartlett, Thomas (ed), *Life of Theobald Wolfe Tone* (Dublin, 1998)

Truxes, Thomas M., *Irish-American Trade 1660-1783* (Cambridge, 1988)

Wheeler, H.F.B. and Broadley, A.M., *The War in Wexford* (London, 1910)

Williams, Ronald, *The Lords of the Isles* (1997)

JOURNALS AND PAMPHLETS

Analecta Hibernica XV 1944

A Portrait of a Traitor by His Friends and by Himself (B.Library 8132.df.2

Co. Kildare Archaeological Society, Volume XV (1971) No 1

Fitzwilliam Pamphlets (B.Library 8145.df.5)

Haliday Pamphlets 780 no 2

History Ireland Vol 6. No 2

History Today Volume 48 (6)

Irish Historical Studies XV 1966: MacDermot, Frank, Arthur O'Connor

Journal of the Cork Historical and Archaeological Society (1948, 1949)

Notes and Queries, 10 June 1851

Paroles sur la Tombe de M. le General Arthur Condorcet O'Connor, 8 December 1852

Speech of the Rt. Hon. William Pitt, (B.Library 8145.ee.20)

The Irish Sword Vol VI no 25

INDEX

Abercromby, General Sir Ralph,
     158, 161, 168, 172, 173
Aberdeen, 207
Adair, Robert, 220
Africa, 8, 18, 19
Allen, John, 170, 225, 251
America, 8, 11, 16, 18, 19, 94, 233
American Declaration of
     Independence, 29
America, United States of, 29, 44,
     46, 92, 202, 203, 241, 243
American Revolution, 52, 61, 62,
     150, 151, 267
American War of Independence,
     24, 29, 30, 38, 43, 72, 73
Amiens, Treaty of, 216
Amnesty, Act of, 188, 196
Ancient Britons, 146
Angers, 117
Anglo-Irish, 11, 13, 19, 21, 38,
     161-2
Angus-shire Fencibles, 206
Anne 1, Queen, 13, 38
Antrim, 131,133,153,183
Arago, MF, 266
Ariadne, 216
Armagh, 125, 139, 157
Arms, manufacture and importa
     tion, 65, 95, 112, 135, 139,
     140, 152, 162
Arms, search for, 146, 152, 161,
     172, 231
Arms, right to own, 30, 65
Army, British, 27, 30, 70
Army, French, 186, 227

Army, in Ireland, 133, 146, 157,
     161, 167, 173, 185
Ascendancy, Protestant, 11, 38, 74,
     77, 80, 88, 103
Asdee, 16,17,20
Aston Smith, 205
Augereau, General, 227
Austerlitz, 231
Austria, Empire of, 70, 71, 110,
     157, 231
Ayrshire Militia, 208

Baldwin, John, 12
Ballinahinch, Battle of, 183
Ballineen, 4,7,12,13,47
Ballinroe, 54,239,259,262
Ballymaloe, 19
Bandon, 7, 12, 15, 17, 19, 23, 24,
     136, 145, 166, 184
Banishment Act, 198, 202-4, 210,
     216
Bantry, 23, 48, 138, 139, 145, 161
Bantry Bay, 136, 137, 138, 234
Barrington, Sir Jonah, 188, 251
Barrymore, Lord, 215
Barthelemey, 111, 145, 163
Basle, 111-4, 117
Belfast, 61, 76, 83, 91, 117,
     120,122, 133, 136, 146, 183,
     188, 195, 202, 206, 215, 216
Belgium, 71
Bell, Hugh, 168, 170-1, 176-7,
     218, 222, 239, 247
Beresford, John, 66, 68, 85, 86, 87,
     159, 168, 276
Berkeley, Bishop, 36
Bernard family, 12, 20
Berthier, Prince of Wagram, 228,
     250-1, 260
Bessborough, Lady, 219, 220

323

O'Carolan, 76
O'Connell, Daniel, 214, 218, 254-7, 263-5, 274
O'Connor, Arthur, born, 4, 7; education, 14-5, 23-7, 29, 255-6, 271; descent from O'Connor Kerry, 15-6, 20, 269; changes name, 20, 54; and Roman Catholics, 20, 26, 52, 64, 88, 120, 128, 144, 158, 256, 263-4; and Richard Longfield, Lord Longueville, 23, 31, 40-1, 48, 59, 66-8, 80, 83, 90, 141-2, 199; at Trinity College, Dublin, 34-6, 40-1; and philosophy, 36, 211-2, 272; and Volunteers, 27, 30-1, 70; and American War of independence, 24, 31, 43; death of sister, 32; oratory, 36-7, 112; memoirs, 1, 258, 264, 271-2; and Dublin parliament, 37, 39, 40, 65-6, 85; and science, 27, 33,35-6, 72, 266; and property, 41, 51, 54, 104, 144, 199, 214, 218, 222, 232, 238-9, 246, 252-4, 259, 262, 271; meeting with Charles O'Conor, 28; republican principles, 30-1, 36, 98, 228, 250, 256; and father, 21; and mother, 14, 25, 27, 41, 211; and law, 41-3, 54, 120, 140, 277; in England, 41-3, 54, 79, 84, 92, 96, 159, 164, 166-182; religious attitudes, 24, 26-8, 32-3, 41, 82, 126, 211, 245, 255-6, 267, 273, 277; and Appolos Morris, 27-30, 42,

47; and economics, 35-6, 42, 49, 50, 54, 67-8, 83, 107, 121, 164, 187, 266; visits France, 44-6, 52, 69, 70, 110, 116-122; and Edmund Burke, 46, 82-3, 90; poetry, 28, 206, 213; and RB Sheridan, 46, 96, 100-1, 106, 164, 167; in Switzerland, 45-6, 111-3, 222, 272; as High Sheriff of Cork, 57-8, 64; heir to Richard Longfield, 48, 91, 96; views on British rule in Ireland, 26, 41, 98, 277; views on Greece and Rome, 31, 50; political views, 48, 54, 60, 63, 66, 96-100, 106-7, 145, 165, 194, 200, 261, 273-4; articles, 40-1, 49; and free trade, 49, 66, 121, 164; and Saxons, 50; character and appearance, 51, 54, 74, 81, 95, 107, 140-1, 151, 214, 221-2, 237, 242, 245, 251, 253, 265-6; as barrister, 54; lives near Kinsale, 54; and agriculture, 45, 54, 246; agent for Lord Kingsborough, 56-7; as MP, 58-9, 72, 75, 85; and Sir Francis Burdett, 67, 79-81, 106, 122, 132-3, 139, 148, 151, 164, 177, 179, refuses job from Pitt, 68-9; and Lafayette, 70, 71, 219, 223, 236, 260, 271; views of French Revolution, 71-2, 82, 97, 110, 228; in Belgium, 71; and political science, 72-3, 228-9, 261, 266; pamphlets: *The Measures of Ministry*, 73,